Canada Made Me

Norman Levine was born in Canada and grew up in
Lower Town ...
since 1949 except for one year (1965-66) during ...
which he was the first writer-in-residence at the
Uni...

Date Due

a yo...
who ...
the ...
writ...
halli...

MAY 2 7 1980	JUN 0 9 1998		
ILLO			
ILLO			
Feb. 5/81			
ILLO			
mar 11/81			

53389

Canada Made Me

BY NORMAN LEVINE

Deneau & Greenberg

To
MARGARET

Siena made me; Maremma undid me.

THE DIVINE COMEDY

It is well known that one's native land
is always recognized at the moment of losing it.

ALBERT CAMUS

CONTENTS

	THE EMIGRANT SHIP	11
I.	OTTAWA	38
II.	INTO THE BUSH	73
III.	A RETURN TO THE MINE	84
IV.	WINNIPEG	95
V.	SOCIETY IN SASKATOON	124
VI.	NOTES IN EDMONTON	135
VII.	THE PACIFIC COAST	147
VIII.	FISHING	161
IX.	THE CARIBOO	183
X.	STOP OVERS	201
XI.	IN MONTREAL	212
XII.	QUEBEC CITY	237
	THE TOURIST SHIP	263

AUTHOR'S NOTE

The idea of writing this book on Canada came while I was living
in St. Ives, Cornwall. But I did not know how I would go about
doing this trip, for one would need both time and money.
Instead, I found that whenever I came up to London I would go
into Canada House, look over some of the old newspapers,
magazines, listen to the sound of the voices, look at the faces,
just sit and watch. And when I found I couldn't go and make
this trip, I began to do it imaginatively. I wrote down places
I would visit, often just for the sound of their names. I filled up
notebooks with what I would do in the morning, where I would
go in the afternoon. I walked through Montreal from the docks
to the airport; in Ottawa from Rockliffe through Lower Town
and out into the country. I wrote about the seasons. I went back
to the Bush, to Ile-aux-Noix, to the Laurentians, Toronto,
Quebec City, the West where I once did my flying training. And
I began to people it not only with the things I could remember
that happened to me in Canada as a child and a young man,
but with incidents and people that I had since met elsewhere;
and then going on from there . . .
    But that book never did get written.
    There was, as in Henry Miller's *Air-Conditioned Nightmare*,
a need for making the physical journey. I felt the need to make
a reconciliation. I didn't want to run away from the country as
I had originally when I sailed in that freighter on that hot June
day in 1949 from Montreal. 'Unlike most prodigal sons I was
returning not with the intention of remaining in the bosom of
the family but of wandering forth again, perhaps never to return.
I wanted to have a last look at my country and leave it with a
good taste in my mouth.'

THE EMIGRANT SHIP

VIA WATERLOO

I LEFT London on a Sunday morning. The sun was out. After a night's rain a cold fresh smell by the Embankment. At Waterloo Station a lump of men, women and children stood by a chalked notice at the entrance to platform 12. The notice said that the boat-train would be delayed an hour. There was nothing to do but wait.

I went into the buffet for coffee. The coffee was weak and tasted of chicory. The smell in the room was of someone being sick. I took the coffee outside and sat on a bench under the long buckled glass roof, steel trusses and pigeons. The four-faced hollow clock. The minute hand vibrated then settled down. One could kill time easy here. Bookstalls, tobacconist, shoeshine, buffet, and the wooden bench. But there was no peace. A noise, continuous, like water going over stones.

Beside me sat a crippled old woman. Two small half crutches. A rug over her knees. She told me that she arrived before seven and that she was going to New York for St. Patrick's Day. I went and bought some Sunday papers for her and for myself. Someone was killed climbing in the Alps. Clashes in the Middle East. We traded. Another murder. A robbery in a bank. Someone put her head in the gas oven. I could hear a clipped woman's voice giving out the weights from the weighing machine. A record played a march. A train gave several loud bursts, the steam flat against the dirty glass roof. The crippled woman sat on the bench, a fixed expression of patience. Her body upright, leaning forward, motionless. She reminded me of a heron. An eye veil widely meshed. I could see the eyes plainly. They were brown with violet around the brown. An orange-coloured lipstick was put on badly, too much on the top lip. Her face looked untidy, as if she did not have enough time in which to make it up or not enough skill to cover the suffering that was showing open. I went back for another cup of coffee. The buffet was crowded.

It was easier to drink standing by the steaming urns, the metal tray with the undried spoons, the glass shelf packed with sausage rolls, then to shove one's way out. But the boat-train finally did come. And we did arrive at Southampton. And later that night we sailed.

THE PASSENGERS

In the cabin were three young Germans. Two were going to New York and one to Chicago. The two to New York were just out of school and they were going to 'uncles'. They wanted to be engineers. They didn't like leaving Germany. *Es ist nicht gut für Deutschland ihre Junge zu verlieren.* The other German was in his thirties. A cabinet maker. He was going to relatives in Chicago. *Mehr gelt.* He said, in German, that his wife was already in America. He wanted to celebrate before leaving so he got drunk, borrowed a car, had an accident, and could not leave on the same boat as his wife because he was in jail. He slept underneath me. The two boys slept opposite. There was a small dresser. A sink that did not have hot water. One of the school-boys said that there was no hot water anywhere. That the lavatories were blocked. That the ship had only one plumber. That one must be careful on the floor as it was painted with a red paint that came off on everything. On the socks, on the feet, on the shoes.

Wie sagt man, das Land ist sehr gut?
The land is very good.
And they brought out their notebooks. And I spelled the words out.
Wie sagt man, können sie sagen wo ist die Strasse?
Can you tell me where this street is?
Und wie sagt man, alles ist wunderbar?
Everything is wonderful.
They were both tidy. They placed their new leather luggage at the foot of their bunks. They made their own beds. Notebook, pyjamas, under the pillow. Shaving things, toothbrush, in separate leather holders. Clothes carefully hung. Armbands to keep up their shirt-sleeves. Pipes ran across the ceiling and they hung up their winter coats on hangers and hooked them on to the pipes so that there was a kind of curtain between their bunks and ours. We were in the first cabin forward. The sea was calm. But I could hear the water slapping ominously against the side before I went to sleep.

Next morning after breakfast, walking around, I realized how much she was an emigrant ship. Families herding together. The lack of comfort. The suspicion between those who came on at Bremerhaven—some three hundred Germans and other Europeans who had been living in Germany since the war—and the fifty-odd passengers who came on at Southampton, mostly British immigrants and returning American and Canadian tourists. On the first day the Germans resented us as intruders. They knew the ship. They were familiar with its routine. Three young men paraded up and down the promenade deck in S.S. uniform. Black jackboots, wide black breeches, black shirts. That didn't help. Neither did the waiting outside the two working lavatories.

In the afternoon we passed Land's End. A fist with knuckles spread apart pierced with stone. The Wolf. Sennen. A few mine chimneys. St. Just. And nostalgia for what one was leaving behind. But it became hazy. Mist. Then fog. The land disappeared. Loneliness.

My five fellow passengers at the dining-table were all men. A sick-berth attendant going to marry an usherette in Montreal; an Irish doctor; a former policeman from Southend; an American student returning to university in San Francisco; a young shy aircraft mechanic from London. Only the doctor and the policeman had jobs to go to. The doctor to a hospital in Saint John. The policeman had joined the police section of the Royal Canadian Air Force.

The sick-berth attendant was a Teddy Boy called Irving. He had blond hair brushed up from both sides to form a ridge at the top that protruded in front of the forehead like a helmet. From the beginning the trip to him was a big joke. As life was a big joke. He spoke rapidly in short phrases. 'Here these trousers one quid.' And he would rub his trousers in his hand. Then show his yellow socks and pointed brown shoes. 'Cheap only three quid.' If a girl went by he would look at her legs. And cluck to himself. He hoped to get a job in a hospital. But he wasn't worried. So far everything had been a big bluff. And he knew how to handle it. If any food was placed in front of him that he did not know, he would ridicule it. Just as he did George, the elderly table steward. 'C'mon slave. Bring on the soup.' There was always the film. The cheap magazine. That he remembered. But there was nothing nasty. A chuckle. A cluck-cluck. The humming of a sentimental popular song. He was in his element on deck at night jitterbugging with Blondy, a short dumpy

English girl with large hoop ear-rings and a continual vacant expression. He had picked her up on the boat-train. She was going to meet her husband in Edmonton. When they danced Blondy did most of the work. Twisting, shaking, turning, swaying her thighs from side to side so that her skirt flared and folded as she changed from one direction to the other. While Irving stood in one small spot, pivoting, a continual grin on his face, his legs moving inwards to half her rhythm, the legs crossing as if he wanted desperately to go to the lavatory and could not wait.

By evening rumours began. That we were going to Liverpool. Another, that we were going to Dublin. I wanted to believe the second for I had not been to Dublin. The ship was dull. The plumber had a few more lavatories working. But it was difficult to find a comfortable place to sit down. Those who came on at Bremerhaven were united against those who embarked at Southampton. One could not sit down in an empty place in a lounge without being told, in German, that it was taken. The cabin was hot and of not much use. Every time I went down there I was involved in an English vocabulary lesson. The Irish doctor had once had a practice in Dublin. He went to see the purser, who confirmed that we were going to Dublin and agreed reluctantly to let a few of us get off the boat 'as a special favour'. One was back in service life. One had to wangle.

DUBLIN

The doctor, the American student, and myself walked down the gangplank at nine next morning. After the dreariness and the monotony of the boat, Dublin quickly appealed to me. It began to rain. The American bought some linen handkerchiefs and shamrocks for souvenirs. The dirty macintoshes. Second-hand bicycles. Small boys pushing carts. It reminded me of a country market town with all the farmers from the districts in for a day's shopping. The doctor took us to O'Connell Street, the Post Office, then by the Liffey, into a secondhand bookstore with nationalistic papers, and finally to the Abbey Theatre—you couldn't get near it for the stacks of parked bicycles against the door and the side. It was enough of a Cook's tour for the time we had. While we were walking down Grafton Street the doctor kept repeating, 'There's somewhere I must take you. I think it's here . . .' But every time we turned off and went down a side street, he was less sure. Finally he brought us to a bar for a drink.

We had several brandies and an excellent cup of coffee. The waiter gave us coloured plastic cocktail sticks with a harp or a map of Ireland at the top for 'souvenirs'. Then some pamphlets. He opened one near the middle. It was an extract from *Ulysses* about Davy Byrne and Nosey Flynn talking about Bloom. But the Davy Byrne of Joyce's time was not around us. And neither was the good talk. It was replaced by chromium plate, mirrors, low chairs, glossy souvenirs, business men, and other tourists like ourselves drinking and looking at the badly painted murals on the wall. It had all the slickness and the anonymity of those bars around Piccadilly and Shaftesbury Avenue that cater for the tourist and the business man who wants to be comfortable and Bohemian.

We started a pub crawl and in the first pub met a fellow-passenger. He was tall, thin, and delicate; in a camel-hair coat, a pink silk scarf. The purser had told him that he was the only one allowed off the boat 'as a special favour' because he came from Dublin. He joined us and began to take us to deserted pubs in side streets the doctor didn't know of. He said he had grown up in these streets. But you could see that he was unable to return, even for a visit. He began to weep. He wanted to have it both ways, and he knew he couldn't. He started to confess. We were anonymous and he knew he was safe. What had taken him away from here was poverty and shame. To remain away he had to disguise his background. So he began to imitate until now he spoke English like a B.B.C. announcer. A few more whiskies made him feel better and be began to discuss the relative merits of various liquors. He said he was a bartender and that he was going to New York to work in some exclusive club.

When we returned to the wharf two ticktack men approached us. They wanted us to go back with them and 'have a nice Irish girl'. We told them that the boat would soon be sailing; anyway it was too early in the day. They insisted. They had a car. We could have sex in the car. The more aggressive one looked like a caricature of Francis L. Sullivan but shabbily dressed. When they realized we were not interested they begged for money.

A LUXURY CRUISE

It was difficult, at first, to believe you were back on the same ship. There were streamers from the pier to the decks. Cars drove up. Well-dressed men and women in tweeds not knowing quite what to do, how to say goodbye. The German band kept playing again and again *When Irish Eyes are Smiling*, and *Auf Wiedersehen*. Finally the streamers snapped. We pulled away leaving behind a dark cluster of people by an empty wharf waving handkerchiefs and hands.

Four hundred Irish had come on board while we were in Dublin. They were going to New York for St. Patrick's Day. Using the boat as a hotel, they would watch the parade, go to Mass in the Cathedral, then return with the boat to Dublin. It had been advertised in the Irish papers as 'The Luxury Cruise of the Irish' and the shipping company had provided a cruise director, an Irish priest, a band, and a Shamrock Queen. For that first day their optimism and ignorance of the ship displaced the gloom I had known before. The stewards appeared more helpful. The ship's officers mingled with the passengers. I had a drink with the ship's doctor. He was middle-aged, German. He said he had been a Nazi but that was past. He preferred the small talk, joke, another drink? It did not cost him anything, he said. He agreed with what you said. Why not? It was easier. Another drink? He had a wife in Hamburg. 'She has no idea what goes on on board.' Then he said his strongest opinion. 'Those who cry the most saying goodbye, screw the first.'

But there were too many people on board. And it did not take long for the Irish to realize that they had been cheated. Most of them were elderly, making their first crossing, and had saved up the £100 for the complete journey. A few had won competitions which offered this 'cruise' as the prize.

On the second day out of Dublin we went into a storm and things became chaotic. Vomit was everywhere. The stewards were understaffed. They went around throwing sawdust until they could clear it up at night. But at night the decks remained full. The old women were frightened and refused to sleep in their cabins. They were more comfortable on deck stretched out in deckchairs wrapped in blankets, telling their beads. The Irish priest—a country priest, white hair, a handsome flushed face, he had played rugby for Ireland and wore a blazer with an Irish crest and the white collar—went around assuring them that the boat would not sink. The storm had broken much of the German's isolation. There still remained the problem of language. The young boys in S.S. uniform paraded less frequently. Then the storm got worse. Over the loudspeaker a record was playing. Then a whine as the needle skidded across. They tried another one. It began to hiccup. Then no more music from the loudspeaker for the rest of the trip. The wind increased. It began to rain. The stewards pulled the windows up on the promenade deck. They wet the tablecloths in the dining-room and placed wooden frames in which we had our dishes. But every meal brought its accidents.

The first few days remained the most incongruous. The Irish dressed for dinner. They had paid for what they believed was a luxury cruise. They had seen films of how life aboard a ship should be. They had bought clothes. Rather than admit that they had been swindled they wanted to pretend. On board ship everybody is rich. No responsibilities. Sit in the bar. Drink with the satisfied feeling that you are getting things cheap. Twenty cents for a double brandy. Twenty cents for a package of good cigarettes. But they were cheated. By the misery, the poverty, and the squalor of the emigrants. By the storm. By the condition of the ship. Pretend. But it is difficult when the black market goes on. A knock on the door. Do you want to buy a watch? An American girl has a camera stolen. On C deck a woman will sleep with you for ten shillings. And boredom won. At first it was a question of endurance, of not getting sick. But the storm went on too long even for that. One became resigned and sat huddled in a blanket on deck and slept or else watched how the others accepted the boredom and the monotony.

The cruise director tried his best to keep up the pretence that it was a cruise. He was a scented, failed, English actor. The kind you avoid at a party. He tried to make the activity on the ship follow the pattern of a Billy Butlin camp. Everything had to be organized. Always there had to be something to do and prizes to be won. There were films in the evening in the dining-room; but pillars got in the way. There was horse-racing on deck; but people spoiled it by being sick or else a wooden horse fell as the boat pitched. He tried a dance; but that had to be called off because of the storm. He became frantic and more nervous as event after event either failed or ended badly. Small things—unimportant things like typing out next day's programme which he knew would be cancelled—he would dramatize until for him they became a matter of the greatest urgency. He walked around in a dinner-jacket, always in a rush, a bewildered man with a large green plastic button marked 'Cruise Director' hooked in his lapel.

The storm continued. And I began to enjoy the roughness in a perverse kind of way. Things became simple and uncomplicated. The group of Irish singing sentimental and rebel Irish

B

songs on deck after breakfast; the priest doing his rounds like a
doctor then returning to the first-class bar for a double whisky;
the Shamrock Queen showing herself once a day, officially, in
a white dress with a green shawl—dark, seventeen, a self-conscious product of a finishing school—she walked with her
mother around the promenade deck, through the lounges, then
returned to the first-class part of the ship. The greatest difficulty
was to be by oneself. If you went to the bar for a drink you were
just as likely to find bottles falling around you, glasses crashing,
the chair you sat in go sliding across the length of the room.
The cabin was also useless. There was no ventilation. The sink
made vomit noises until it became blocked. Then the water ran
on to the cabin floor.

Next day seemed less worse than the one before. One became
conditioned. To not shaving, to suddenly seeing someone sick,
to the blocked lavatories with the scribbles on the wall showing
the basic positions for copulating. Or else a walk down to the
stern to watch the huge lumps of water pound the ship. She
heaved like a see-saw. Every time the propeller came out of the
water, the ship shuddered.

At night in the top bunk it was difficult to sleep. The boat
rolled and pitched violently. I could hear the water crashing
against the side and over my head. The wump, swish, and the
ebb. Wump, swish, and the ebb. That went on. And in the morning I woke to the gong, to water on the floor swilling ankle-deep,
dyed red by the cheap paint. The cabin stuffy. The sink blocked.
A voice from behind the swaying curtain of winter coats *Wie
sagt man* . . . and the wump, swish, and the ebb.

I began to lose count of the days. About the ninth or the
tenth day the wind lessened and the cruise director brought out
the Irish band to entertain the passengers on deck. It was led by
a short stocky clubfoot man with an accordion. He was nervous
and anxious to please. They had a singer with them, a pimply-
faced boy, and he sang imitation Al Jolson songs. The band
played imitation Glenn Miller. The audience was enthusiastic.
A gawky girl, a passenger, was asked to sing a sentimental song,
The Blind Boy. She sang a Spike Jones version of the song,
ridiculing it; the Irish did not like that at all. They remained
soft, sentimental and stagey. They were still fighting the
English. But that night the storm became worse. The boat hove
to. The old women stayed on deck with their beads. At breakfast
next morning the doctor told me that he had been called in by
the ship's doctor. A woman had died during the night from

shock. A window on the promenade deck blew in and some passengers were badly cut.

The Irish priest said a special Mass for the dead woman. She was an Italian married to a Hungarian, and with their five-year-old boy they were emigrating to Canada. The man was penniless. The priest organized a collection among the cruise passengers and collected over a hundred pounds. From then on whenever the dead woman's husband or child appeared, people stared and talked. They had become the ship's celebrities: like the boxer on board, the priest, the band leader, the Shamrock Queen.

EUROPEAN TIME

At teatime you could sit anywhere in the dining-room. I asked the German sitting opposite me if he could tell me the right time. He said he only had European time. I asked him what time it was in Europe. He pulled back his jacket sleeve. As far as I could see up his arm there was a long succession of wrist-watches strapped on.

*

Meals still kept up a certain sophistication. There was the formality with the food and the talk. The American student had returned from a six-weeks 'pilgrimage' of England. He said he had been to see Wordsworth country, Hardy country, Brontë country, Shakespeare country. And he had filled up notebook after notebook with 'raw material' for his proposed thesis on 'The Influence of Place'. As long as money was coming from the university he was in no hurry. He said he had enough material to keep him busy for the next ten years. Whenever he came to the dining-room he carried a book with him. And if anyone said anything that he thought profound he would say, 'I must get that down in my notebook before I forget.' And out would come the Biro and the small black book. He liked to display his ignorance as if he was proud of it. He was short, feminine, black hair with a streak of grey in front that he pressed with his hand into a wave. He made a great deal of fuss about cleanliness. Examining the knives and forks and spoons before he used them. 'George. George. This knife is not clean. Thank you, George.' Once he said he was getting homesick. George overheard. 'Homesick. It is a luxury, my friend, for those who are romantic and don't want to grow up. Wait, my friend, until you have been

around and seen some more of this world.' It was the only time
he spoke out sharply.

Usually when George finished serving our table he would go
to another table and eat his meal. He said he came from Stettin
and he refused to sit and eat with the German stewards. He was
like the professor in *The Blue Angel* before the egg is cracked on
his head and he begins to crow. Only instead of saying 'Cri Cri
Cri', George had said 'Yes, sir' too many times to too many
different people. Now he did not care. He would write down on
pieces of paper what we wanted, then go to the kitchen. But if
he dropped a plate or came back as he often did with a wrong
dish or to the Teddy Boy's 'C'mon slave', he no longer appeared
vulnerable. Neither did he pretend to make a fuss and fawn over
us for the price of the tip at the end. Once when only the doctor
and myself were at the table he began to talk. He said he was
captured by the 4th Canadian Army in Holland. 'The Canadians
were very good to me. They treated me like a raw egg.' I asked
him why he did not emigrate. 'You can't plant an old tree in
new ground.' The doctor asked him how were things now. 'We
say, "How you make your bed that is the way you sleep".'

*

But the serious talk, whenever it got down to it, was always
of money.

Most of the immigrants were going to relatives. They had
little money or belongings. They were told how good the wages
were and they decided to come. A Pole who lived in Hamburg
since the war sat in a deckchair, unshaven, glassy-eyed, working
out on pieces of paper, at so much an hour and so much for
overtime, how much money he would have at the end of his first
month in Canada. Another was debating what name he should
change his present one to. There were others who wanted to forget. A broken marriage, an affair that didn't work out, failure,
unhappiness . . . it was better to be separate from the places and
the streets and the people who were reminders of the mistakes
and the messes one made, and ran away from.

I woke up on a cold March morning to the sight of trees, tall
industrial chimneys, cylinders of Esso gasoline. A slate sky.
Snow flaked white from it. The sea had a mild swell. But the
soundtrack to all this was gone. It was like seeing a foreign film.
I expected some kind of recognition to appear as we moved
towards the land. But it continued to approach silently and

monotonously like the funeral of someone you don't know. Snow was on the tugs. Slush on our open decks. The ship looked dull, used, and tired. Like a nightclub in the daytime. On the quay, men in lumberjack shirts and ski-caps with flaps over their ears began to take off the heavy luggage. Newspapers were brought on board from Halifax. They told us that we were two days late and that we had the roughest crossing for the past six years. But already that seemed not important. The crossing was over. All that remained was the ritual of exchanging addresses with people you had no intention of writing to; signing one's name on menu cards; looking at snaps the ship's photographer was selling. And while we waited to disembark the shrinking down continued. Until what had been larger than life-size was reduced to a few tired lumps standing by the rails in the slush.

WAITING TO DISEMBARK

What was it that pulled me back? I didn't know. But it was there; a restless energy that I could not understand, that had driven me from wherever I was, gnawed at me until by every means possible it had brought me back. But now that I was here it left me uncertain and hesitant. For all its squalor and absurdity the ship was safe.

But we waited too long. The uncertainty, the hesitancy, increased. The lounges were dark, empty, the fans not going. An old copy of *The Times* that had been bought in Dublin lay torn in a chair. On deck, in the slush, heaped in a sprawling mound, was the luggage from the cabins: cardboard boxes with rope around them; wicker chests with large steel locks; knapsacks; expensive leather cases. The cameras were out taking pictures through the snow of a caravan sight of brick and steel fixed like a lot of frozen garbage. And while we waited I wondered why I felt so reluctant to get off the ship.

Perhaps it was the image that I did not understand. Though I called Canada home—and by Canada I meant only parts of Ottawa, Montreal and the Laurentians—I felt no particular sense of belonging there. But then neither did I feel I belonged particularly anywhere else. Was that one's inheritance, a rootlessness? Or maybe it was just curiosity that drives one back to see where one had grown up in? But that kind of journey can be done leisurely, in comfort, and in old age. Or was it something more personal? A kind of personal destructiveness that one is condemned to carry. Of going back to places that one left innocent, knowing that now one's equipment has changed.

But once down the gangplank, 'the present opens its arms', and these thoughts went. One could no longer afford the luxury of being a passenger, of going around recording the oddities of the other passengers. Now, one had to take risks.

FROM THE GANGPLANK

I entered a large drill hall. I was marched with the others inside a tall wire cage that was open at the top and told to sit down on a wooden bench. Around the walls of the drill hall hung the shields of the various provinces. Four Union Jacks hung down from the walls. They were all faded, two had moth holes. The drill hall was divided by toilets into two squares. A sign in between the toilets said WELCOME TO CANADA in seven languages. I told the nearest standing official that I was a Canadian. He told me, in German, to sit down.

When it was my turn to go from one side of the drill hall to the other I had to show my papers to another official who sat behind a wooden desk not far from the toilets. Ahead of me was an elderly man, well dressed, with rimless glasses, straight white hair—and with that unageing North American face. He looked very gentle. He was talking to the official whose unshaven face betrayed no sign of interest.

'I'm a native-born Canadian and I believe there's an immigrant here who won't make a good citizen of our country.'

'Why do you say that?'

'I saw the way he was actin' up on the ship, gettin' drunk every night, cuttin' up. He's no good. He's not the kind we want here.'

Somebody was crying. A child was crying in its mother's arms. A short man with many documents in his hand kept biting his lip, he looked anxious, as if he had something to hide. He went to see the passport official. The official was bored.

'Where's he now?'

'On the far side sittin' down.'

'Will you show him to me?'

'I most certainly will.'

The short man was trying desperately to say the right things, and smiling, and sweating. His wife, taller than the man, and

stout, kept on shaking her head, everything to her was Yes.
Their small boy was there a hand on each shoulder. Then the
official stamped their papers. The woman behaved as if she
knew this was going to happen all the time, but the man
couldn't hide his feelings. He wanted to tell someone; he was in.
I continued to sit on the bench and wait. The child continued
to cry. A tall blonde girl in dark slacks, from Berlin, who knew
no English but had pantomimed coquettishly with every male
who had spoken to her on the ship, sat by herself on a bench,
and wept. No one paid her any attention. Everyone looked exhausted. At the end of the benches like a pack of watchdogs
stood dark-uniformed officials.

I had been away before and I never had to worry about re-
entry. It was a formality, like punching a clock, signing one's
name or standing up at the end of a film. If there was any un-
pleasantness, one forgot quickly; they were not organized. I
remember the last time coming down the St. Lawrence. Standing
by the rail. Watching the small French villages with the
dominant wooden white church, hands in prayer, and the
inverted thistle-tube steeple, the expensive summer resorts, the
brightly painted bungalows, cows grazing; approach then go
behind us. Sun behind trees. And the ducks flying over like one
of those calendars. Sun sets. River yellow. Then blue. Then cold.
Then the moon. The river narrowed. A side of the land rose near
and dark like a fjord. Danced on deck to a four-piece band;
students working their passage. Cold blue lights amidships. And
from the loudspeakers the clink, small talk, giggle, breaking
through the dance music from the lounge. A star climbed slowly
up and down the rigging. Officials had come on board. It took
a few minutes behind a curtain near the forward bar. It was
done discreetly. Then you returned to the dancing on deck, the
line-shooting, the giggle, the blanket, the star slowly up and
down the rigging . . .

My passport was stamped in silence and I went through a gate
in the wire enclosure and into a narrow tunnel where two middle-
aged women, in blue uniforms, stood behind a long wooden
table. One asked me in a Scottish accent what I was carrying in
my briefcase and in my typewriter. I told her. She didn't believe
me. She opened my typewriter, upside down, shook it violently.
Then she made me open my briefcase: a crumpled tie, a toothbrush, a few books. She asked me what kind of books I had.
There was a copy of W. S. Graham's *The Nightfishing* and a
dog-eared Penguin of Graham Greene's *The Lawless Roads*.

'Are they dirty books?'

'No.'

She picked up the Penguin and looked at a few pages.

'Did you buy them or were they given to you as gifts?'

'I bought them,' I lied.

'How much were they?'

'A pound each.'

It did not matter what absurdities you answered. They were solemnly marked down on a piece of flimsy paper. Sometimes the machine became human. While I was questioned by one, the other interrogated an Irish nurse. She found a small bottle of vitamin tablets in the nurse's purse. She didn't believe that they were vitamin tablets and made the girl take one. As the girl swallowed the tablet the grey-haired woman quickly over-turned the purse and spilled what was inside on to the table. The girl began to weep.

I walked down the sloping tunnel to a door, opened it, and immediately three men shouted out if I had my rail ticket. I told them I wasn't sure where I was going. Two ignored me and continued shouting to everyone who opened the door, while one insisted that I get a ticket for somewhere. I told him that I was going to fly across Canada on a flying pass. Did I have it? No. I would have to pick it up. He insisted that I get a ticket for somewhere. A young girl, ash blonde hair, a short fur jacket, came down the ramp. They asked her for her ticket. She said in broken English that she did not have enough money for a ticket to Toronto. They would not let her go by. The Irish doctor quickly passed the hat around until there was enough money for the girl. I told the man I would have to cash a traveller's cheque. He pointed to a wicket in the wall of the room.

I went to the counter. Two hands held stretched open a news-paper, legs on the table. I rapped with a coin. Nothing happened. 'Can you cash me a traveller's cheque?' Still no movement. Then slowly the paper was put down. He was a timid-looking man in a grey suit. Bald, stocky. Pink blotches in his face and on his neck. Underneath his eyes and chin were layers of creased skin making him look like some plucked fowl. He reached down and took out a small revolver from his desk, came to the wicket, placed the revolver on the counter in between him and myself.

'Now we can do business.'

I showed him my cheques.

He counted them, then examined them.

'Pound cheques. They're no good.'

I turned them over. On the back they were rubber-stamped valid in any country. He again picked them up with exaggerated slowness and reluctance. Finally he said, as a special favour to immigrants, he would give me a certain rate. I now understood the necessity for his performance. His rate was low, and I told him. He said he was giving me a better rate than any bank could. I didn't believe him, but I had to have some money. Later, in a bank in Ottawa, when I cashed another cheque I realized the profit he was making.

I waited in this room for the doctor and the Irish nurse and watched the three men shouting like outside barkers at a circus every time the glass door of the tunnel opened. It was now over three hours since I entered the drill hall.

One side of the room was partitioned off for several offices. Some sold railway tickets. Behind the others sat middle-aged women with blue ribbons pinned to their blouses and sweaters, as if they were pedigree cattle. They sat there, doing nothing, looking bored. Signs above them said that they were the representatives of the various churches in Canada. The only one who came out to meet the immigrants was a lay-sister in a grey habit. She asked me if I wanted a rosary. The doctor and the Irish nurse arrived. The lay-sister asked the nurse where she was going. The nurse said Quebec City. The sister said it was too bad that she was going there for it was full of French people.

Our first sign of welcome came after we left this room and as we were going down another ramp into a shed. Against a background of piled luggage and bewildered groups of tired immigrants, a pale, narrow-shouldered man in a shabby brown suit, trouser cuffs soiled from the slush, held out his hand, shook our hands, but said nothing. He gave each of us a sample box of corn flakes. And with the box a card written in four languages.

WELCOME TO CANADA, AND TO THE MANY GOOD THINGS IN IT

To introduce you to one of the very fine things this country offers, we are presenting you with this package of Kellogg's Corn Flakes—the world's favourite breakfast cereal. You'll find big packages of Kellogg's Corn Flakes (they're very thrifty) and other Kellogg grain cereals at grocery stores. Meantime, welcome and good luck.

He also gave us pamphlets that said a Bank welcomed us to Canada, a telephone company, and if we wanted to develop a Canadian habit we should buy certain patent medicines.

We were through. The doctor and the nurse and myself walked through the shed to the cafeteria at the far end of the building and had some coffee. Except for an old woman who sat behind the cash register, hunched over, knitting, and a thin colourless woman in a faded green uniform behind the counter, the cafeteria was deserted. It was warm. Outside by the window I could see the frozen sides of a train, snow thick on the roof and icicles hanging down from the edges. We didn't talk. We just sat there, smoked, and drank several cups of coffee.

BIOGRAPHY

He joined our table. He looked Syrian or Greek. A fat generous face, brown skin, full lips, nearly bald. But you could tell he was young. There was hardly a line in his face. He asked me if I ever went to Soho. I said I did. He said he used to work at the *Casa Pepe*. He was annoyed with himself for being seasick for the whole trip. The first day he found a young German girl. 'She would have been so easy to stuff. But I couldn't get out of my bunk to save me.' He cursed himself, he cursed the storm, he cursed the ship. He said he was born in Burma of Greek parents and had been moving about the world since he was seventeen. His plan was to come to Canada, to see what it was like, 'make a packet', then return to England in three or four years. 'Are you going back?' I said I was. He brought out a small blue notebook from his jacket. 'Then let me give you some addresses. None of these girls are over nineteen.' And he began to write in my notebook. Ann (redhead) and a Fremantle number. Very hot. He underlined hot. 'Molly is a nurse.' And he wrote down a Flaxman number. 'Moira, she's a sex maniac. I'll put down S.M. in brackets so you'll know.' He kept on going through his book. Maureen (blonde); Pam (air hostess); Peggy (model); Florence (hot), this one likes mirrors, you can bugger this one as well. Just feed them gin. That's all it takes. About four or five gins. Now do you want some queers . . . ?' Then the doctor and the Irish nurse came back with more cups of coffee.

*

I suggested that we go out for a meal. It had stopped snowing and the sun was out. We walked from the railway station on the road away from the slush, our breath smoking in the cold still air. At first I didn't feel the cold or notice the glare from the snow; but there was a sudden lack of tension between oneself and the outside. The sky seemed further away.

It was as if one had moved from a small, cramped, squalid, semi-detached house into a sprawling, full of light, empty, mansion. And there was a sharpness in seeing things, as in one of those transfers that one had as a child. Where you stuck the dull-coloured side to a piece of paper and then with spit you began to rub the back, peeling off thin grey flakes, so many dead skins, until you curled the last skin back and there it was fixed, a wet patch of gay colour. Only this time the colours were white, white-blue, grey, and black. And as we walked up the slushed slope towards the main street I suddenly felt the cold tighten across my forehead and the harsh glare from the snow. Then I noticed the silence. Not only as the absence of noise, or of smell, or the fact that few people were about. But everything appeared boarded up. It was as if some animal, a white enormous snake, had crawled in and filled up with its weight every possible surface, smothering and stunning all the life out of the place.

A church bell clanged somewhere. We continued to walk up the slope away from the railway station. Behind us gulls were wheeling over the docks, flakes chipped from a winter landscape.

We came to a main street. Churches and cemeteries beside traffic lights. Large gravestones sunk in the snow, entire fields sown with them. The dead, like a conscience, dominated the drab street with its small business stores and restaurants on the other side. The doctor and the nurse were busy window-shopping, comparing prices with those they left behind. I had forgotten one of the reasons why they had come.

We walked on until the stores ended ·then doubled back through frozen shabby side-streets. Whole streets were boarded up by the snow and the cold. It was a climate that rejected man. And yet I felt strangely at home in it. This is what one belonged to: the cold, the snow, the frozen emptiness.

I saw a sign off the main street, *Steak House*. We went down steps. A small rectangular room with three lines of booths; two on the sides against the walls, and one down the middle. On the floor were torn newspapers to soak up the slush and the dirt that the overshoes brought in. In the back, between swinging doors that went to the kitchen, a squat shiny, nickelodeon played loud. A couple of young boys in leather windbreakers and crew cuts stood beside the machine nodding their heads to the rhythm. The proprietor sat behind the cash register by the front door picking his teeth with a toothpick, a look of contempt for his customers. About half of the booths were occupied by young girls: stenographers and typists. They sat there slowly sucking cokes, drinking glasses of milk, coffee, and carefully eating pie with ice-cream and staring at the room and at each other with long empty stares.

We ordered steaks and French fried potatoes. And with it came the cold glass of water, the serviettes in the chromium holder, the nickelodeon selector on the wall, the toothpicks in the glass, the plastic table-top. The doctor and the nurse kept looking around the room. The nickelodeon boomed on. The heads beside it nodded. The stares continued in a kind of slow motion. The food came. We began to eat and to get warm. And for the first time since we left the ship they became talkative and relaxed. This was new, and they were not disappointed. I could feel the hardened blobs of chewing gum stuck underneath the table. And neither was I.

When we came out the slush on the sidewalk had frozen into hard crusts. We found our way slowly over the icy sidewalks to the railway station. But the train had gone. There wasn't another one until tomorrow morning. I telephoned T.C.A. and luckily my air pass had come through. I would be able to fly to Montreal later that night. But for the doctor and the nurse it meant spending the night in Halifax.

We began hunting for a hotel. The few large ones were either full up with conventions and business men, or else they were too expensive. They suggested that we try the smaller ones. These turned out to be converted houses in residential streets. We walked from one to the other. It was late afternoon. The harsh light and the cold made everything raw and hard and clear. Heavy-looking, plain houses with wooden verandas, snow heaped against them, a path cleared in the snow, enough for one person to reach the ice-covered steps, long icicles from the roof. Hard packed snow on the sidewalk and snowbanks between the road and the sidewalk and hardly anyone walking. A few cars went by with a clatter, chains on the back wheels; and cars stuck on the slopes, at the traffic lights, the back wheels spinning on the ice. We continued to walk from one small hotel to the other, getting colder and more discouraged and it was getting dark. The same icy wooden steps, the icicles above us as we rang the door-bell. The receptionist (inevitably a drab elderly woman) when she found out it was to be for a man and a woman, even though they asked for separate rooms, she became suspicious, said they were full up, or else made the price too high. Finally the doctor got a room in the Y.M.C.A. and the nurse one in the Y.W.C.A. In the street we met the Shamrock Queen and her mother. They were going to the airport to fly to New York to be certain of arriving in time for St. Patrick's Day Parade. The doctor and the nurse went to see them off. I was very tired and I went to the doctor's room to lie down.

I woke up feeling worse and shivering. I wasn't used to the sudden changes of temperature, the below-zero weather outside and the dry central heating in this room. And even though I had opened the inside window as high as I could and lifted the bottom slot open of the outside window, the room was stuffy and the air dry. My throat was sore. I felt flushed and I began to sneeze. I blamed it all on the shoe that I had got wet during the day walking in the slush. The sock was soaked and I didn't have another pair with me.

So I wandered around Halifax trying to find a clothing store open, but all the stores were shut. I returned to the Y.M.C.A. The doctor had not come back. I asked the young boy at the reception desk if he could tell me where I could buy a pair of socks. 'Try old Pop down the gym.' I went down to the basement and opened a door. There were strangers' laughter coming from the shower, youths in jockstraps, shorts, getting dressed, undressed; talking to each other. The smell of sweat, small patches of water on the floor. I asked for Pop and someone said: 'First door to the left.'

Behind a worn wooden counter sitting on a chair, timid, white haired, trying to fix a combination lock for a boy in a white sweatshirt and canary-coloured shorts. He was the Pop that I remembered. The one that never lets you down. Pop at school, Pop at the boys' club, at the university, loyal to every generation that passes through. And then at the end, the pen, the small cheque, an honorary member. But while he was there tears in his eyes every year at the annual dinner weeping unashamedly as we sang 'Lord dismiss us with thy blessing. Those of us who are gathered here.' And Pop wept because of some physical disability. I could see he had two fingers missing on his left hand.

He sold me a pair of white gym socks and I went back to the doctor's room, threw the old ones into the waste-paper basket, put these dry ones on. Then I went out to have something to eat. The street was silent and deserted. It was bitterly cold. I could feel the cold tight across my forehead and the tension in the empty street. The packed snow had a frozen crust that glittered and crunched as I walked. And the houses appeared even more boarded up, as if you would have to go through several layers before you found something living. Someone had made a long slide in the sidewalk and with a run I went down it. That helped. I could hear the whistle of a boat. The stars and the moon were out. And the intense cold seemed to have contracted everything, bringing the Atlantic and the frozen wastes of land to the west, even more convincingly close. Down the main street. The only people walking besides myself were two service police, army; then two more, navy. Young boys, tall, well built, their breath smoking in the cold air. At the cinema a girl stood inside the glass door, her face against the glass like a corpse. I went into the first small restaurant and had a couple of hamburgers and coffee. Several young boys in navy uniform were flirting with the girl behind the counter. I felt flushed and began to sneeze again. Two more cups of coffee and it was time to go to the hotel by the railway station, where a taxi would take me to the airport. I went to the payphone, on the wall, to ring up the doctor. It was out of order. Outside, back in the cold and deserted street, I felt like a vagrant. I took a bus in the direction of the hotel. When I got there a long black limousine was waiting with five silent men inside.

*

The firecracker exploded. Below my window behind the engine, coloured lights appeared as the aircraft banked over Halifax. I could pick out orange lights across a width of black— the bridge we went over—then white and red clusters. Not a true red but like a cheap technicolor film or the reflection of a café's neon in a rain puddle on the road. And black, black everywhere else, severing the coloured lights at their head, blacking out the snow, the cold, the emptiness of those streets. Click click click, the coat hangers jingle in the back, a domestic touch. Head aches. Would you like some coffee? An aspirin. And she takes the small white pillow from the chromium rack above my head and puts it on my knee and pours coffee from the pyrex pot into the cardboard cup with the cardboard handles. I burn my tongue. Then she comes round again: *Newsweek, Time, Reader's Digest, Life, Maclean's,* the Halifax paper. I take the paper, it is nineteen below. I read about the luxury cruise of the Irish . . . the roughest trip . . . two tons of shamrock in the hold . . . the engines drone on like a dentist's drill . . . it is completely black below . . . my foot goes to sleep . . . the coat hangers jingle . . . Molly is a nurse . . . a girl with no chin singing 'His grave is green but not with grass, And you'll never lie beside him' . . . it is completely dark below . . . *wie sagt man* . . . blobs of chewing gum.

STOP OVER

We landed in Montreal near midnight; a blizzard was blowing. I decided to get as quickly as I could to Ottawa, to my parents, and shake off whatever it was that I had caught, then plan and begin the journey. But there wasn't a flight out until tomorrow. I rang up Mrs. R. She had a rooming house in Westmount. I was grateful that her son in London had written to let her know that I was coming. She said that all the rooms were taken but that a Greek girl was away for a few days and I could sleep in her bed.

It was a narrow wooden house, high, undecorated, with a steep outside staircase, the steps icy and covered in snow. A secluded dead end street opposite a playing field and by the railway tracks. The house beside it was exactly the same, in the front window a sign ROOM TO LET. I knew this area, a kind of no man's land. It had a good address but it was hidden half way between the wealth of Westmount and a slum.

Mrs. R. was a small Jewish woman with a harsh nasal voice. She reminded me of a small bright bird; a sparrow. It didn't matter what she said she made it all sound like a comedian telling jokes. As long as she was talking she appeared confident. It was only when she was a listener that one noticed the vulnerability; the melancholy look in the eyes, the clumsiness of her generous gesture. She had placed on the kitchen table a leg of cold chicken and some sliced tomatoes; but I wasn't hungry. While I was telling her news of her son, a girl came in. Mrs. R. introduced her as Rosemary, the German girl from upstairs. She was in her middle twenties, straight blonde hair down to her shoulders, coarse features; she looked as if she had been used by other people. The face was pale, shy, defensive, and the generous body had started to lose its shape, her belly pushed out from the brown skirt that was too tight and too short. But one could feel immediately a heavy, lazy sensuality emanating from her. And with it an innocence, a kind of trust, that asked to be violated. She said she had arrived fifteen months ago from a small town in Southern Germany. Her only contacts, so far, were at night school. She said she didn't like Montreal, she wasn't meeting enough people. I started to cough again and they both became concerned. Rosemary, who spoke a broken English, said she knew a German recipe which was good for colds, fever and the grippe. Mrs. R. brought out lemons and honey and Rosemary made strong tea and then mixed all the ingredients together. It tasted hot and sour. Then another occupant of the house came into the kitchen. He was thick and graceless in a drab second-hand blue suit that was too small for him. He grunted good evening, the face unshaven, sullen, and fat. He went to the refrigerator, took some food from his allotted corner, grunted again and went out. Mrs. R. said he was a Latvian who had been with her for the past ten years. 'My boy friend, he can't leave me,' she said and laughed without much amusement. 'He's got only one passion in life and that's food. He'll keep stuff under his bed that's so rotten it's growing things. And the stink when I open his door. But . . .' and the shrug that followed, the hunched narrow shoulders, said eloquently, that's the way of the world : 'He's always first with the rent.' I could hear a gramophone playing in the room next to the kitchen and a distant squeaky voice : 'When the sun has gone to rest, That's the time that we love best' . . . 'That's Frank,' Mrs. R. said. 'He's a mechanic with an aircraft factory and he gets records and papers sent over from Scotland. The guy's been over here two years and he's still home-sick.' We listened to Harry Lauder coming through the thin wooden partition. Rosemary stood awkwardly by the sink, then with a shy sleepy smile said goodnight and went upstairs. As soon as she had gone Mrs. R. told me that Rosemary had just had an illegitimate child, that she was anti-Semitic, that she had no job, and was broke. 'I'm sure that if our roles were reversed and she was in my shoes and I was in hers she would have kicked me out long ago.' How easy it is to tell recommended strangers intimate details of one's life when you know there's no responsi-bility to be faced. We talked on. She told me of her operations, showed me the gallstones kept in a small glass jar; that she used to work in a nightclub but now was working in a respectable clothing store 'for a couple of gangsters'. Then another person came in shaking the snow off his coat and hair. He was young and aggressive, tall with curly black hair, too well dressed and an easy confident smile that said he was not to be trusted. He was a French-Canadian from a small town in the Gaspé, working in the Government, and he stood inside the doorway of the kitchen combing the snow out of his hair and looking in the mirror. He occupied the best room in the house. Mrs. R. had slowly retreated with all her possessions from three rooms, to two rooms, until now she lived in the front room which she kept locked. The French-Canadian and Mrs. R. kept up a small talk, flattering one another. He had just come back from a date. Mrs. R. said:

'How did it go?'

'All right but she was no chicken.'

'Was it Lucille?'

'No, she was busy tonight.'

Then he appeared to lose interest in what he was saying.

'You like this suit? I got it last week.'

It was a black drape with scratches of silver thread in it and thin lapels. Mrs. R. said she liked it.

'I got twelve other suits, thirty-six shirts, ninety-two ties, nine pair of shoes.'

He was reluctant to leave the kitchen and kept talking about himself, about films he had seen during the week, about movie-star scandals. He just stood there in the doorway, not knowing how to go. While Mrs. R. humoured him, I took four aspirins and went to bed. But I couldn't sleep.

I couldn't shake off the crossing. Every time I lay down I began to feel the pitch and the roll of the ship. I tossed and sweated. Suddenly I felt cold. I searched the room and found one of the Greek girl's sweaters. I put it on. The stale smell of someone else's sweat wasn't unpleasant. But it was too small. And it didn't seem to help.

DEFINITIONS

I woke up next morning restless and flushed. I looked out of the window. It was still snowing. My plane to Ottawa wasn't until late afternoon. I planned to return later to Montreal, on my way back, and stay here for some time. Now, I didn't want to see anyone I knew. So I rang up an official in the Montreal Board of Trade. I had promised a young army officer in Cornwall that I would go and see this man to see if he could help him get a job. He wanted to leave England. He had just had an unfortunate experience. His girl friend had left him for someone else who had more money and who had attended a better, minor, public school.

I wasn't in the man's office ten minutes before he began to lecture me on Canada. What did I mean by living away when Canada needed all her writers at home? I was in no mood for a sermon. And I thought I would gradually change the subject by asking him what did those advertisements BE A GOOD CANADIAN mean, put out by Seagrams. I had seen them again this morning on the streetcar. Before, they had a green parrot saying these words, now there were pictures of smiling bank-managers, smiling farmers, smiling salesmen. He stood up as if he was going to make a public speech. But he was betrayed by his physical presence: the round plump face, the glasses, the weak eyes, pink like a mouse, and the pot belly making his trousers seams fan out as if he was smuggling something inside. 'A Good Canadian is one who sees that he earns enough money . . .' The voice drawled slowly on full of small-town wisdom, . . . 'so that he is able to do the same things and live the same kind of life and maintain the standard of living that his friends are enjoying.'

I remember a night in 1944 in the blackout. Walking down Shaftesbury Avenue towards Piccadilly. Stopped by a voice in the doorway of a shop: 'Can you give me a light?' The match flares. She sees your face. You see hers. She noticed the Canada flashes on my shoulders. 'Canadians.' She laughed good-humouredly. 'Nothing but big cocks and dirty underwear.'

*

Coming out at the Place d'Armes I met by chance P. (So much happens by chance that I wonder if that isn't what makes the pattern of one's life.) P. suggested that we take a taxi and go to the Press Club in the Mount Royal Hotel where we could have a drink. We used to share a room during our first year at McGill, a dismal, sour-smelling house in Prince Arthur Street run by an untidy ginger-haired woman, a Catholic with a wastrel of a son, on whom she doted, and who had the habit of urinating in the kitchen sink whenever he found the toilet occupied.

We drank brandy and talked about what we had done during the last seven years. He had joined the C.B.C., had put on weight,

married, three children, a small house in a suburb, a small car.
He said he would have to leave in an hour to interview a general
about the Canadian army. I asked him about his poetry. He had
written free-verse poems as an undergraduate which were published in the university's literary magazine. 'I don't even read
poetry today,' he said quietly.

That was one of the things I liked about him. He was never a
phoney. At the time when those who came to McGill after the
war, without money or family influence, and ruthlessly began to
charm, to sell themselves, P. never quite fitted in. All he had
wanted was to continue in the Academy. He would have been
happy with his slippers, the pipe, the glass of beer, the fire going,
and books on all the walls: an insignificant lecturer in some
provincial university in the States. But that passed him by. He
needed a higher degree, and to get that he needed a Fellowship,
and you don't get a Fellowship on second-class honours unless
you have cultivated the right references. We talked about people
we knew. Then the conversation lagged. Both of us were reminders of something we had betrayed in ourselves. Or perhaps
one had merely become faithful to a new set of experiences.

And then after several minutes when the conversation had
tried several subjects without much enthusiasm, and there were
silences, I wondered if he was thinking along the same lines
as I was, remembering bits and pieces: the drinking bouts and
the talk in the Shrine, writing poetry in that sour-smelling room,
discussing life, swotting up before an exam with benzedrine that
the medical student upstairs gave us, then walking very clear-
headed through Montreal to the top of the Mountain at five in
the morning and watching the sun rise, taking the girl upstairs
to the abortionist on Park Avenue, then later reading in the
paper how the doctor was caught in another case and hanged,
telephoning late at night, 'I'm here and I've run out of money',
then getting dressed and coming over with what was left of the
Government monthly cheque. The confidences, the worries, the
ambitions, the lies, the things one loved, one hated, one feared,
that one confided . . . and now we had nothing to say to each
other. 'When we met this morning,' he said, 'I'd just come back
from my mother's funeral. Not that it was a sad occasion, for
she'd been an invalid for as long as I can remember. But it does
mean the end of something, and I can never take that easily.'

After he had gone I sat there drinking brandy and not enjoying it. I vaguely hoped that the brandy would help to get rid of
the hot and shivering sensations. I remembered how I stopped a

cold once in London with a half-bottle of Hennessy; besides
there was nothing else to do. I still had over an hour to wait
before I could take the limousine from the front part of this
hotel to the airport. The room was deserted. The barman looked bored. A figure
whom I hadn't noticed before came over to where I was sitting
with a glass in his hand: grey hair, crew cut, overweight, bow
tie, rimless glasses. He looked too much of a type that one sees
but does not notice.
'You don't look well,' he said.
'I don't feel well.'
'Have you had the treatment?'
I held up my glass with brandy in it.
'No, not that. I've got something better. Follow me.'
I followed him to the bar. He told me to face the narrow wall
which was hidden in shadow to the left of the bar. 'Closer,' he
said. 'It won't bite you.'
I waited. I didn't know what to expect. Then lights went on
and the wall, a few inches from my face, was lit up with enor-
mous breasts, nipples, buttocks, legs, shaved groins.
'Pretty good,' he smiled.
'Pretty good,' I said.
I returned to my seat. He followed.
'I've got something else that helps to give me a pick-up when
I feel down. And if you don't mind my saying so you look pretty
down to me.'
He brought out a black pen, pulled off the handle; inside the
glass tube, in some liquid, was a nude rubber girl about two
inches long. He tilted the pen as if it was a seesaw and the girl
opened and closed her legs. Then from his coat pocket he took
out a nutcracker; the two handles were made out of wood and
shaped as a pair of girl's legs. He took out a hazel nut and put
it between the legs and gave the cracker to me. 'Go on crack it!
It's no good just holding it. You gotta crack it; you'll feel better.'
When I came out the fresh air hit me and I felt drunk. The
snow was coming down thick and the wind made it slant. A
tight feeling of pressure in my head. I did not want to close my
eyes. When I did, I felt everything turning. I kept them open
and saw the snowflakes. I could see no sky, no buildings, only the
white falling from the grey, falling silent around me and on me.
I walked to the corner and went into Ben's to have a smoked-
meat sandwich. The man behind the counter cutting the meat
was without eyebrows; I remembered him. From Ben's I went

out again. The snow was falling wet and thick. I began to lose all sense of direction. I felt as if I was skiing down a steep hill in a blinding snowstorm at Fairy Lake, then a sick sensation in my stomach of falling through space as in an aircraft just as it stalls. Later, I realized that I had hardly moved but had stood unsteadily in front of the Mount Royal looking up at the sky which I still could not see, for the wet snowflakes kept pelting down soundlessly on to my eyes.

Of the drive to the airport, the flight to Ottawa, the drive to my parents, I can remember very little: the sinister look of cars coming out of the snow, the fixed black eyes, the driver of ours continually stopping and going out to clean the snow from the windshield even though the wipers were going steadily; warm inside, the smell of burning tobacco; a sleigh (with a wooden box on it) harnessed to a dog standing on the sidewalk of a street in N.D.G. and a boy in a Montreal Canadian sweater delivering newspapers from the box. The other passengers, two men, well dressed in black, tailored winter coats, homburgs, angora scarves, both smoking cigars. One is reading *Time*. 'Ron, did you see that sign? It says "The Fastest Car Wash in The World".' 'Where was it?' 'Back along Decarie.' 'Remind me to give them a try next week.' And the loneliness of the airport. The wind blowing the snow across the runways. Ground staff in parkhas, hoods up like frozen monks, by the abandoned tractors. The long, light corridor. The taxistrips with the young evergreens and the brilliant blue light beside each tree at the base. A blue dominating the entire winter landscape like in those miniatures that are kept in glass cases in the British Museum with the small curtains across. Then along the frozen canal, the trees like snakes, white snakes devouring the black. Back along familiar frozen streets. By the school. My parents. Home, food, drink, and quickly to bed.

I
OTTAWA

LOWER TOWN

ONLY it wasn't a bed. My parents had rented the spare room and I lay on the chesterfield in the living-room inside a folded sheet in my dead uncle's maroon pyjamas, expensive New York dressing-gown, and blankets, feet over the end. My mother called the family doctor. He thought I had some kind of pneumonia virus that I would get over in a couple of weeks. A couple of weeks was too long. In any case I didn't have much confidence in him. He was short, plump; a well-fed baby face. Charm with him was automatic. The only thing not in keeping was his voice, which was clear and resonant—you expected it to come with a larger body, a different person. Whenever he spoke I thought of a ventriloquist who had carelessly picked up the wrong dummy. 'So you've become a writer,' he said. Getting old did not show many cracks, only around the eyes; the hollows were in permanent shadow. 'Didn't someone say that writers are like doctors, only interested in sick people?' 'Yes. And somebody else has also said,' I replied, 'that the important thing is not be cured but to live with one's ailments.' I didn't feel like talking. He did. He went on about England: wartime England, a few hospitals, a few leaves in London, the Lake District; did I know Aldershot, the Cumberland Hotel, Warrington? He asked me what I thought of socialized medicine. I said it was a good thing. He said it was bound to come to Canada, but he hoped not in his lifetime. I hadn't seen him for over fifteen years and this was the longest conversation we ever had. 'I remember your room with those Beehive hockey pictures,' he said. 'Primeau, Jackson, Conacher, Sweeney Schriner, King Clancy . . . you had them all over your wall. You told me then you wanted to be a professional hockey player.'

I remembered him coming to see my sister. After examining her, he gave her a large bar of chocolate for being 'a good girl'. When he had gone we went up to her room. She gave me a piece

38

of the chocolate and ate the rest. Not long after I watched the
long, thin, white-yellow worms come out of her mouth, like
pieces of living spaghetti, and lie slowly twisting on the floor.
For the next five days I tossed and sweated on the chesterfield
in the living-room.

*

My parents had moved from the house I knew to this top-
floor apartment. In this small room, lying on the chesterfield
against the back wall and connected to the dining-room and
through there to the kitchen—I had an observation post of the
entire flat and to the street below. I could see anyone who
opened the front door. There was the television set against the
wall opposite me, the two chairs in front, part of the chesterfield
set, a bookcase by the TV with a few pre-war Book-of-the-Month
Club selections supported by two glass unicorns. The room was
stuffy, the air dry. Even when I opened the slots of the outside
windows and turned off the radiators. And if I opened the balcony door the wind blew the loose snow into the room. A rubber
plant stood in a large clay pot by the balcony almost touching
the ceiling. A stick was sunk in its earth, the stalk tied to the
stick in several places by torn pieces of linen. It had been with
us as long as I can remember. The bottom leaves had begun to
shrivel and turn brown. I can hear the insistent muffled sound
of the refrigerator coming from the kitchen, then silence, and
you wait expectantly for it to begin. It does. And you find yourself seriously playing this game trying to guess when the next
silence will come or the next hum. Above me on the wall was a
water-colour of St. Ives. A friend of the family moving from
Ottawa to California gave this picture to my parents. The sketch
was done from the Malakoff looking down to the harbour. It's
a picture postcard of a hot summer's day looking down to the
harbour, and the cottages going away from the front. 'A lot of
teeth, false teeth, without a face, one set behind the other; when
the sun comes out you can see the gaps between and the per-
petual grin.' And yet it seemed so absurd. Coincidence always
shows up the absurd like some cruel joke. That in this room with
only one painting it should be of this particular fishing village
where I had lived for most of my time in Cornwall. I told this
to my parents. It did not really interest them. Their curiosity
was confined to what is local; what they can be part of. Neither
they nor the owner knew what the watercolour was. It was just
decoration; it had no title. Around six in the morning when it is
still dark Harry quietly opens the door. The passage light shines

on the outside mat of the flat opposite. On the disorder of rubbers, galoshes, the plastic overshoe coverings like used contra-
ceptives that women wear to protect them from the slush. Then
he shuts the door and I can hear him in the lavatory before he
goes to his room. Harry had a room with us in the old house
and when my parents moved Harry moved as well. I remember
as a child sneaking into his bare room when he was out, the iron
bed, the green chest of drawers, a sour smell of soiled clothes;
and looking at his stamps that he kept jumbled up in an old
cigarette tin. He still has an asthmatic cough. He works behind
a sandwich counter in a small café that is open all night. He
hardly speaks. He looks bloated. He sleeps until noon. I can see
the street, silent, empty, frozen. Low roofs, snow lying thick on
top, icicles hanging along the edges. Lumber in a backyard. An
old truck without wheels lies buried in the snow beside the lumber. Against the sky the stone cross of the Catholic church on
St. Patrick Street. At night it is outlined by pink neon tubes.
And throughout the day and part of the night the sound of
train whistles. Only it was not a whistle. It sounded like the
bass part of a mouth organ; two notes repeated and held. And
somewhere else it was answered. The same deep mournful chord.
A cross between a foghorn and an organ. And it brought back
more than anything else the inarticulate loneliness and the
emptiness of this place.

*

All day visitors have come. Mrs. Pleet is an attractive small
woman, a widow, with bright dark eyes and black straight hair
of which she is proud. She has a large house. All the rooms are
rented to recent immigrants. She sleeps in the living-room on
the couch with her possessions: the samovar, the silver pestle
and mortar, the silver candlesticks, old photographs, and the
embroidered cushions of large flower petals. She came over from
Berlin in the 1930's. We talked about London. For a year she
had lived in a street off the Gloucester Road before coming to
Ottawa. She spoke nostalgically about Sunday afternoons in
Kensington Gardens hearing the band, watching the children,
the dogs, the expensive prams pushed by nannies. When I asked
her if she wanted to return to Berlin. 'What have I got there?'
she said. 'Nothing but graves. I left graves behind. You don't
worry about graves too long.'

Mr. Morgensterren has been a fruit pedlar until a year ago,
when a car ran into him and paralyzed his left arm. Because of
this accident he now has a steady income for the rest of his life.

He lives with his son and daughter-in-law in Westgate; but his friends are down here. He comes down on Sunday afternoons. 'I want action,' he said. 'I come all the way down here for some action.' Then the four of them sit around the dining-room table and have a quiet game of casino. Mr. Morgensterren is short and bald with a sad clown's face, a spare body. Whenever he speaks he shouts and begins to act. He likes to tell stories against himself. How he arrived in the Union Station in 1921, with a yellow label tied around his neck. How someone who met him, from a Benevolent Society, gave him a small leather case with shoelaces and boxes of matches and told him to go from street to street knocking on doors. The only English words he was told were: Please. Two for a nickel. Thank you. No change. Then he acted out what happened when a bottle of ketchup was placed before him for the first time. He drank it. But there was no humour when he put his good hand into his trousers pocket and drew out some dollar bills and went around the room introducing them to everyone as 'My friend, Uncle George.' He slapped the dollar bills. 'My best friend Uncle George.'

Then there was Capello. He was a rags pedlar. He also knew something about horses, so that if anyone had anything wrong with their animal they got hold of Capello who came with a stomach pump and saltpetre. He rode through the suburban streets with his horse and wagon. Bed springs, mattresses, rags, sacks, bottles, were piled behind him. And as he went slowly from street to street he sang in Italian, cursing the street, the country, the people. 'Thieves. Thieves. Nothing but a bunch of thieves live here . . .'

*

I like the lower towns, the place across the tracks, the poorer streets not far from the river. They represent failure, and for me failure here has a strong appeal. On my first day out I walked along St. Patrick Street. Slush, mud, streetcar tracks on the road. And slush and snow and mud on the sidewalk. Between the sidewalk and the road, low hard grey-black snowbanks. Every time a car or a truck went by it splashed the dirty melted water from the road on to the sidewalk. It was strangely quiet, flat, and drab. The only optimistic patches were the large billboards standing on stilts in the vacant lots with their doll faces and yard-long smiles advertising soft drinks, cars, cigarettes, and shoe polish. Sometimes a large gaily-painted car, or a truck, drove by, crunching the snow and the slush and splashing water. Or a red streetcar, like a mechanical goose, swayed along the tracks. Otherwise it looked like a cemetery; only it was second-hand, washed out. And the drabness was heightened by the intensity of the harsh light and the freshness of the air that I could feel cold in my throat.

The houses were not built to last. The owners who lived away did not trouble about repairs for the rents were too low. And those who lived here and owned their houses had moved in too late. They were run down, sinking in the ground. Solemn boxes with wooden verandas. A dull brown dark green broken by a narrow yard that widened as it skirted behind the house. Then another repetition of wooden veranda and shabby box. I saw two houses in no worse condition than those beside it being pulled down beside a filling station to make room for a second-hand car market. There was no outward sign of possession or pride. A few had their outside walls painted so that the wood looked like imitation bricks. But the paint had worn off. There was a bit of land, in front, separating the veranda from the sidewalk. Around this bit were the small green boiler pipes for railings. And inside the railings, an old boiler, part of its centre cut out for a flower box, rested on a pair of rough wooden trestles, all smothered in snow. Some houses had in their front rooms a grocery, a tailor, a laundry, a barber shop, Chez Maurice ('no free reading'). While in the back, behind the curtain, lived the family. You could tell these houses by the tin signs nailed to their sides or hanging on a piece of iron, creaking in the wind, giving the name of the owner and advertising Pepsi-Cola, Sweet Caporal, Alouette, Kik. Most of the signs were in French.

Towards the river. Down King Edward Avenue. Black trees in the middle, their branches dripping. Dirty snowbanks around the trees. The best place to walk was on the road. At the corner of Guigues there was a large three-storey red brick house, squatting, very ugly. A *Chambre à Louer* sign nailed to the outside door. The double windows were few and small so that the massiveness of the brick was exaggerated. It looked like a house afraid of the light. On a slope between the side of the house and the sidewalk were two tin-covered wooden doors lying flat on the ground. They lead to the cellar. I remembered how I used to slide on these doors in winter. And skate in between the trees of the Boulevard after a rain when it froze at night and the ice weighed the trees over until the branches touched the ground like enormous silver brooms; if a wind came along it set them crackling. Now I could hear only French around me. On another street a house was practically smothered by the snow. News-

papers covered up empty windows. Rocking chairs on the verandas were thawing out. And parked in front of these drab
wooden shacks were the large bright cars with the huge back
fins with three sets of tail lights.

By the small park, the sour tunnel, the Black Bridge, the river
was frozen hard. Trees were black. The snow piled high in the
park made the green benches small and sunken. All around
the snow was thawing, losing its whiteness and its solidarity. The
surface texture was that of a watermelon flesh, only black and
dirty as if someone had blown coal dust across. Boys in windbreakers and flying boots walked by. Some children were playing with alleys in front of a veranda. Three others dressed
warmly in winter helmets stood on the road. One of them was
counting out

> My mother and your mother
> Were hanging out the clothes.
> My mother gave your mother
> A punch in the nose.
> What colour was the blood?

The finger pointed, a child replied. White.

> W-H-I-T-E spells white and you
> Are straight out of this here game.

Then I came back by the frozen river, passed the convent, the
iceyards, the Good Shepherd Laundry, water running from the
roofs. Crossed over drab St. Patrick Street, by the Catholic
church, the French supermarket; and I was back to where one
had grown up.

*

A letter from Morocco: You ask why I left Canada. Well, in the
first place, I think I left for the sake of a change. As far as I can
remember I intended to return and settle, and then I gradually
forgot about it. Any emotional feelings or ties I had to Canada
were to various small regions, but I had become attached to other
small regions where I was, and these counted more for being near-
by. On the whole, I don't think Canada ever excited any warm or
patriotic feelings in me; perhaps it did once when I was a child,
but the feelings died easily. In general it was just a thing that
issued postage stamps and dollar bills, and set up customs offices
next to American customs offices. Mind you, I have no rancour,
I don't feel that Canada has cheated me of anything, I feel quite
kindly disposed towards it. But I find that in the place where I
am expected to have patriotic feelings there is a little void. This
is an entirely personal deficiency, and has nothing to do with
Canada: I have discovered many such little voids in myself as I

have grown older, and I don't expect other people to have them as well. But when I go back to Canada, and I hear people waxing enthusiastic over the country (generally, when I am there, a little bit aggressively, with little glances out of the corners of their eyes challenging me to contradict them) the same kind of yawn comes over me as when someone tells me about his stamp collection. Then, on a purely practical level, the climate is atrocious, except for a few months of the year, and there is absolutely nothing one can do in Canada, except go fishing, that one can't do better, or more profitably, or more comfortably, or more easily, elsewhere.

Most people live in the country they were born in because it is much easier for them to do so. The problems of language, and earning a living in a foreign country are generally insuperable for the great mass of people unless they are forced out by famine or wars, etc. Moreover, most people are conservative, and prefer their national customs, their national dishes—their culture, in a word. For my part, most of these difficulties of moving don't exist. I enjoy learning foreign languages and I have a personal predilection towards the exotic. And coming from a country which has no culture (ours is still a mixture of other cultures which hasn't fused into anything separate, and the elements of the mixture are principally Anglo-Saxon and Scotch, hence rather dreary) it is perhaps easier for me to find myself at home quickly in a new culture. And since the world is still reasonably large and reasonably various, it is obvious that a rootless person such as myself, if he looks about for a while, will find somewhere that suits his personal taste better than the place where, through no choice of his own, he was born.

Then there is another, purely personal reason (I guess there are a million more, of varying degrees of importance) why I don't seriously intend ever to live in Canada. It represents my childhood. And I can trace innumerable actions, likes and dislikes to a revulsion against my childhood.

MURRAY STREET

It looks much the same as the streets beside it. The same dull shabby boxes with wooden verandas and the walls so thin that you can hear every word that the neighbour says. The dung-yards frozen hard in winter and crawling in summer with white maggots from the wooden manure boxes; the gloom from the warm smelling horsestables; the rats; the washing lines.

It cuts right through Lower Town. At one end is Anglesea Square (a treeless, grassless, dusty playground); the Bishop's Palace with the young priests pacing up and down the stone porch; the two Catholic schools. East of the Square is a small park. Opposite the park, a large barn, the end of a streetcar line. Not much further is the Rideau River. At the other end of the street, past the synagogue, the Boulevard, are the wooden shacks, the poor French, the rough taverns. This end of the street ends the same as the other with a park and a river. And clustered near it is the centre of Ottawa the tourist knows: the Chateau Laurier, the Parliament Buildings, the By Ward Market, and the Basilica.

As a child and a young man Murray Street was 'home'. Not the entire street, but the one block next to Anglesea Square where most of the fruit and vegetable and rag pedlars of Ottawa lived.

'Good morning, Jake.'

'Good morning.'

'Cloudy outside?'

'Yes, it certainly is cloudy all right.'

'Are you using the sleigh or wagon?'

'Sleigh.'

'Snow will be all gone from Bank Street.'

'There will be enough, besides my wagon's stuck. I took a look at it this morning. It's frozen up to the rim in ice.'

'We can pour water, hot water on it.'

'There's too much snow inside, and I'd have to grease her again. I'm using the sleigh.'

'Nadolny and Pollack are using wagons.'

'I'm still going to use the sleigh.'

He said this with a note of finality. He took a crushed cigarette.

'How is your wife today?'

'Not too bad. She is very tired these days.'

'It is the cold.'

'Yes, it is the cold. She should be down in Arizona. The doctor said the climate is better and cleaner. But it costs money and she doesn't want to leave the children.'

'She doesn't have to be away long.'

'Long enough for the cold to go by. At night I can hardly fall asleep. She starts to cough and cough from her stomach just like old L'Appotive laughs and gets red in her face and makes a noise when she takes in air. I run downstairs and get her a piece of bread. Her face is still red . . . and she coughs and coughs . . .'

'Doesn't the bread help?'

'Sometimes.'

'Can't you send her away for a short time?'
'It costs money and you have to make out papers.'
'Money.' He said this philosophically.
'And now there's to many pedlars. It seems that everyone who can buy a horse and a wagon becomes a pedlar.'
He finished his cigarette.
'Care for a game of casino?'
'No. I have to go and clean the sleigh.'
He got up.
'Think Charlie will be in with the potatoes? He gave me an extra bag last time.'
'Did you tell him?'
'No. He makes enough money as it is.'
'But he is a good man.'
'One of the most honest you can find.'
'But like all farmers, dumb.'
'Like all farmers.'
'Goodbye, Jake, see you in the market.'
'It's still cloudy outside. I suppose it will snow.'

*

Yet at the start they knew nothing about fruit, vegetables, rags, or horses. They were shopkeepers, small business men, scholars. They came at the beginning of the century, driven out by persecution, from Poland and from the provincial towns and villages of Eastern Europe. From the very beginning it was a question of survival. It did not take much money to buy a secondhand horse, a secondhand harness, a wagon, from one of the dairies or bakeries. Then in the market a couple of bags of potatoes from a farmer and whatever fruit was in season. And you rode through the city streets not knowing the language, knocking on doors with your basket of samples; or else just shouted out one's presence.

And they remained pedlars. They were kept down by the indifference of the outside community and by their own inability to make contact with it. Instead of self-pity, they joked, they cursed, they rode their wagons through the streets playing schoolboy games amongst themselves, making bets who would be first home or at a certain café, or raced through the streets with their empty wagons at night. And they had their religion. Most of them were Jewish, a few Catholic. Religion did not end in the bare synagogue with the small badly painted Zodiac around the front of the women's balcony. It was there in the

drab houses, the rich food, the smells, the candles, and also in
the street. I remember a service by the river. Twenty men standing in a late autumn afternoon in the park, by the shore, sil-
houetted against the sky. The muddy water passed by and under
the Black Bridge, the Hebrew Chant, the sound of birds and
frogs, bulrushes, leaves, sky. As a child one did not understand
or as yet question; but this felt right. And then at Corpus Christi
the Catholic procession through the streets. The men and women
on the sidewalk kneeling and crossing themselves as the white
canopy with the golden embroidered edges was carried by, the
cross held underneath. And in front and behind the small girls
in communion dresses, their Hail Marys going through them
like a wind through a wheatfield. While those on the wooden
verandas, behind the lace curtains, watched in silence.

There was no pretence about them. They had little ambition.
They lived life instinctively. They didn't belong to Ottawa or
to Canada; they never fitted in. It was Lower Town and Murray
Street where their lives were; the place was like a village. But I
doubt if there was anyone in the city who knew the streets of
Ottawa physically as well as these men. They were out in all
weather. I remember seeing my father's hands in winter; the
skin was hard and split open in several places by the cold.

But their wives were different. It was she who was bored staying behind at home looking at the street through lace curtains.
It was she who nagged, who worried about the practical side of
life. And it was the wife who goaded on the man to give up the
horse and wagon for a truck; to make money, to move away
from Murray Street to a better district. And the men reacted
instinctively to this by taking longer to go through the streets,
coming later home. Then they ran away from home and got
together in a room and played cards.

The sleigh changed to the wagon and back again. A horse
died. It was replaced by another secondhand one. While they
waited for their children to grow up. But their sons and
daughters betrayed them.

It began at school, where learning took a secondary place to
that of moulding one to want to belong to 'the outside'; not to
Lower Town, or Sandy Hill, or New Edinburgh, but to something larger and anonymous. And this was repeated in the newspapers, in the films, on the radio and in school. I can still remember those afternoons when we had to go up to the front of the
class, in turn, and pretend we were selling something: a car, a
washing machine, a house, while our teacher criticized our

technique. To 'get on' meant turning one's back on Lower Town
and the values it represented.

And the sons and daughters moved away from Murray Street
and began to cover up their tracks. They changed their names.
They charmed. They imitated. Lower Town was failure. Their
parents were failures. And their own success was doomed by the
reminder of failure that they carried with them.

*

Letter from Israel: For me the most striking thing about Murray
Street was the manner in which our Jewishness managed to isolate
and insulate us from the usual qualities of a lower-class, near-
slum neighbourhood. The drunkenness, wife-beating, poverty, ill-
ness, drabness, the lack of meaningful ceremonial, of cultural
artifacts—we felt and heard these things in the dimmest and
most fragmentary of ways. Our identification was simply not with
the non-Jewish aspects of the street: on the contrary, it was the
patriarchial set-up of our tight-knit Jewish family pattern, the
religion, festival, synagogue which emphasized our apartness,
gave us our values, sensitized us to our isolation and to the cultural
values by which we could overcome the street. If Hashomer
Hatzair was a cry against our families, it was also a positive shout
against a society which our Jewishness primarily prevented us
from identifying with. It wasn't our poverty (and we really weren't
so badly off) that separated us from the community; it was our
Jewishness. For me at any rate this seems to be the determining
factor in my relations not only with the Street but with life in
general.

*

Now. A pair of eyes look out from behind double windows,
lace curtains, at the empty street, out of habit. For there are no
horses, no sleighs. The few old men who still live here look sick
and tired. They sit on the wooden verandas bundled up in heavy
coats and scarves and caps, or else inside by the stove in the
kitchen, asleep. Most of them still have to work. Too weak to
peddle they go on as nightwatchmen, or else sweep up store
floors after closing. What I admired about them, their gaiety,
their jokes, their obscenities, their ability to lash out instinctively
at life, their gesture of going against the grain, was gone. And
it left in its place a doddering uncertainty. They mumbled about
the success that their children were having. But you could see
by their insistence, the repetition of the same words—'wonderful job', 'getting ahead', 'doing well', that they didn't understand. A community that human injustice had thrown together
was breaking up: by dying out. And those who replace them—

the immigrants since 1945—come to Lower Town better
equipped. They are old hands at survival. The black market, the
camps, have done their work. Murray Street is only a stopping-
off place for them; one of many. In a few years they will have
forgotten that they were ever here. And it is also made easier for
them by the rootlessness and the restlessness, which has drained
the Lower Town of its young and left behind these husks of men
and women. They have lost something. Something that one, too
late, understood and valued. And now, from here, it is gone.

That evening I began to plan my journey. I would remain in
Ottawa another few days then set out westwards to Sault Ste
Marie and from there go into the bush, then to Winnipeg,
Saskatoon, Edmonton and northwards. Then west to Vancouver,
Victoria, the interior of British Columbia. The return crossing
would be through the cities along the southern part of Canada,
through Montreal and Quebec. I had already realized that the
more difficult places to write about would be the places I knew.
While those I hardly knew, or had never seen, would be com-
paratively easy. The quick impression is always safe. There is
nothing there to destroy, or to betray, or to feel any sense of loss.

BIOGRAPHY

The catcher's mitt, the fingers like a webbed foot; pitching
strikes and balls over a plate marked in the sand with a stick.
Selling exhibition tickets on Sparks Street opposite Zellers: 'Six
for a dollar, mister.' Going for blotters and bookcovers before the
school year started. Heney's coal always gave, so did Hope's the
bookstore and Trudel's hardware. . . .

Slapping our sides as we galloped in the backyard. The warm
smell from the stables. I'm Tom Mix. I'm Ken Maynard. I'm
Buck Jones. I'm Hoot Gibson. I'm Bob Steele. Firing over the
bales of hay, the parked winter sleighs, sprawling by the fence
with the wild cucumbers growing, then coming out of the yard
into the open with our peashooters and elastic-firing guns to hide
behind the Morning Glories hanging down the sides of the
veranda or behind the Four O'clock hedges inside the front
garden. . . .

Ivy and Virginia creepers on the grey stone school building;
handball in the square; putting up the wooden boards for the
hockey rink, flooding it, then scraping off the snow. Ketcherson
throwing chalk; Matthews running his hand up your leg and
teaching us Gilbert and Sullivan songs, English folk songs, negro

D

spirituals, that we sang in the Chateau Laurier, for the Rotarians and Chamber of Commerce luncheons. Miss Owen reading us poems from Pauline Johnson, *The Song My Paddle Sings*, and weeping as she read. In the elocution class Miss MacDonald pushing up her breasts, while we chanted

> The north wind doth blow
> And soon we'll have snow
> And what will the robin do then poor thing?

Then back to the house. To the large plate of Lutkas; the stone jar of sour cucumbers with the large stone on top in the summer kitchen; the barrels of apples, the fruit in season, the leaky ice-box. Cold Putscha in winter with the sliced hard-boiled eggs frozen in it, sucking the hot juices out of the bones the night before. Chopped egg and onions, chopped liver, greeben, with the white, black, and rye bread. The wonderful food smells of a Friday night. Watching my mother pluck the chicken that I had seen have its throat cut, singe the skin, then open it up and leave the flesh and bones to salt overnight, drawing out the blood, on the wooden bushel-cover by the sink. The taste of cold gefülte fish on a Saturday morning. Going to the synagogue. The men in their element, in their best clothes, relaxed, playing games : lifting up seat covers, passing the snuff around, tickling each other on the back of the neck with the fringe of the prayer-shawl, that would later be their shroud; losing their tempers as they bid for the *aleeahs*; the private arguments shouted out so that everyone could hear; Cantor Baker looking like King George V and singing out of the side of his twisted mouth. And once looking when I was cautioned not to—'You might go blind'—and seeing about a dozen men on the steps in front of the Ark, their large prayer-shawls thrown over their heads hiding their faces and most of their bodies. They pushed the shawl away from them with their hidden hands and began to sway and turn around lifting their feet, chanting the Nigun, all out of tune. They looked like ghosts but one knew that under this shawl was gentle Mr. S., who came on Friday evenings for his glass of Jewish tea and biscuits and talk, and under another was Mr. Z., who had a stand in the market and brought my mother eggs and butter. . . . Then back to the house to more good food; the mandlen, the kreplach, the knaidle, in the chicken soup. The roast of lean meat with prunes and potatoes. The fat helzul, the lockshen kugel, the golden-red tzimmes. The pickled herring with onions in the synagogue basement after Maariv on Satur-

day night. The Sabbath *was* different from the rest of the week.
On Sundays it seemed to rain a lot and the men played cards,
the women went to the synagogues in the afternoon and gave
teas. On Monday one was back to the procession of horses and
wagons coming out of the yards, the women sitting behind lace
curtains and watching the street.

And summer holidays. Driving down to Vermont. My aunt
smuggling in a bottle of Canadian whisky in her pants. Swimming in the lake before breakfast. The farm in Bowesville. Pitching horseshoes. Going in the cornfields tasting the young corn
when the teeth are still a chalk white, sucking the sweet milk.
Going behind the horse and cart, the corn taller than I was,
pulling the ears off, the tight-wrapped green leaves, throwing
them into the cart. Making tobacco out of the top hairs and
smoking it in a cheap clay pipe. Listening to the gramophone
in the next farm:

> I have no use for the women,
> A true one can never be found;
> They'll use a man for his money
> Then laugh in his face at his fall.

In By Ward Market. The wagons, horses, trucks, stands, pedlars, panhandlers, farmers, bums. Watching the bananas cut
from the stalk, then placing the hands in a box on the wagon.
The crates of strawberries and raspberries; squeezing empty
boxes and making them smaller, then turning over the full-
packed boxes into these smaller ones and skimming off the sur-
plus berries, for profit. The deep purple baskets of blueberries;
the freestone yellow-flesh peaches behind green fishnet; the bags
of Golden Bantam corn, each cob with seven rows of teeth; the
bushels, the boxes, the bags, the scales and gallon measures . . .
the large umbrella strapped to the side of the high red wagon;
the white heavy horse. At the Rideau, Shirley Temple tap-
danced and sang:

> On the good ship Lollipop
> It's a nice trip to the candy shop.

And my mother going regularly to the dinnerware nights, coming back with another dish, another saucer, another cup. The
A. J. Frieman's Birthday Sale: 'Count the number of pebbles
in the window.' The water in the boiler by the kitchen stove
crackled as it got hot. And after the bath my mother combing
my wet hair with the hard double-edged fine-tooth comb, crack-

ing the small insects with the back of her thumbnail on to the
flat centre of the comb.

Then High School. Riding the new blue C.C.M. bicycle down
the Driveway to Second Avenue. Learning bookkeeping, typing,
filing, shorthand; how to write in the easy-to-read commercial
style, how to clean nails, shine shoes, how to sell. And as a special
treat the teacher took the class to the Capital to see 'Destry Rides
Again'. At the morning assembly the orchestra played:

> I'm no millionaire
> But I'm not the type to care
> For I've got a pocketful of dreams.

We stood in the large auditorium listening to the short
announcements, the smell of stale cosmetics; the orchestra
played again and we sang:

> When it rains it always rains
> Pennies from Heaven.

Going to the river, watching the men with long saws cut the
ice in blocks then put them in sleighs with sawdust, the horses
pulling the loaded sleighs, the sound of their bells on the
harness, icicles from their lips, their breath smoking in the cold
air. . . . Learning to ski underneath the trees in Rockcliffe, the
picture-postcard slopes, thick white snow, evergreens, silence. . . .
Playing hockey outside the house on the road under the over-
hanging street light, snow mounds for goalposts, a piece of coal
for a puck. When a truck or a car went by the game stopped and
we remade the goalposts. Then outdoor rinks. Clusters of taped
hockey sticks over the shoulders with the skates, shin-pads,
gauntlets, felt tongues. Getting dressed in the warm wooden huts
around the iron stove, tin pipes across the ceiling, then going out
to sweat in the cold air underneath the lights.

Hitch-hiking to Montreal. Standing by the large cemetery at
Eastview and getting lifts to Hawkesbury, the mounds and smell
of sulphur. Walking through villages, the mosquitoes biting,
the French-Canadian restaurants with outside screen doors on a
spring, the rocking chair on the veranda, the pickled eggs in
glass jars, the large bottles of Kik for six cents.

Bits and pieces, like signposts. One remembers songs, photographs, tastes, smells, faces, things left unfinished . . .

The small library on Rideau—the double-parlour of a house
like a Chinese laundry—the naked bulbs, the unpainted wooden
shelves, the books without covers. A dark French-Canadian girl,
who was much older, gave me my first book. I came back often,

thought about her before going to sleep. I wanted to do things to
her, but I was too young. Instead I picked daisies in the park
and pulled the petals and tossed coins: this year, next year, this
year . . .

Up those dingy wooden steps above the small shoeshop on
Rideau Street. The room with the blue-and-white crêpe paper
along the wall, the ping-pong table, the canteen. Dancing the
Horah, winding like a watch-spring right around the room. Hearing talks on Marx, Engels, Dos Passos, and listening to someone
who had been to Paris, and to London. Acting in plays, inter-
pretative dancing, scouting in the Laurentians. The piano, the
canteen, the ping-pong table: a place to get away from home.
Saturday Night. Listening first to Foster Hewitt's hockey broadcast from Maple Leaf Gardens, then later that night to Toscanini
and the N.B.C. symphony orchestra from New York. Archie,
Chaim, and myself, in the dark, falling asleep, waking up to
static and the green cathode eye, each one feeling the other out
as to who fell asleep first.

'I heard all of Mozart's D Minor.'

'I must have fallen asleep during En Saga.'

'The last I remember was the start of The Faun.'

Putting on the double windows, the double doors. Smashing
the ice in front of the house, knocking the icicles down with a
broom, freezing an ear, helping my father bring in the frozen
bags and baskets from the sleigh into the cellar. Standing on
the veranda in the dreary Spring days with the snow breaking
up, in my windbreaker, all dressed up, but where to go?

To work. In the large stone government building by the Driveway. Punching the fairground clock, you expected a fortune card
to come out telling your weight. Filing linen tracings, running
errands, pretending one was learning something about architec-
ture. And coming back to thick hamburgers, listening as one
ate to the 'Happy Gang', to the bad jokes, the four pieces trying
to make a lot of noise. Bert Pearl singing There'll Always Be An
England; a tin penny version. And in the evenings, after the
softball game, when there was nothing to do, going to the
Chateau Laurier, standing inside the lobby and watching other
people going somewhere: the Hollywood magazines, the newspapers from London and New York and Vancouver. Then down
the sloping tunnel underneath the street to the Union Station,
and the Post Office, and sending letters out. . . . How one de-
pended on letters, even then.

And the immigrants coming continually over, staying in the

rooms a few months, then moving on. The local Jews getting rid of all their unmarriageable daughters to these newcomers while their own sons went to Montreal where there was more choice. The war had been going a year. It was still remote. A recruiting drive. Commandos in full equipment were to swim across the canal by the Union Station. I saw them slink across the railway lines, hug the side of the canal like a shadow and then they dropped quietly into the dirty water, one after another, and only a few came up, the rest remained stuck in the mud and the slime at the bottom.

At night, on the corner, standing in groups, drinking cokes, too hot to go to sleep. The lit-up clock of the Peace Tower against the sky above the houses. Walking through the hot streets to Parliament Hill, to Bowles Lunch, with the bums asleep by the wall, having a cup of coffee and a doughnut, coming back. The whole street sitting outside on the verandas. Sometimes a horse broke loose from a stable and ran out. But more often you could hear the loud flat coughs coming from the stables. A horse lying down unable to get up. Capello came with a stomach pump. 'The horse got the heaves. Once they got the heaves they're finished.' Outside the rocking chairs rocked, someone on a kazoo played *Bei Mir Bist Du Schön*. You could hear bits of talk coming from the dark verandas, and a gramophone playing:

> It's a Barnum and Bailey world,
> Just as phoney as it can be

Nelson Eddy, *At the Balalaika*; Alan Jones with his *Donkey Serenade*; every Christmas, Bing Crosby; and at Easter, Irving Berlin. The midnight shows on Sunday. The Tremblay concerts once a year with Barbirolli conducting. And Glenn Miller, Cab Calloway, Benny Goodman, Shep Fields, The Dorseys, Harry James. After 'Orchestra Wives', decided to become a trumpet player. Bought a secondhand nickel-plated trumpet and began to play across the backyards and the stables: *Praise the Lord and Pass the Ammunition*; *Sleepy Lagoon*; *Abide With Me* . . . One's world was movies, sport, radio, songs, funnies, chewing gum, The Book of the Month Club selections . . . and the street.

Then flying out west. Flying over the prairies and the lakes and the grain elevators with the small town by the railway line. Dropping white practice bombs on the foothills. Going into a small town for a steak, a dance, a pick-up at the Trianon above the garage with the Chinese lanterns. Then back to the dreariness of the camp, the long room of double bunks, and those over from England, Australia, New Zealand, lying there nostalgic.

> I want to have a paper doll that I can call my own,
> A doll that other fellows will not steal;
> Then those flirty-flirty guys with their flirty-flirty eyes
> Will have to play with dollies that are real.

Then to England.

And what remains vivid after these years is not the boredom of the flying stations; the incongruity of a string quartet playing with our meals on Sunday afternoons; the blobs of brilliant colour of a night raid on Hamburg. Nor the briefings, the waiting, the take-offs, the long ten-hour trips. But the aloneness of flying at night above the clouds on a cross-country trip; and the intensity of a few careless brief encounters.

BRIEF ENCOUNTERS

For the next few days I let things happen as they came. I walked through the streets, met people I knew, had a few drinks in the beer parlours, cups of coffee in the restaurants, took streetcars and buses and walked.

It was still a small town. A safe provincial place overflowing with boys and girls from still smaller towns who come here to take unimaginative jobs in the Civil Service.

You can see the young girls walking in twos at night waiting to be picked up and the boys in secondhand cars patrolling the streets looking for them. It is still the film, the dance hall, the drive in off the highway, the bowling alley, radio, and now TV. The place is busiest in the morning when they go to work. The lower grades with their lunches in small brown-paper bags punching the clock. The higher grades carrying briefcases, driving cars, 'signing in' on a piece of paper. Then waiting for the next pay cheque and the next pay cheque and eventually the pension. A large black headline in the *Ottawa Journal*: CIVIL SERVICE PAY ON TIME THIS WEEK. But in smaller print: more clashes in the Middle East; another house burned out because of electric overloading, cheap wiring, three people dead; a collision on the highway outside Ottawa, 'Police said looters ignoring dead and injured in the car fled with almost $1000 worth of wedding presents' . . . 'Two young boys were brutally slain . . . the woman was beaten and stabbed to death'... And yet with all the violence going on the appearance outside is one of nothing important really happening, of indifference, dullness, and boredom.

And a sense of space, that continually reduced the importance of the human being. You didn't have to go very far to feel it. It was there in the centre of Ottawa. I could see the Gatineau Hills outside the Chateau Laurier, by the War Memorial, and the Union Station. I could feel the pressure of those vast frozen spaces to the north. I could feel it at night when the place was deserted. Cars driving by, hardly anyone walking. A couple of telegraph boys, cigars in their mouths, running down Sparks Street, jumping to the CAR STOP NO PARKING signs and hitting some of them. A drunk lurched down Rideau Street went into the passage of a neon-lit clothing store and was sick. I could hear the mournful sound of a train whistle somewhere in the distance and the tension in the air of the frost setting in. Darkness was coming. But it was held back by the snow on the roofs and on the road. A clothes line with frozen washing hung in a back-yard; the washing frozen in its folds. At an open crossing: LOOK, LISTEN; a steel mechanical arm kept moving, hiding and showing a red disc, like a heartbeat.

*

I walked towards the market. An old man in a shabby grey coat, unshaven, was standing on Dalhousie Street asking for a dime. But he was having no luck. A schoolgirl in a new blue woollen winter outfit and a red chook was going into every out-side telephone booth, tilting back the return slot. But she was having no luck either.

The market was one end of Lower Town. A square block of stores: cheap clothing, pawnshops, fruits and vegetables, fish and meat, joke stores with the false teeth, the itching powder, the signs burnt in wood 'She wears mink all day and fox at night'. The stores on the outside of the square are mostly run by Jews, and the stands that face them by French-Canadian farmers. When I was a child and I was told that someone had a stand in the market, it seemed a large enterprise, something ahead of the horse and the wagon. Now, a couple of orange crates piled up like bricks to a counter level, then a few planks across the top for the tomatoes, the eggs, the braids of garlic, the jellied meats in the small glass jars, the washed carrots, the flowers. Beside the stands were the farmers' trucks: Billing's Bridge, Cyrville, Kars, Manotick, Gatineau.

I bought some apples very cheaply from an old woman who only had apples and eggs. To protect her from the wind she had stretched an old sack nailed to two pieces of wood, placed to windward. She was short and swarthy, wearing many sweaters,

rubber boots, a brown kerchief on her head, and an apron folded
from the bottom back to the top was fastened around her waist
for her money. All around her in the mud lay broken eggshells,
the yolks pierced through the mud like hundreds of canary
wings.

In William Street I was passing the pawnshops, the cheap
clothing stores—with the pullers standing in the doorways like
prostitutes; all you had to do was just take a look in a window
and they were after you, coaxing you to come inside—when a
large blue Cadillac stopped ahead and sounded its horn. I recognized L. We both grew up on Murray Street. He said he had
nothing to do: would I like to go for a drive.

He drove me around Rockcliffe, the Driveway, out to the
Experimental Farm, to the airport at Uplands, then back to his
large house in Sandy Hill. He left school at fourteen and went
out to the farms buying up cattle then selling them to the but-
chers. Then he started his own butcher shop, then moved on to
salamis and smoked meat. Now, he said, his business was one of
the largest in Canada. He was thirty-two. He had married C., a
sad, thin girl, with sad eyes, who looked as if she was ready to
fall apart. They had two children. Then she died unexpectedly
from cancer. Everyone I had spoken to felt sorry for L.

In his house he offered me a cigarette, black paper with a gold
tip. And some cherry brandy.

'Boy have I got troubles,' he said. 'I advertised for someone to
look after the kids in the *London Advertiser* and I had more
than three hundred replies. I picked one of them. She came
over. And in a couple of weeks we were at it. I couldn't come
home without having to jump into bed with her. I used to dread
the thought. I got really desperate. Then I found out that in
New York you can get some ground sunflower seeds.' He disappeared and came back with a large jar that said *Heinz Pickles*.
'I put it in this jar, you never know who might open the fridge.
Here try some. This will make your pecker stand up to no end
of punishment.' It tasted oily and pulpy like that of sunflower
seeds. 'You'll need to take it at least a week before you get results.
But even then I was getting it too much. It got so that I dreaded
to come home. Finally I had to send her off for a holiday in
Mexico, and hope she meets someone there.'

'What about C.?'

'She. Hell, we were unsuited to each other, but we pretended.
Days used to go by when we wouldn't talk to each other. I know
what the town is thinking, let them think. This girl is class. She

cut my toenails, shined my shoes, manicured my fingernails. She taught me how to dress, how to behave. That's what we need here, you know. There's lots of us guys with money in the bank, making hand over fist. All we need is a dame from England whose got it, but is more or less broke. What's the use of having beautiful manners if you've got nothing to eat? She wants money. We give it to her. And she makes us into gentlemen.'

But he was cheated. And he cheated right back.

BIOGRAPHY

He was quiet and placid. So placid that he seemed to be continually asleep. Yet he asked the most personal kind of questions right away. He was full of apparent kindness, and a friendliness, that became so obviously fake that it ceased to be embarrassing. He made money in everything. He had a block of flats built, then quickly sold it at a profit. He made money out of lumber deals, scrap deals, rag deals, and now meat. He had no sense of loyalty. Anything that was confided to him he would quickly tell to someone else. He had spent too much time going out in the fields to the farmers, when he was young, making money. And now that he had it, he was bored. Behind that face with the slight top moustache, the crooked front teeth, the large head going into the stocky body, there was hardly a visible neck. Behind the expensive suit, the English shoes, the American shirt, the not-too-loud tie, the manicured nails. Behind that exterior of charm and friendliness, there was nothing, only indifference.

We sat there drinking brandy and smoking the black cigarettes.

'When I'm in England I'll buy a car and give it to you when I finish touring the Continent.'

'And I'll dedicate a book to you.'

'I'll send you food parcels from Canada with salamis, smoked meat, salmon, cigarettes; all kinds of crap.'

'And I'll send you copies of everything I get published.'

It was easy to be generous, to be pleasant, with things neither of us intended to do. Some promises one keeps, or tries very hard to keep. Others one may have had an intention of keeping at the time but then other more immediate promises turn up. There are some one has no intention of keeping.

He won this game. I soon ran out of things I could promise. And he used money to get things.

When he came over to London he was lost. His housekeeper
was taking him around. She didn't go further than the small
Morris, the saloon bar, the drive to Brighton for a weekend.
She had knocked around an American airbase during the war
and when the war was over she went from one man to another.
But they soon got tired. She did not have much more to sell than
a very secondhand kind of body.

But with L. she represented culture, class, good manners.

She came from Eltham. The small semi-detached, the bath
with no hot water in the summer, the top window with the back
of the wooden dressing-table facing the street, the curtains
drawn to keep the sun from bleaching the furniture and the
wallpaper, the all day shining the car on Sunday, the dog taken
for his walk; and the little meannesses that come with not having much money, worrying about appearances, and continually
playing safe. And she also had the hard-faced unhappiness of
being in her late thirties, unmarried, knowing that she was on to
a good thing, and it was slipping away.

He controlled her with his money, but he didn't like her. If
that's all class was what did he make money for? So he told her
all the obscene Jewish words which he would get her to say in
front of his friends. That was one way to get even. He told a
story. When he came to London he had to go to the toilet and
found there was no paper to wipe himself. He didn't know what
to do. The only paper he had were one-pound notes. So he used
one of them. She was furious. 'You could have used your underwear and bought four pair with that pound.' She went on trying
to please him by saving his money for him.

In London he kept praising Canada, saying what a wonderful
country it was. From Israel he wrote: 'Honest to God. Coming
to Israel is better than an orgasm.' And he remained the kid of
the backstreets. He wanted to go to Soho, not for a meal, or a
drink, but just to walk by a couple of prostitutes. As soon as we
turned off Shaftesbury Avenue he became worried: 'Where are
they?' I pointed out two on a corner. He crossed over the street,
deliberately, and he began to walk as if he was walking up to get
some sort of prize. When he passed them, without looking at
them, he had a large grin on his face as if a photographer was
there and had asked him to smile, and this moment was fixed.
He would go back to Ottawa and tell the boys. 'I remember the
time in Soho with a couple of pros.' And he kept on saying:
'The world is a happy place.' He continually wanted to be reassured that one was 'happy', 'well off'. But if you told him

differently, if you showed him things, he refused to accept them.
'What's the matter with you, getting morbid? You've got your
health, you're young. What else do you want?'

On his last day in London he rang up: would we all like to
make a splash night on him, go to the ballet, or the Festival
Hall, and then to the Dorchester, the Ritz, or the Savoy? We
said we would leave it up to him. We spent our last pound at
that time on a baby-sitter and got all dressed up. But there was
no theatre or music. We ended up in a small restaurant in White-
chapel eating hotdogs, chips, and cokes. He was looking around
the place seeing if he could make a deal with one of the stores
there to import some of his products.

*

The thaw has set in. From the balcony of my parents' apartment I can look down to the street where we used to live. A man
in a leather windbreaker is breaking up the ice with an axe in
front of his veranda. In front of another house a stout woman
in a white kerchief is smashing the snow, then shovelling it on
to the road where the cars and the trucks will go over it; where
the sun will further reduce it; until it flows down the drains.
At night the melted water freezes and the roads and the sidewalks become dangerous. But by next morning it begins to flow,
churning with the sand that was thrown on to the sidewalk and
the road during the winter. Then the water disappears, and only
the mud is left to dry, to become dirty sand that the wind whips
down the street.

*

People I meet, especially those with whom I used to play ball
and hockey, keep on asking: 'Isn't it good to be back? This is
the country now you know. . . . Why not stay here and make
your pile with us . . .?' But they don't believe it. They want to be
reassured by hearing you say Yes. They have read the newspapers, the advertisements, gone to the films. And they have to
reconcile what they are told is the envy of the world with
the emptiness, dullness, and the boredom of their own lives.
And they preferred pretence: the continual inflation of claims;
the sentimentality of the advertisements. It left them passive,
pliable. And gave them a veneer of optimism, of confidence that
was so thin of real experience and yet led them to believe that
their resources were deep. And when the luck did run out and
the chips were down and one had to fall back on oneself . . . how
one was tricked. For all the comfort: the fine homes, deep freeze,

the gadgets, they were resentful; they felt they were being cheated, though of what they didn't quite know.

And those who did try to break out from the emptiness and the boredom had little choice. So much here is extrovert, that to get out one has to push it still further. To smash through with the accelerator down, to daydream, sex, or the small acts of cruelty. Or if one had enough money, one could do it through pleasure.

I met S. He has been in Ottawa since 1948. He came over from a D.P. camp and he started work as an apprentice for a tailor. While he was learning the trade he took extra work home. In two years he was able to buy his own store. He met his wife at night school. She also works in the store. They have two children. He moved from Lower Town to Sandy Hill and now he was having his own house built near the Experimental Farm. He drove me over in his car to see the foundation; a large hole was in the earth filled with water. The road had potholes. He was very pleased. On the way back he brought out proudly several small pieces of paper from his pocket. They were notes from his children. They only saw them on the weekends. They had hired a German girl to look after them. 'Daddy I love you. You are the BEST Daddy in the World' . . . 'Thanks for the Teddy Bear' . . . 'I got three stars two gold and one red . . .' I asked him why didn't he ease up and take it slower. He said he was doing it for the kids so that they could have a better chance than he had.

I had on a pair of grey corduroys that I bought in Penzance before leaving. 'You know,' he said, 'you shouldn't go around in things like that here, people might mistake you for a greenhorn.'

*

I was glad to leave Ottawa. Murray Street had not changed. But the fruit and rags pedlars, those who made one's world, had either died or moved away. I had called the place home; but it had no real hold.

FLYING OVER THE GREAT LAKES

The airport was desolate. Snow melting. Grass and turf showed through the snow and water in patches. The sun hard to see into. The plane taxied down the runway. Small evergreens, snow, water, turf, the control tower with the coloured glass, the painted red and white squares, came out behind the trailing edge. Passed a grey hangar, parked jets in front marked 'U.S. Air Force', the tricycle undercarriage, the large blacked-out nose, the high tail.

Telegraph poles, slushed highway, a cluster of wooden houses by the golf course covered in snow. Taxi-ing quietly. Little vibration. Only the stewardess's kitchen unit shakes. The plane stopped by the runway in use and the engines were revved up. I could see the flap moving. I could hear the low whistle-whine of the radio. The sun caught the glint from the propellers at the top, the metal wing, the rivets, the sign NO STEP. A half turn to the runway and without a pause the roar of the throttles opened and the black tyre marks of other landings became streaks of black lines.

The plane climbed, turned. Cars, small coloured bugs, seemed to be drawn by the road. Patches of fields went slowly backwards. The snow on them looked fake, as if it was covering of soiled cottonwool and there wasn't enough to cover everything: the urine colour of a thawed field with last season's grass; the flooding in another. Then the lakes. Small frozen lakes, all shapes, with their backbone of islands. The black trees on the islands lifting them up out of the grey-white ice like a risen loaf.

The plane climbed through the clouds and through turbulence and then levelled out above them. Snow, trees, fields, lakes, islands, were no longer visible. Only thick white clouds brilliantly lit up, whiter than the snow, were below. And no sense of movement. One was only conscious of the nearness of the metal, very sharp in focus, the nacelles, a pair of nipples, turning, the thousands of small shiny bolts, the metal wing trembling against a blue cloudless sky. The sun was hot, the air inside the plane stuffy, my foot had gone to sleep . . .

And then the clouds had gaps between them and the plane slanted down through a wide gap and levelled out underneath the clouds. The ground was no longer a map of irregular lakes and islands and small hills and fields, but a white-black plain very neatly laid out. The roads ran east and west, spaced evenly, every three fields and another long black line in the snow to the horizon. Sometimes a clump of trees broke up that straight line, sometimes a lake. But the line continued on the other side as far as I could see and it pulled the white-black plain together. On the snowfields the slow-moving shadows of the very white clouds.

Lake Huron was completely free of ice. And the edge of the land entered the water in a series of rocky shelves; they were a brilliant emerald green in colour underneath the water. After the miles of black and white with the occasional olive green of a thawed field one was suddenly back to vivid bright colours. The water of the vast lake was green, then blue, and patches of black in the blue like splashes of ink. Over Georgian Bay, thousands of islands, neat pieces rising out, a white fringe around them, set in the blue water. The larger islands were joined together by sheets of ice, a piece of white skin. Georgian Bay was very much like a poster. The large curves of land, the thick growth of pine trees, the land carved out as a roast. Now one could understand better 'The School of Seven' and the poster-quality of their paintings. For this repetition of water-lake-land-trees had the appearance of a good poster. Over Manitoulin Island, Gore Bay, and a small clearing hacked out of the bush, the neat square fields lying out flat to the trees. How easy it was to see man's method of conquering nature, imposing his rage for order, using mathematics.

The land here was pock-marked with lakes. Thousands of small shiny bits of black glass set in the bush, thick black with trees. There was so much black. And patches of snow; blue, green, water, and muddy brown earth. Then the islands. Thousands of them with their centres swollen with trees. Where the land was more than the water—lakes. And where the water was more than the land—islands. After a while it made no difference.

The plane landed in the country in a strip on the American side. A small airport surrounded by evergreens thick with white snow as after a heavy fall. A cafeteria, a few bored passengers waiting, hotdogs, an air hostess with Max Factor make-up and full red lips sat by the counter smoking and stared vacantly outside.

We drove in a taxi to the Canadian side. Michigan Highway 2 U.S.; signs, but otherwise it was exactly the same as the side one knew. The same car advertisements on the billboards, birch trees, motels, mail boxes at the side of the road. The sidewalk in slush, the backstreets covered in snow. A Lutheran cemetery. Signs to go to church.

Then we came to the ferry. The ice in the river was broken up into large slabs. They reared out of the water, coffin-shaped shrouds. People came off the ferry and went to the U.S. side. Cars with Ontario licence plates drove on. A customs man came along with us (he came with us from the airport as we were held 'in bond'); we could not leave the taxi until we arrived at the dropping-off point on the Canadian side.

THE SOO

We were brought to a tall narrow hotel on the main street of

Sault Ste Marie from Soo, Michigan. After leaving my bags with
the young boy in the T.C.A. office I went next door into the
hotel to have a beer. The waiter was English, hair parted in the
middle, greased down. The place had large comfortable booths
against the walls and small round tables and chairs in the centre,
subdued lighting, stuffed heads of moose and deer and bison
mounted on the walls. I ordered a Labatts. He brought a bottle
and a glass. The beer tasted cold.

Opposite me, at one of the tables, sat a small Indian woman.
Her glass was empty. She was brown and wrinkled. A small
spare body disguised by odd bits and pieces of clothes. Nothing
seemed to fit. On her head, pushed to the back, a bright yellow
hat like the ones young girls wear at private schools, with a red
velvet ribbon tied under the neck. The black hair coming out
from the hat lay in twin braids on her shoulders. She had brown
cotton stockings; even though they were held up above the knee
by green elastic bands, they sagged. Her short legs did not touch
the floor but dangled and crossed themselves in front of her.
She looked at me. Prominent rounded cheekbones, a flat nose.
She smiled, leaned towards me and whispered. 'Be a sport. A
drink.'

I made a pretence of fumbling in my pocket and said I missed
the bank. She sat there as if she did not understand what I had
said. 'Be a sport. A drink.' She tried to flirt. But she couldn't
even wink right. She closed both her eyes tight, then opened
them suddenly and looked pleasantly surprised. I thought, what
the hell, I'll be broke soon in any case. I waved to the waiter and
pointed to where she was sitting. He shook his head. I waved
and pointed again. He came over shaking his head, and looking
worried. 'She has had enough,' he said nervously. 'We must not
give them too much or else they go crazy.' I tried to argue with
him, but it was no use. All this time she sat there perfectly relaxed, laughing with her dumpy body, winking with both eyes,
an uncomplicated bundle too large for the suit that was buttoned tight around her middle. She looked ridiculous in her
clothes: the schoolgirl hat, the crimson silk scarf at her throat,
the sagging cotton stockings, the stone-grey suit too small for
her. But there was so much warmth and gaiety coming from
her, she looked as if she hadn't a care and was enjoying all this
enormously. Then two other men came in and sat down in the
booth next to me. Again the childish wink, the thin whisper. 'Be
a sport. A drink.'

I went out of the tavern hotel and walked along the main street to the Algoma Ore building to see about going up to the Mine. The man in the company's office was tall and wore a box-like suit. He had the appearance of an athlete turned salesman. Straight blond hair combed back without a parting, a well-fed face. But there was something deceptive about the way he talked. For his mouth, when open, seemed unnatural in that position as in those films where animals are made to speak like human beings. I showed him my credentials. He read them, said I would be able to get a train early tomorrow morning. 'Things have improved a lot since you were up there. We now have a train going up once a day.' He walked to a large map on the wall. It hung there framed. The bottom had a large blue area marked *Lake Superior*. Smaller pieces of blue were scattered all over the map. 'The only other way is by seaplane.' He tapped a spot in the top left corner. 'But there won't be a plane for at least another month. The lakes are too dangerous. There's either too much floating ice or they are still frozen, but not strong enough to take a landing.' I asked him whether they had gone through with the road to the Mine. 'No,' he said. 'The Government keeps promising, but nothing much has been done.' I said I would take the company's train.

I went to the river to the Algoma Central Station to get my ticket. But all the doors of the old building were shut. A notice said: *Tickets sold only between 6 a.m. and 7.15 a.m.* There was nobody there. A few Indians in bright lumberjack shirts walked along the tracks.

I began to walk back to the main street when I saw a house that had a BED AND BOARD sign in the front window. I went up the walk, the wooden steps, and rang the bell. A young man in jeans and a heavy lumberjack shirt opened the door. He was unshaven and he had bad teeth.

'Have you a room for one night?'

He looked me up and down and without turning around yelled out: 'Mah, have we got a room for a night?'

There was no reply. He disappeared inside and I could hear them arguing.

He returned and led me down the hall and opened the door of the front room. A sour smell came out of the darkness. I could see three rows of camp beds across the room. Men were lying in some, grey blankets over them. The window blind was drawn over the only window in the room. He pointed to a bed.

'You can have that one.'

'Have you anything else?'

E

'There's one up in the hall.'

We went up the stairs. An old iron bed was at the head of the stairs flush with the wall beside the open door of the toilet. Two grey blankets lay on the bed.

'How much is that?'

'A buck. They're all a buck.'

As we went down the stairs he said, 'Are you going on the A.C.R.?'

'Yes, I am.'

'You wouldn't get me to go on that for love or money.'

'Why not?'

'Slides. This time of the year it's full of slides.'

He cackled like a radio ghoul. 'You wouldn't get me to go on that railway if you paid me.'

I made up the first excuse I could think of by saying that I'd left my luggage in another place and if I didn't come back it meant I had found another room; and wondered why I didn't come straight out and say it wouldn't do. As I went down the wooden steps of the veranda he called out: 'By the way what's your name?'

'Levine.'

'Levine?'

'Why?'

'Just wanted to know. I'm going to watch the papers. Nobody gets out from them slides.' And again that forced ghoulish cackle followed me down the street.

Back along the main street, gusts of wind blowing sand from the sidewalk into one's face. I saw a sign Y.M.C.A. off a turning. An old thin man was washing the floor with a mop. The woman behind the desk was short and fat and had a mouth full of badly fitted teeth. She was unable to close her mouth. I asked her for a single room for one night. She said it would be two dollars for the night and a dollar deposit for the key. I took the key and walked along a dark passage. A room without a door and a small kitchen where the men cooked their food. The stove was black, covered in grease; garbage, opened tin cans, spilled over the pail and lay on the floor. Old beaten men, unshaven, walked around in their winter underwear, slippers on their feet. Some wore shirts and leather windbreakers and rubber boots. There was a smell of things going rotten. I finally found the room, but someone was in there lying fully dressed in the bed. I went down and told this to the woman. She said it was the only one she had available.

I went out and walked further up this side-street. One wooden house with a large veranda had a cardboard sign ROOM TO LET nailed to a veranda post. Above the bell button was a plate. *L. M. Kalma. Music Teacher. Qualified.* I rang the bell. I could hear the bell ringing inside. But the brown winter door remained closed. I rang and knocked and waited. Then I heard steps.

The woman who opened the door was small. She had a dressing-gown on over a nightdress. Her hair was grey, fuzzy, and held in place by a net. Though it was late afternoon, the fact that she had obviously just come out of bed did not seem as startling as her face. The eyes were there. So was the mouth. But where her nose should have been there was a flat surface of scarred flesh with two small holes.

'You caught me undressed,' she said.

I told her I wanted a room for one night. She led me through the dining-room into a back room. A square room with a window and a large fourposter bed. 'It's a feather bed. They are much better than spring or rubber. The feathers, they sleep with you like another person.'

My first impulse was to make some excuse, leave, and find another place.

'The clever doctors, to them I should be dead.'

She said this without sadness or humour. Probably she had said the same words many times. She told me where the bathroom was, asked me if $2.50 was not too much for the room, and placed on the kitchen table a leg of cold chicken and sliced tomato that she had taken from her ice-box. She insisted that I sit down and eat. I ate the food while she talked. She talked as if we had known each other a long time. I now found a strong physical attraction to her face.

Later, in the evening, when I returned with my bag from the T.C.A. office, it was difficult to recognize her as the same woman who opened the door. She had on a dark dress instead of a dressing-gown. She wore a false nose attached to a false piece of skin that stretched from one ear to the other and, by wearing glasses, held it into place. Face powder and rouge generously put on only helped to show the falseness. I preferred the scarred face with the two air holes to this manufactured monstrosity. In her attempt to look normal she looked ugly, like some witch.

*

I went out and walked along the main street. I had been here eight years ago but I remembered very little of it. And yet it all seemed familiar.

No one is really a stranger in Canada if he was brought up in a small town. They remain so much the same across the country: a vast repetition, not only of the Main Street, the side-streets, the railway track, the river; but the same dullness and boredom.

A few movies, restaurants, small stores; the Italian, Finnish, French and Slavic sections; the black lunchpails; the crowded pool rooms; the side-streets with their poor wooden shacks, mongrel dogs and children; and streets by the railway without sidewalks, deep in mud. Unshaven faces, shabbily dressed, beaten men not speaking English, walking aimlessly along the street, a few Indians. And the miners, the lumberjacks, the trappers, down from the bush on their annual holiday, coming to the Soo for their 'big blow'; spending it in the Y.M.C.A.; or the boarding-house with 'the little woman' they have shacked up. Or else getting gloriously drunk for two weeks. It was a rough labour force, a few stages back from Ottawa.

An old man stopped me on the main street. He had one leg and moved with crutches. He waited at the lights. 'Can you help me across?' I walked with him over the street. After thanking me, he wanted to talk, to find out where I came from, what I was doing, where I was going. 'This place is full of foreigners,' he said. 'Not like us. I'm an Irishman, at the old people's home.' He waved a crutch towards the end of the street. 'If I had the strength I would kill all these foreigners that are here. They're not Canadians. I don't like them. My name is Patrick. If you have a chance come and visit me. I'm at the old people's home. But this place isn't Canada. It's full of goddam foreigners.'

I was tired from walking and went into a drugstore to buy a local newspaper, then into a restaurant to have some coffee. The restaurant was the standard kind: juke box in the corner, the open wooden booths, the fixed circular stools at the counter; while in the corner booth by the kitchen the proprietor with his cronies was playing cards and talking loudly in Polish. The menu was mimeographed.

THE NEW ALPHA GRILL   SOO ONTARIO CANADA

Bless us O Lord and these thy gifts which of thy bounty we are about to receive through Christ our Lord. Amen.

Fried whitefish $1.00
Fried fresh herring $1.00
Grilled T bone steak $2.75
Roast lamb $1.00

Besides the card players in the back booth there were two young boys in leather windbreakers sitting in a booth ahead of me having milk shakes. They tried to flirt with a waitress, a young dark girl who stood behind the counter looking vacantly at the room. She was unco-operative. Finally one of the boys went to the counter and said to the girl, 'Toss you for a record in the machine.'

The girl remained silent. She looked Italian.

'You're chicken.'

'Yeh, I'm chicken,' she said solemnly.

He grinned to his partner, walked over to the juke box and put some money in. The music blared out. The waitress remained standing behind the counter staring vacantly at the room.

I looked through the newspaper. News stories were repeated on different pages, to fill up space. Typographical errors were everywhere. When a column came to an end and it did not quite fit into the next one 'bits' of information were put in.

OLD SHAVE
People in Mesopotamia 5,000 years ago had efficient razor blades of volcanic glass with slate handles.

GREAT COMPOSER
Franz Schubert, the Austrian composer, died of typhus in 1828 at age 31.

LONG LINE
The railway terminal at Crewe, England, has more than 1,000 miles of track.

WIDE RANGE
George Sand, French woman author born in 1804, in turn wrote romantic, socialist and pastoral novels.

But one found the absurd in the local advertisements, with their jingles, slogans and gimmicks. In the paper was a three-quarter-page advertisement for LEMAY'S FURNITURE. On top was a large black headline:

COURT IS STILL IN SESSION AT LEMAYS
The Great Price Murdering Trial is Still On. But the Judge Is Lowering the Bail for Each Convict Still Further. Come and Make Your Selection Now.

There was a large picture of a man behind bars. A well-fed moon-round face, a hooked nose, a spotless white shirt with a flashy tie, black bushy hair. He looked like the proprietor. Then came the advertisements.

They say we were intoxicated Because We Were Stretched Out. SPACE SAVERS. Any lawyer would take this case. All colours and the bail was 69.50. Now only 59.50.

We got off easy for being stool pigeons. HASSOCKS. We find it pays to squawk as bail was lowered from 3.99 to only 2.99.

2 pc CHESTERFIELD SUITE. Please help me lead a new life by bailing me out . . . They sent me up for loitering. I'm Cocoa Brown in colour with a Silver Metallic Fleck. Previous Bail 199.50. Now 150.00.

KIDDIES ROCKERS. We were convicted in juvenile court. But we want our freedom. The bail is 5.75.

MEDICINE CABINETS. We couldn't cut the bars, so the judge cut our bail to 5.00.

I felt tired and decided to have an early night as I would have to get up early to catch the train next morning. On the way back to my room a man stopped me in the street, he could hardly talk English, he tried unsuccessfully to sell me a radio ridiculously cheap which he said he won in a raffle.

But it was no good. I was tired and I couldn't sleep. The bed was comfortable. But I lay there listening to the very loud alarm clock that the landlady gave me and which I placed out of reach on the floor set for six in the morning. I could hear the sounds of boat whistles. Until midnight a piano was going from the house next door, and after that the other roomers came in and I could hear them walking about upstairs. The landlady had said she only had 'Canadians'. Up until last year she had immigrants. They were all right, she said. Only one left without paying his rent. I tried to go on with a poem about flying. But it remained stuck after the first two lines. I thought of how we came into land: the shadows rose, the 3D shapes, the shine from the railway lines, the windsock like a worm that has been cut. Impressions; full of inessentials. What one couldn't get used to, at first, was this way of looking that distance gave. How easily it erased the human being. One became again a detached observer watching a map roll out.

It was this distance that released us from being involved with the violence below when we dropped the bombs. All we worried about over the target was first ourselves, then getting a good picture, an aiming-point. One was taught indifference as a game. First in the trainer, the map of Germany rolled out slowly below and we pretended we were bombing the cross-hatched cities with the dark blue winding rivers. Later in the three-dimensions with the other planes besides us stretched out, their long slimy egg-trails churning behind the trailing-edges, we didn't care. Whatever was human below was made insignificant and shallow. Distance was the buffer, a way of looking that separated our action and its consequences, that allowed us to repeat this performance without having any doubts, or pity, or feeling in any way involved.

And later, at night, when there was no flying, about five or six of us piled into a taxi and went to Scarborough. To the Victorian hotel with the cold rooms and the shilling-in-the-slot heat. And then to the bar. Who picked who up? After a few drinks, maybe a meal, it was back to the room with the shilling heat, the gloomy drapes; and sometimes it was to her room. And while she put in her Dutch cap, you lay waiting in the cold sheets, the small light from the lamp on her dressing-table, the cold cream, the jar of vaseline, and beside it a cheap photograph enlarged of a middle-aged man in uniform fixed smiling in the frame. 'That's my husband,' she said. 'He's a long way from here. They've stationed him in India.' She said this without regret or malice. Just a matter-of-fact statement to explain the presence of a photograph on the dressing-table, as she came into bed.

The clock was loud. But I knew that if I muffled it I would not wake up in time. In the end I pushed the clock over to the far side of the room. It continued to tick like a dripping tap. I couldn't sleep. The room was too warm. No windows were open. I tried to raise the one by the bed. It was stuck. I tried the one near the door; but I couldn't move it. In any case I saw that the outside windows did not have an air slot. I lay awake listening to the clock and the train and ships' whistles, and worried about money. How long could I make what I have last? I began this trip with an advance of £125 from my publisher. Most of it was gone before I left England. The way I would have liked to make this journey was to do it in leisure and not have the tensions, the anxieties, the waste, due to lack of money. But I also knew that if I waited for the right conditions to come along I would probably never make the trip. And there was an urgency about the need to make it that I could not entirely explain.

The alarm went at five to six. I got out of bed, dressed, and went upstairs to shave. The lights were on in the hall. In a room with the door open I could see a man lying on top of his blankets in winter underwear, asleep, his lights on. The bathroom and the toilet were crowded in a small shabby room. The toilet had not been flushed and had orange peel on top of excrement. I shaved in cold water. Then I left.

It was cold. No snow, but a cold wind. Main Street was deserted. A man was sweeping the sand from the sidewalk by the post office on to the road, but the wind threw it back into his face. The sand was dry and loose. The cold wind whipped it into gusts down the street. I walked to the river and to the Algoma Central Station. Ahead of me a girl, in her late thirties, in a fur coat, was getting her ticket to the same place as I was going.

II

INTO THE BUSH

THE MAN in the Algoma office was right; there were improvements. Though the machinery had changed—instead of the old steam engine there was a new diesel freshly painted with a large black grizzly bear on its sides—the two coaches carrying the passengers had not. Their insides were still like old worn-out billiard tables with large patches eaten out of the green. The seats were hard and uncomfortable. Gas brackets hung from the ceiling. In the centre of the ceiling a couple of naked light bulbs. Two men got on dressed in heavy lumberjack shirts and tall boots laced high up. They spoke in French. They went through the first coach that was going to Wawa and into the second one.

In the first coach there were five of us, all sitting in separate seats. Opposite me was the girl in her fur coat. Her top lip protruded and was pinched just underneath the nose as if she had had an operation there. She was plump, her eyes inquisitive, but when you looked at her they became defensive. Behind the girl was an elderly couple, both short and stout. The man had coarse straight white hair cut short on top of his head. His head looked much too big for his body. He wore a cheap secondhand black suit. He took off his jacket and showed fireman's braces holding up his trousers, and a loud tie of painted palm trees. His wife was taller, a shapeless body, a sad tired face; she had a print dress on with a clasp *Mother* pinned to the dress by the neck. Behind me, in the last seat of the coach, was a well-built middle-aged man, a handsome Slavic face, high cheekbones, a long thin nose, wearing a cheap blue suit.

We started to move at 7.15 with the familiar two deep notes. I could see the muddy river, the logs piled high on the banks; snow melting everywhere, leaving stains as it turned to water and the earth to mud. The place looked like a junkyard. Old buckets, tyres, cardboard, twisted wire, old rusty tins, mounds of rubbish. On the other tracks were freight cars and tankers;

73

an Algoma Central attached to one marked Chesapeake and Ohio, another to Missouri Pacific. Past old brick buildings with narrow windows and mud around them. And men in old coats, overalls and windbreakers and ski-caps walking to work with black lunchpails, driving to work in new brightly painted cars, parking them outside the grimy buildings, and going inside. The coach smelled of disinfectant.

In less than five miles from the siding we were in thick forest. And the rest of the morning and early afternoon was one vast repetition.

We crossed trestle bridges, curved by small partly frozen lakes, and moved slowly through miles of pine, hemlock, spruce, and birch. Sometimes the trees were so thick they did not let the light through. Every fifteen minutes there was a stop. Eton. Frater. Canyon. Magpie. Cases of milk bottles were taken off from the baggage car for the logging camps deeper in the bush away from the line. Often the train did not stop, it just slowed down, while the conductor held out to the waiting man on the ground a small bundle of newspapers, a mail order catalogue, a circular, a few letters. And by these whistle stops hemmed in by the trees were a few shacks painted a dull brown, smoke coming from the chimneys, an outhouse not far away. But then the trees swallowed the clearing and the perimeter of stumps. And then more trees and more trees and the melting snow between the trees like an animal skin that was shrinking as it dried up.

We moved from a crest of a ridge with a river below, the ice breaking up, thick massive blocks jammed one on top of the other while the muddy water flowed swiftly around and under the ice. Then down through a valley with large rocks above us. And icicles hanging from the rocks thick and long and tapering to a fine point which was turning into water. On one side of the slope where the sun was shining, the snow and the ice was melting and the water came down as a torrent and over the track, washing away the top layer of soil in its path, uprooting trees and rocks. The sun had not yet touched the other side of the slope and the water which had flowed yesterday, then froze during the night, remained frozen: a streak of thick grey ice with small trees and rocks locked in the ice on the lower slopes while the top hung down with massive grey icicles. It would run again later in the day, then freeze again during the night.

Then more trees, close together, very thick and straight, especially the pine and the spruce, hiding the light. Then we stopped again by a few log cabins, the snow piled high on the roofs and a tall Finnish-looking woman in a heavy coat and flying-boots came through the snow and met the two men in lumberjack shirts who got off the train. Then back through tunnels of evergreen, by rocks, water, ice and snow.

The scenery for all its magnificence did not excite me. It had the beauty of something primitive, hostile, and indifferent. There was no warmth to be had out of this landscape, it hadn't been lived in. To try to understand it, one would have to reduce it to human terms—it represented wealth—that meant possession, and man reduces this hostility and indifference by hacking into it, cutting straight lines and curves, imposing the only sense of order that he knows.

'T'rawnah-Star. T'rawnah-Star. Funnies. Western. Get your last read. Get your last read.' A small boy, Italian—the shrewd face looked sixteen or seventeen, but his short spare body made him look younger—came through the compartment wearing a white apron and carrying magazines and newspapers and shouting. The Slav in the back was sprawled out in his seat snoring. The girl had long ago taken off her fur coat. It was warm in the coach. No ventilation. We shared a bar of chocolate. She said she was a Scottish nurse going to work in the hospital at Wawa. She had worked in the bush in Labrador and in Newfoundland and she was coming here because the pay was better and it was a little closer to civilization. I told her it was isolated.

'It couldn't be as cut off as the logging camps in Labrador or the one in Newfie,' she said. 'Sometimes we didn't get mail for weeks.'

We watched the trees go by.

She said you could tell a spruce by the bit on the top that always faced the same direction. She had picked that up from the loggers in Newfoundland. We sang a few songs: *A Wee Dock and Doris, The Nut Brown Maiden, My Bonny Lad.* She had a soft resonant voice. Her face was very pale. She asked me if I was married. I said I was. She said she had had a boy-friend, he was an engineer in the R.A.F. He was killed in the war. The old couple who sat behind her came over and listened while she sang. They were going to visit their daughter in the bush. He used to work for the railroad, and they gave him a free pass when he retired so that now they come up twice a year to see their daughter. They were Irish and they both had badly fitting store teeth. His clicked when he talked, while hers appeared to float in her mouth.

Outside young birches moved in the wind. White praying

branches and peeling bark. Their fragility stood out in all this massiveness. They were white and stark, snow about them.

By noon the journey had gone on much too long. It was too much the same. The coach was stuffy. The retired couple had slumped in their seats, mouths open, asleep. The nurse fell asleep leaning against the window looking outside. The total distance was 183 miles, and we had travelled half of it in nearly six hours when the young boy in white apron came walking through again. 'Anybody want to eat? Anybody here for lunch?' I went to the head of the coach. There were four tables with chairs and a small kitchen partitioned off by a dirty black curtain. Stacks of funnies were on the floor, Western stories, Dime Detectives, Love stories; and a large cardboard box overflowing with opened tin cans. The boy came out from behind the curtain. 'You want tomato or vegetable soup?' I said I'd have a hotdog and coffee. He over-boiled the hotdog in a large pot and brought me a cracked cup of stale coffee. Then he went back to his funny.

At Hawk Junction we had a ten-minute stop. Young boys were waiting for the train and as soon as it stopped they climbed in, ran through the coach, went into the toilet, drank the water out of the glass container at the head of the coach until it was dry. Then they threw the paper cups, and fought each other for the choice seats by the windows.

I went out to exercise my legs. Everything was still. The air cool and fresh and the smell of trees. The light clear. The forest spilled over its silence into this clearing. It was the largest clearing that we had come to. The trees were all around it. And huddled inside were wooden houses, a few had signs saying that they were hotels and general stores. Some men in overalls and windbreakers were standing by the back of trucks at the siding watching the train, the kids and the passengers. A couple of black mongrel dogs were playing in the snow. It was like most of the other stops along the line, a railway-workers' settlement.

When I returned inside the kids had squeezed into all the empty seats. They were playing a game of 'going somewhere'. One said that this time he was going to Toronto. Another said that this time he was going to New York. Another one said he was going to Montreal to see the Canadians play for the Stanley Cup. Several others agreed to go with him. Then the brakeman came on board and, without being told, they climbed off, stood by the siding, threw snowballs at each other, and watched as the train pulled away.

The landscape had remained so much the same for so long

that one hardly took notice of it now, but after Hawk Junction
the train began to climb a sharp gradient and to go even slower.
And as we approached the crest, the landscape suddenly
changed.

It looked like a battlefield. One of those melodramatic pictures
of the first world war. Trees, with branches and leaves and bark
and pine needles, disappeared. And all that remained standing
were scattered black charred trunks. Sometimes there was only
half a trunk, split, broken, burnt; and stumps around it. And
they stood up from the rock; black gaunt vertical lines; a grey
and yellowish-grey rock broken by patches of white snow. And
where the snow melted, the water was the colour of rust. All
vegetation was killed by the sulphur that the wind carried from
the Sinter Plant. You could see the direction of the wind. It was
like a scar in the landscape. In the distance, on either side, I
could see more hills with the blue-black outline of growing trees
on them. But here everything was dead. The rocks the colour
of ashes and the burned-out remnants of trees sticking up like
a field of gibbets. And it seemed as if we were deliberately crawling through this cemetery until we came around a bend and I
saw the Mine rising like a large back tooth that was decayed and
split in its centre.

THE MINE

I first came to the Mine on a hot June afternoon in 1948. With
two others from university we decided to go and work the summer in the bush where we knew the pay was good and where I
would be able to save some money, as I wanted to come over to
England.

We did not get to the Mine until sundown. The train was slow
and made this journey only three times a week. A cream
coloured bus with a blue sign 'Algoma Ore Properties' painted
on its side waited by the siding. Some men were inside. The
driver sat like a sparrow over the wheel, a jockey cap on his
head. He wore an orange sweater with 'Helen Mine' in blue
across the front. 'Students?' he said. We told him we were. 'Hop
in.'

We came to a lake with wooden houses on one side and a dirt
road. The bus stopped by a General Store. Several men with
black lunchpails climbed in. They called the driver Jack in
various accents. He punched small cards that they held up as
they entered the bus.

We drove around the lake and up a hill. Above us a steel
cable carried large buckets of iron ore from the Mine to the
Sinter Plant. We stopped at the top of the hill beside wooden
buildings. I asked the driver where the office was. He said to
follow him. He carried a mailsack over his shoulder.
'Where you from?'
Bob and I said Ottawa; Ian said Montreal.
'Play ball?'
We said we did.
He remained silent as we went through a wooden gate and
into a frame building partitioned off for several offices. The bus
driver dropped the mailsack on the floor and a girl came out of
one of the partitions. 'Hi, Glorie. Students.' And he went out.
She came to the counter, unsmiling, and took some paper. A
skirt and a sweater, and on her sweater at the neck she wore a
black cross. She took our names and home addresses. Then she
told us to go to the cookhouse, the next building away, and ask
the cook for our lunchpails.
We crossed the rough ground and saw a man with glasses,
grey hair, stripped to the waist, holding a white apron. He stood
by the cookhouse near several large barrels filled with garbage
and looked towards the horizon. It was a stiff sky and all the
hills were black.
He brought us into his office and gave us black lunchpails.
'It's all right,' he said. 'It will come off your first cheque.' He
spoke with a Scottish accent. Then he told us to scratch our
names on the lunchpails with a nail, that supper was at 7.30,
so that we still had half an hour to get a place to sleep. We
walked out through the dining-hall. Twenty large unpainted
tables, benches on both sides. The first table near the door had
chairs and flowers and a sign STAFF ONLY. He showed us a
wooden building about thirty yards away, at the edge of a cliff.
'Go to room nine and ask for Jim Wordle.'
The cable stretched over the cookhouse and I could hear it
creak as the buckets kept passing overhead. Where the cable
crossed between cookhouse and office a steel net was suspended
above the ground.
We found number nine in a plain building smelling of paint.
Outside the door a bundle of dirty laundry was tied together by
a shirt. Some time passed between our knock and the door being
opened. At first I thought he was a boy, then he switched the
room light on, and I could see that he was old, unshaven, and
sleepy. He could not be much more than five feet, a thin frame

covered by a dirty white shirt buttoned tight at the neck, collar
crumpled, and grey trousers that were too small. He wore no
shoes but heavy woollen socks. His fly-buttons were undone.
We told him what we wanted. He went to a cupboard and
pulled out a large piece of cardboard. He sat down on his bed
and began to examine the large writing on one side of the board.
I looked around the room. It stank of old age. Shelves covered
an entire wall. In these shelves toothpaste, soap, razor blades,
shoelaces, and chocolate bars, were propped up in the open boxes.
Above his bed, pasted to the wall, was a map similar to the one
hanging in the company's office in Sault Ste Marie. Covering
most of the map's face were pictures of boxers, hockey players,
movie stars, old Christmas cards, pin-up girls, and an old
calendar advertising Life Insurance.

'Yours will be forty-two,' he said to Bob and myself, and to
Ian he gave No. 43. 'You'll be with a Finn. He's away in the Soo
having a blow.' He said this with difficulty for he had no teeth.
They were sunk in a glass of water by his bed. He licked the end
of the pencil and printed our names large on the cardboard.
'You can get most things from me.' He showed us the cupboard
built into the wall where he returned the piece of cardboard.
Inside sprawled hundreds of paper-backs and magazines.
'Mystery, cowboy, sex stories, funnies, no need to pay. It'll come
off your cheque.'

Number 42 was a square room freshly painted white with one
window directly opposite the door. Two iron beds, two
dressers, all new. A light hung from the ceiling. I tried to raise
the window but was able to move it only a few inches. I could see
a side of a hill right below us and what looked like a small lake
which was dry. The outside air tasted cold and fresh. Bob and I
unpacked and had changed into old clothes when we heard a
bell tolling. There was nothing urgent about the sound. A slow
sound, silence, then the sound again. We went out of the room
and looked out of the window in the passage. Men were pressed
tight to the door of the cookhouse. Others were running towards
it. Suddenly the door opened and those that were there disappeared inside. By the time we reached the cookhouse the tables
were crowded with men eating. Late-comers, like ourselves, were
running from one table to another until they found a place on a
bench.

At my table they were speaking German. The only one not
speaking was deformed. He sat opposite me. Stubbles for fingers
on a wrist which was raw. A large red handkerchief, tied around

his head, went underneath his chin. He used this handkerchief to hold his jaw together. To eat he would loosen the knot above his head and with one stubbled hand he would slide the food from the table to his mouth while the other worked the jaw up and down.

'You a Canadian?'

A few nicotined-stained teeth, wide gaps between.

'Yes.'

'Look at these monkeys eat.'

As a platter of food was placed on the table, often before it reached the table, hands snatched whatever they could get. In less than ten minutes it was all over. The men, still chewing, stood up from the benches and went with their dishes to a large sink in the kitchen where a thin Slavic woman took the plates and plunged them into greasy water. An arrow painted on the wall behind her showed the direction to the kitchen door. By the door black lunchpails were lying open on a table. I saw the men who were going on the next shift look for their pails, then examine the lunch inside.

Outside, the men stood in silent groups by the side of the cookhouse. On the side of the cookhouse facing our bunkhouse a wooden booth was built on to the main wall. It stuck out like an ear. Steps without handrails led to a door. Someone shouted. 'Here he comes.' I saw Jim Wordle coming from the office to the cookhouse, his hands full of letters and newspapers. He gave the letters to the first man then went up the ladder to the booth and flung the papers inside. 'Shout them out.' Another man took the envelopes and began to call out names. Letters passed from hand to hand. After all the names had been read out several times, the D.P.s went through them again.

*

The three of us were put on shovelling muck for the first few weeks, then promoted to operate a machine. There were about a dozen students here for the summer, from different universities, mostly undergraduate engineers. We were the smallest group. The largest were the D.P.s and the various kinds of Canadians.

The D.P.s had been hired at the camps in Europe. They had to pass a medical and sign a contract that they would work at the Mine for three years. Then they would be free to go wherever they wanted. Very few could speak English and the only common language was German. They marked off each day on their home-made calendars with an X. A few had their wives with them. They worked as waitresses in the cookhouse. But they lived separate lives. They slept in different bunkhouses. They met if, by chance, their one day a week off coincided.

There was a Polish film director, Konrad, who had his front teeth knocked out by the Nazis. He taught me the words of the *Horst Wessel* song. There was the fair-haired architect from Lithuania with his prize edition of *Faust* that he kept carefully wrapped in several pieces of paper, in despair because he could not see himself coming out of here alive. There was the plump Polish philosophy student working in the blacksmith's shop, reading Nietzsche and Goethe. There were teachers, ex-army officers, tradesmen. The intellectuals amongst them suffered the most; at least they were more lucid about their despair. They did not go drinking or bootlegging or play crap on pay-day or go fishing. They remained in their rooms lying on their beds, writing letters to Europe. And waiting, like the others, for the next shift, the next meal, the next pay-cheque.

Most of the Canadians who were here were born in Europe. They could not understand why university students came to a place like the Mine. We told them, to make money. But they thought: if you have education you can make money without having to do labouring work. That was why they were saving up money so that their children could go to university and not have to come to places like this. Our presence confused them. Those who had their families with them lived in the company town by the lake; the bachelors, at the camps at the Mine. There were seven camps at the Mine. Each camp consisted of one bunkhouse. And the bunkhouses were divided into small rooms; two men to a room.

The management lived in wooden bungalows on top of the hill. They were mainly Anglo-Saxon and Scotch; various engineers from the small towns of Ontario. Quiet, dull, provincial. A few came from South Africa and Australia. There was one Englishman who had been in Canada about ten years. He said proudly that when his children were born he had some water flown over from his church in Sussex for them to be baptized. During the summer when their daughters came here on holiday from the private schools, the students were then invited to picnics along the lake, to dances in the wooden bungalows that went on late into the night when you walked outside and saw the sky shot through with Northern Lights.

But the highly-skilled miner, the one who worked at the rock-face, was a transient. The bush telegraph worked amazingly

F

well. They would arrive with their kitbags as soon as there was an expensive level to be cut, a slope, or a drift. They stayed as long as the bonus made it worth while. Then they would be off to another mine. They were professionals. They took pride in their equipment and in their work. Their only other interest was making more money. When the pay-cheque came every two weeks they would come back to the bunkhouse drunk on bad whisky they called rotgut, screech, poof. Then disappear. They were not very talkative, or articulate. Of all these men the only one I got to know was Max.

BIOGRAPHY

He was born in Poland. He came over to Canada in his early twenties. He still spoke English with a heavy accent. He was big with a barrel-chest, a bullet-head accentuated by having the grey hair cut short. He had a strong face with black thick eyebrows and dark eyes. He always looked worried. His room was across the corridor from mine in the bunkhouse and we often sat on the same bench at the dining-table. On one of my days off I went up to the Mine.

The day was hot. The earth between the rock was dry and cracked open. Patches of grass were scorched brown. Small black flies came in clusters and bit the skin. The only sound was the creaking noise the tramline made. Past the office building, a dirt road led to the top of the hill where the open mine stood ugly and massive. The peak of the hill was peeled back, stripped, hacked out, the colour of rust. All around me, as far as I could see, were a series of similar hills with blue lakes set in them. But they were untouched. The rock was grey-blue and intact. And scattered trees sprouted from their sides and tops.

Max was sitting with a few others outside the dryer, fully dressed to go underground, looking towards the horizon. 'You know,' Max said. 'God must have made this boosh all right. Look at the hills and the lakes. It's good boosh. The best boosh I have seen.'

Once we went out blueberry picking in the dips of the rock where the grass was burnt. He led the way, scrambling over the hot surfaces of the rock until we came to a ridge, and there was a fine patch of ripe blueberries. We picked and ate the blueberries, then we took off our shirts and lay in the sun. I asked him why he had come here. He did not answer right away.

'I come to the boosh because I got a wife. When I meet her I only want a poke. Then she tell me a baby made. So what the hell. In the end we marry. But it's a big swindle, fixed from the start. I only wanted a poke. But what do I get in the bargain? I get a wife, a child. She tells me now I got responsibilities. I say to hell. I don't want to be with her. When we are together, we say nothing except quarrel. I like her in bed. But not for a friend. So I come here. Make good money. Send her more than half. Then I miss her. Three or maybe four months and I begin to forget what a bitch she is. So I go back. But I know right away it's no good. We quarrel. I come back to this boosh. This time I stay . . .'

*

For the rest of the summer we ate, worked, slept, and watched the dollars mount up every two weeks. On days off we cut each other's hair, went blueberry picking, fought the black flies and the mosquitoes, escorted the daughters of the management for canoe trips on the lake, picnics; or else just lay on the bed and looked up at the ceiling until it was time for the next shift or the next meal.

We had to take a day off a week (union rules allowed only forty-eight hours a week, the union was affiliated to the one in the United States) but nobody wanted to. If we could only work that extra day we would get time-and-a-half. The union leader was called Bogie, a nearsighted, slow-moving, timid man. A French-Canadian who went around with an oil-can oiling the moving machinery at the charge bins, the conveyor belts, the crusher, and the coke plant. He also had a sideline. He was the representative of a mail-order catalogue firm in Winnipeg. If you wanted anything you went to Bogie and he would measure you up for a suit, or get you a pair of shoes, a tie, socks, underwear.

At the end of the summer we each had over four hundred dollars with us. We bought a bottle of rotgut and drank it. We smoked cigars. We took the seaplane back to the Soo.

III

A RETURN TO THE MINE

THE PLACE was deserted. It was cold. A few gulls flew slowly down hill. The only sound was of the tramline creaking overhead. I had a slip of paper that let me have food and accommodation on the Company's account. I went to the only bunkhouse that was being used; all the others were empty. There was a pool table downstairs, a small counter where you could buy soft drinks, coffee, cigarettes. A juke box.

There were four people in the room. A couple of young boys in slippers: German immigrants speaking in German as they played pool. A short dark French-Canadian in a yellow-and-black lumbershirt was talking to a young boy, going bald, behind the counter, about the N.H.L. play-offs between Detroit and the Canadians. All new faces.

The room I was given had a window facing the hills and the open mine that was no longer being worked. Two iron beds, a plain unvarnished table battered about, a dresser built into the wall carved up with initials and dates. Steam pipes came from the wall across the room and into the next wall. A radiator was by the window. Half of the wall was ripped open and a large piece of brown paper was tacked up over the damage. A Polish cleaning woman made one of the beds for me. I remembered her from the last time. Her husband used to be a driver of a Euclid truck taking the ore from the open mine and dumping it down the side of the cliff. One night he went over with the truck. The company had kept her on making the beds and cleaning the rooms and the toilets.

I took the slip of paper to the cook, but he was out. A young boy was playing in the main dining-room with a puck and a hockey stick. There were only four tables in the room close to the door. Curtains were on the windows. There was no staff table. I asked one of the girls who was laying the table why were there so few tables. 'Most of them have moved into town. They have their own homes, they have married, or brought over their families. Those that eat here are mostly old men and bachelors.'

At 5.30 it was time to eat and I was hungry. I went with the men from the bunkhouse to the kitchen and instead of waiting outside we came in and sat on benches by the walls until the supper was ready. No one spoke. Sometimes the young Germans said a few words. But there was no horseplay, or any sense of urgency. Men came in and brought their lunchpails to the kitchen then sat down and waited.

A waitress appeared with a plate full of roast beef, and as at a signal we went to the tables and sat down. There was still a half rush to get to the benches, but it didn't mean anything, for there was more than enough room. And lots of food. Toothpicks in a dish, ketchup, H.P. sauce, a container with paper napkins. There was a huge bowl full of soup, tinned salmon, roast beef, scalloped potatoes, macaroni, celery, a saucer full of tinned pears, a cake with thick icing, tea in large tall enamel containers. The meal began by a continual: 'Pass the milk . . . Pass the meat . . . Pass the bread . . .' In a few minutes it was all over.

When I came out it was cold. There was no one outside. The snow was dirty. I went back to the bunkhouse to my room and slept for an hour. Then I woke up. The room was very hot. The air dry. I opened the windows and lifted the slot of the outside one. I shut off the radiator. But I could not get to sleep again. I could hear the wind sounding against the side of the bunkhouse. My head ached. In the Soo it was the boat and the train whistles. Here it was the wind.

I went downstairs to the counter and had a coke. A few beaten men sat dejectedly on a bench and watched two young Germans play pool. There wasn't much talk in the room. Only the sound of the balls hitting and falling in the pockets. 'Day off?' 'No. Tomorrow.' Someone came in in a heavy lumberjacket, ski-cap, and told the boy behind the counter that he was going to Blind River. 'They want men, and the money's better.' Apart from a few questions as to where I came from, how long I was staying, they were not curious.

I went back to the room but I couldn't sleep. A radio was on loud. Someone near was groaning all night. Others were coughing. Then the ringing of alarm clocks and men going to the bathroom, which was next door to the room I was in. Doors opening, closing, shift changes. I switched the light on at 1.20, a few minutes past two, and again at four. Yet in the morning I felt strangely rested, more so than for the past few weeks.

At breakfast I saw Max.
'Oh, you're back. What's the matter?'
'Nothing. I'm just here for the weekend. How's life?'
'Oh, it got worse. They're all gone. It used to be good boosh here. Now no more. There in town. Go down, take a look. Lots of women now and children and dogs. I make thirty dollars a day. And I worry about income tax.'
There wasn't much time to talk as he was going on the next shift.
'Maybe I see you before you leave. I'm getting too old. I think I retire soon.'
'Max, you retire when you have enough money,' someone said at the end of the table.
'It's these goddam new machines. No more Jumbos. I liked the Jumbos. But these things. You have to wrestle with them. And they can pin you down.'

THE TOWN

I decided to take the bus into town after lunch, but I missed it and got a lift with a truck delivering groceries to the staff houses. The driver worked with a young boy who carried large cardboard boxes filled with food and milk and tins to the wooden verandas and left them there. There was no one outside. No movement. Except for a gull and the buckets passing overhead on the cables. The driver of the truck was French and he whistled *Jingle Bells* and as we drove over the unpaved road down the hill I could see Lake Superior hinged as a blue eye in between the far hills against the horizon. Then down to the level of the frozen lake.

He let me off halfway up on the single main street. A gale was blowing; the wind whipped the sand from the road. No sidewalk. At best the sand was hardened. I sank in soft slush whenever I tried to go anywhere but on the road. The wind lifted the sand and raised it high so that the sand could be seen coming over the road like snow over the runway. The signs from the café waved in the wind. Taxis hung around. Small wooden hut, men around a stove playing cards. A couple of seaplanes were beached on the shore by the frozen lake. The hills around were layers of rock. Solid rock, a yellow-grey white, with some birches growing in the cracks.

In the back streets kids were bundled up. They had made kites out of cellophane bags. They put string around the mouth so that the bag filled up with wind; the cellophane had advertisements for the local taxi and butcher and grocery. On another street two boys were throwing a baseball. They played an imaginary game. They both had baseball gloves. One was the pitcher. The other called each delivery either a strike or a ball. The pitcher faced an imaginary batsman. And he either struck him out or gave him a walk. Other kids just followed me down the road saying, 'Hi, mister.' They didn't want anything. They just followed a little behind me and to the side saying 'Hi, mister.' Dogs were nosing around outside garbage, and more dogs by the verandas and doorsteps. Apart from the children and the dogs, the streets were empty. In the snow-covered backyards there were old cars, old baby carriages, all kinds of junk, rusting away.

The lake was right beside the main street and it was frozen. There was a café, a cleaner, a jewellery repair, a bank, a movie (it was closed), a taxi-stand, and a hotel. I went into the hotel. It was dark inside. About half a dozen men in working clothes, their black lunchpails beside them. A few in their dark Sunday-best suits. Nearly everyone looked European. I had two glasses of beer and gave the man twenty-five cents.

At a table in the centre of the room a man was furiously rubbing an empty bottle of beer against his trousers, against the inside of his leg near the groin. Then he quickly brought the bottle to the toilet door, to the wood, where the door was hinged. The bottle held. It stuck out at right angles like a sign. Everyone came to have a look. One old man was drunk and, not listening to the shouts, went on into the toilet. As he touched the door the bottle fell and smashed.

Outside I walked again through the side-streets and came back on to the main street. It did not take long to walk through the town. It was a company town. The men could now buy land, build their own wooden houses with the stairs up the back porch, the wooden fences, the washing hanging up by the telegraph poles. It would last as long as the iron was there underneath them.

For something to do, the kids waited for the bus to come. Then rode, free, up to the Mine, the Sinter Plant, and back. It was Saturday and they were free from school. Otherwise the place was desolate.

I returned to the bunkhouse in late afternoon. Those who weren't working on the shift were dressing up to go into town. They had ordered a station-wagon from the taxi in town and they all piled in for Saturday night; the film, then the hotel, or the bootlegger.

Inside it was too warm. I went out and walked around the bunkhouse. This was the only bunkhouse still being used: Camp 5. When I first came here Camp 5 had just been built; it smelled of fresh paint and varnish. Now the glass in the window was smashed, chairs were without legs, holes in the walls, the windows had to be held up by empty bottles. The other bunk-houses were empty. It looked like a small ghost town. Empty wooden houses with faded signs on them Camp 1, 2, 3, 4, 6, 7. Outside my window empty cigarette packages, roll-your-own-tobacco, broken whisky bottles, beer bottles, toilet rolls, old over-shoes, lay in the melting snow on the side of the hill.

I wished I had something to read. I left the few books that I had taken with me at the Soo. So I went and knocked on doors until one opened. It was the French-Canadian I had seen down-stairs when I arrived. I asked him if I could borrow a book. 'Sure,' he said. 'Come in.' He showed me a pile of them on the floor: *Life*, *Reader's Digest*, Westerns, and paper-backs. He picked up a paper-back. *A Virgin in Chicago* by Ace Demarco. 'This one is a good story,' he said.

I went back to my room, lay down, and tried to read. The story began with a cocktail party in a smart flat in Chicago. The hero, young and innocent, had just left his father's farm and arrived at this cocktail party where his boss lived. He found everyone drunk. His boss's wife liked the look of him. And while they were dancing . . . 'He could feel her biting into him, she had nothing on underneath. She made sure he knew that she had nothing on.' The chapter ends with them in the corner of the room, standing up and copulating. . . .

I remembered the small office in Southampton Row. I was taken there by a writer I met in Cornwall. The man in the office was tall, well-dressed, wearing a public school tie. He looked as if he belonged. He was publishing paper-backs. He had read some-thing of mine and asked me if I would like to do a short novel for him. It apparently didn't matter what I wrote. I had to sub-mit nothing to him. He said he would pay me £75 for 20,000 words. All it had to be was 'full of action, don't mess about.' He said, 'Just knock them off cleanly. Don't give too many details of blood, put in lots of sex and murder, and a chase is always good, but have it set in Canada, anywhere in Canada.' Then he said that he printed 20,000 copies of these paper-backs every two weeks and practically all of them were for the Canadian market.

He had several authors, good ones he said, women too, writing for him, but they all had to go under one name 'Ace Demarco.'

I was straight from university and didn't understand. 'Couldn't you give them good stuff?' I asked. 'Even with hot covers?' 'Naw, it won't work.' This time it was his partner. A short, spare young Jew, with a shake. The well-dressed man called him 'Shaky Jake' when he was not in the room. He looked after the covers, the sales, promotion, and publicity. 'The public knows,' Shaky Jake said. 'You can't fool the public. It knows what it wants. We tried a good writer once, straight stuff, but the public didn't want it. We had to change the dust jacket twice before we sold that particular edition.'

They were singing *The First Noel* downstairs. But they didn't know more than: 'Noel, Noel, Noel, Noel. Born is the King of Israel.' I went down the wooden steps to the canteen. The men were just coming back from town, each with a bottle. One had cherry brandy. He, opened the bottle and passed it around.

He looked and talked like James Cagney. 'My name's Anthony. What's yours?'

'Norman.'

We shook hands.

He said he was here a week, a diamond driller, but he didn't like it here.

A voice called out. 'Anthony. What's your other name?'

He smirked. He was blond with a round baby face and froggy eyes that slanted upwards. His chin had a deep cleft in it, like a scar. He was short, stocky, and wore a new suede windbreaker. 'My other name had thirteen letters in it so I made it short and sweet. Anthony King.' He kept on passing round the cherry brandy. Then he began to sing with the young boy behind the counter.

> Down by the Old Mill Stream,
> Where I first met you,
> With your eyes of blue.

But nobody knew any more words. We started *Pack Up Your Troubles*. But that went as far as the first lot of 'smile, smile, smile.' We tried *She'll Be Coming Round the Mountain*. That went for two verses and someone began some children's songs: *Around the Corner and Under the Tree*. But none of us knew what went after 'He kissed me once. He kissed me twice.' Then someone started *Jingle Bells*, and most of us knew that.

The bus had returned from town and the men came into the canteen. One of them was drunker than the others. He had thick lips, a long nose, was bald, and his skin hung in pouches underneath his eyes. He had his bottle wrapped up in a brown paper bag. He was in his fifties, a D.P. I recognized who was here in 1948; the only one who had not left the camp. He began to weave around the room bumping into the pool table and the juke box. The boy behind the counter took the bottle away from him. The man went after the boy. He took hold of his hand. 'You are my friend, Peter.' He began to stroke the boy's hand and to weep. 'You are my friend, Peter.' And he kissed the boy tenderly on the lips, then lurched away, took out his false teeth, and vomited. The boy helped him up the steps and gave him back his bottle, then returned with a rag and cleaned up the spew. The others began to sing *The Old Grey Mare*, but like the other songs it didn't last very long. Then they tried *Alouette* and that didn't last very long either. Someone put a dime in the juke box and it blared out *The Poor People of Paris*. Then the canteen closed and we went back to the rooms, but I couldn't fall asleep.

The room was hot and stuffy, the air dry, plugging up the nostrils. Men kept going to the toilet and I could hear them being sick. Bottles were smashed. I could hear broken glass falling outside on the rocks. Someone was coughing like a hurt animal. A radio was going loudly, a disc-jockey on an American late-night station. Then the alarm-clocks began to ring. And I listened to the opening and the closing of doors as the men went off to the next shift.

SUNDAY IN THE BUSH

Sunday was just another day. Those who didn't work on the day shift had chicken for lunch. There was little talk. No hypocrisy. And there was no trust. Everyone locked his door.

Outside it was cold and windy. The gulls over the frozen lake were blown back as they soared. The tramline with its buckets kept passing overhead. And the continual pressure of this landscape. One belonged to this and was nothing. It reduced all human effort by its indifference and size. Even the old men who were here, though they were involved in hard physical work— they weren't taking any human risks. They surrounded themselves with this no man's land, cut off and isolated. They wanted no responsibility, no human involvement. One had contracted out.

But it had caught up with them. These—apart from the young ones who come here for a few years to make their stake and then go back—these men had come to a dead end. The town was growing. They now had a small hospital, a weekly newspaper, the immigrants had brought over their wives, others married. And the small town was pushing these men away from the security they had, of being cut off. They were being thrown back on to themselves, and they had few resources. Their only chance was to go further into the bush. But most of them were now too old for that.

I had borrowed, *The Scourge of the Swastika* from the boy in the canteen. It was a strange feeling to read this book here. All this account of man's inhumanity to man seemed so remote. What connection was there between the things that one read, the atrocities and the butcheries, and the kind of life that one lived here—the emptiness, the repeating hills and lakes and rocks?

> *This is the staring unsleeping*
> *Eye of the earth, and what it watches is not our wars.*

I went out and walked around the empty bunkhouses, up the dirt road to the Mine shaft. No one else was outside. I remembered how enthusiastic I felt living in this landscape, for the first time, that summer. Watching the morning come over the hills, the purple peeling back from the black; the rime frost on the roofs; the low clouds level with the top of this hill. Now one recognized the hostility and the indifference.

I decided to go down to the Sinter Plant and took the bus. The place, by the railway siding, looked much the same as when I worked here. The same drab dusty waste ground. The ore-dust and coke silted against the windows, the buildings. Grit on the skin. But there were a few changes. A larger shed-like building where the ore was burned with the coke and came out as clinkers tumbling into the freight cars underneath the chutes; large pieces of clinker, blue-grey, falling with flashes of red, like the dying moments of a horse lashing out. I went into the dryer. The smell of human sweat caked and soaked in old clothes. The clothes pulled up on ropes to the ceiling above the lockers. The same small shower with a wooden footboard. And outside a taller chimney pouring out a thick brilliant-white smoke, the smell of sulphur, and the smoke going out over those hills and killing all vegetation. I walked around the Sinter Plant, ankle deep in mud. The things one remembered . . .

Grey dust coming off the conveyor belts like a soft mist, smelling of sour cucumbers, as the crushed ore was carried to the coke plant, as the returns were carried away, the dust coming out of the cracks in the wooden ramps that joined building to building like a cat's cradle. And coming off a shift the grey powder on our faces and clothes. The mask we wore, a thick piece of gauze across our lips, touching the nostrils, like a woman's sanitary towel, held in place by an elastic around our head. Black where the lips touched the gauze and black the inside of the nostrils. Then the shower—the former gravedigger, the former hockey player, the former boxer, truck driver, two from reform school, the D.P.s—and feeling so much lighter, punching our numbers and waiting for the bus to come and take us around the lake up the hill to the bunkhouse. And when things were going right and the charge bins were emptying their ore on to the main conveyor belt and the belt was not too heavily loaded as it went up the steep ramp, so that the chances of it stopping and all the ore backing up and spilling in a heap was remote, I would go out to the waste land by the building and in the water-filled hollows by the railway lines sail matches with the Lithuanian architect to see who would win. So much of the time one had nothing to do but watch machinery moving.

And on the graveyard shift the mice with their pink eyes that came into the building for warmth. I sat down on the wooden box outside the door—the air inside was filled with ore dust so thick that you could taste the grit and see it cloud the light like a fog—and fed them from the roast-beef sandwiches, the pieces of cake, that after a while in the black lunchpail tasted soapy and dry. In the day the black flies, the mosquitoes; we made small fires outside the buildings; but it didn't help. And watching the Northern Lights, the dawn, the hills, the sunken blue lakes. One was continually reminded of the magnificence and the hostility of the landscape and the mundane dullness of the work.

I left the Sinter Plant and took the bus back with those coming off the afternoon shift. The town was deserted. I returned to camp.

The men off work had nothing to do. The canteen was closed. It was too cold to go outside. And what was there outside? Nothing to do but sleep, lie on your bed, and wait for the next meal, the next shift, the pay-cheque every two weeks. Then a trip into town for a hamburger, a movie, a drink, bring back a bottle. And those sitting in the offices in the Sault and in

Ottawa[1] who showed me, so proudly, the progress charts with the lines going up, producing more and more tons of high grade ore, the high wages, say nothing of the boredom, the isolation, and the continual defeat of any form of human relationship.

I can hear the wind outside the window. A full gale. But there is no indication except from the gulls how strong the wind is, or its direction. For there is nothing in its way.

On Monday morning I was ready to leave and I was glad I was going. The last time I was here I was here to make money. In the washroom there was another person also shaving.

'Not working today?'

'No.'

'Day off?'

'No. I'm leaving this morning.'

There was no more conversation.

I took my bag and went to say goodbye to Max, but his door was locked. I went to see the man in the office who gave me the slip of paper for my accommodation and meals. He was in his early thirties, corpulent like an overgrown schoolboy. We talked about the Mine. He told me of the new shaft that would soon be open on a ridge not far from Camp 5. I asked him about the men. He said they were a nuisance. It was costing the company money to keep them here. It would be better if they went somewhere else.

*

The train had started at Michipocoten Harbour, eight miles away. A diesel engine, then a new generator car, and one old coach. The seats were hard. Two fans, not moving, were on the ceiling and two small bulbs. The woman opposite me had her hand in her purse clutching her rosary, her lips moving. Someone behind me was playing a mouth organ.

We went slowly through the same dead land, then passed the small logging camps: the cut wood; the sawdust-pile yellow against the snow; logs piled and sawn, ends like cigarettes in a full pack. A few dogs in a clearing. A clothes-line full of bright washing.

At Hawk Junction we stopped and waited for the train to come from Hearst and to join another coach on to ours. Freight cars at the siding. Big grizzly bears painted on both sides. Across one in a child's scrawl in yellow chalk: *Sandra Kearn loves*

[1] *Sault Daily Star*, April 6, 1956. (C.P.): 'U.S. investors controlled 55 per cent of Canada's mining, smelting and petroleum industry, and 43 per cent of manufacturing industry, the Bureau of Statistics reported today.'

Nelson Armstrong. On another: *Trade with Red China means Jobs.*

About five miles from the Sault the bush ended. There were the mile-posts; the brightly painted wooden houses; the cars rusting on their sides by the houses stripped of everything usable; the junk-heaps in the fields, old baths lying upside down like dead cows; the hotdog stands off the highway.

Then back to the slow brown river with the slabs of ice still floating. The ride to the United States side, across the bridge, with the customs man in the taxi. The flight to Winnipeg. I moved my watch back an hour. It was easiest, at one in the morning, to go to the hotel where the taxi brought us.

I woke at noon to doves making soft insistent sounds between buildings; the sunlight coming through the window blinds; the noise of traffic; and the near faces of stenographers at their type-writers in the building across the back. I took a bath and lay in the water watching the steam race like mice across the ceiling.

It was a large clean room with two windows, a low double bed, several easy-chairs, lights, telephone, radio, and a good writing desk. I went down to the coffee-bar and had two cups of coffee. And I felt content just to sit in an open booth drinking cups of black coffee and being in the presence of strangers, listening to their talk, watching the actions of their faces. It somehow seemed a long time since one felt this particular warmth in just being reminded where one belongs. Outside, the streets looked cold and grey. I went out and walked without any particular destination.

IV

WINNIPEG

AT FIRST it was all width and loose sand blowing and women with bad complexions and the wide streets looked even more empty with so few people walking. I walked along Portage. The snow had melted. The mud had dried, leaving loose sand on the street that the wind lifted. Department stores, banks, offices; they're much the same. But it was down Main Street that one felt quickly at home. The huddles of old men outside small restaurants with the foreign newspapers in the windows, who had lived here for thirty, forty, even fifty years and who still remained Ukrainians, Poles, Lithuanians and Germans. They were the Displaced Persons, the failures. Not the D.P.s who have come here since the war or even the more recent immigrants. They have quickly taken on North American values, discarding their background, their childhood, putting on the thin veneer of conformity, what is demanded of them, in order to be accepted, to be on the way to success.

A sign: *Labour Progressive Party*. A Jewish store with religious goods. A Catholic window filled with a large plaster statue of Christ with blood-drops painted on, dripping. I went into a small restaurant for something to eat. In the back was a large pool room with several tables and the low bright lights, the green reflectors. I sat at the counter. Cough-drops, cigarettes, peanuts, sunflower seeds, Bromo-Seltzer, razor blades, handkerchiefs in cellophane, a sign: *Two Minutes to Prepare any Tin of Soup.* An old man came from the pool room, sat on the stool beside me. Unshaven, a shirt buttoned at the neck, collar crumpled, no tie. He ordered a hard-boiled egg and two pieces of black bread. He salted the bread and ate that until the egg came. The radio was playing cowboy tunes, every song sounded the same, the vowels stretched and repeated at the end of each line. Across the road were the secondhand clothing stores, the Loan Offices. The men coming in from the pool room did not speak English amongst themselves, only to the waitress. They sat at the counter and ate hard-boiled eggs with black bread and butter and salt. Outside, old men passed the window, coat collars turned up; sometimes a family of Indians.

I decided to leave the expensive hotel for a cheaper one on Main Street. Money was getting short and this hotel would be a third of the price of the other. The room was small, dingy, and smelled of disinfectant. No windows. A skylight took up half of the ceiling. But the ropes to the skylight did not move the glass. The only ventilation was a glazed portion of the wall facing the corridor. You could make the top part of the wall open, and the air from the corridor would enter the room. It was barely furnished: an iron bed, a wicker chair, a plain dressing-table without a Bible. Down the corridor was the only toilet, no handle or lock, just a piece of rope that you hooked around a nail.

The only pay-phone was downstairs in the lobby beside the shoeshine stand. A glum schoolboy wearing a black leather winter cap, rubbers, a heavy shirt buttoned tight at the neck, was squatting on a wooden box and cleaning a pair of shoes. I telephoned a writer who was a professor at the university. He invited me over for a party later that night.

When I came out of the telephone booth there was a line of men, in working clothes, carrying lunchpails, that twisted right around the lobby to the door. It was pay-day. Each man carried a cheque that he cashed with the hotel proprietor behind the desk, then went straight into the door to the left: the hotel's tavern. Before setting out for the party, I decided to go in and have a few beers.

'Hey, Porkovitch. Two here.'

A fat placid man in white apron and black belt around his bulging belly, a conductor's change-machine hanging heavily in front of the belly, was walking by the tables carrying a large tray with glasses of beer on it. The room was so crammed with round tables and chairs that it was difficult for him to go by. Men in parkhas, overalls, in cheap suits, in windbreakers, were talking loudly. It was difficult to see because of the smoke in the room. The fat waiter waddled over and brought me a couple. 'Hey, Porkovitch. I said two here!' The voice was drunk and mocking. An old man with a white waxed moustache and a gold chain hanging from his vest sat beside me. 'That man's name isn't Porkovitch,' he said. 'I forget his name. But I know it isn't Porko-vitch.' A young man came and sat down at the same table, his fingers kept tapping away on his black lunchpail. Then his beer arrived. He quickly downed two, then had two more, slowly. He said it was cold outside, in a German accent. The three of us were soon talking. The German had a good-looking face with blond short hair and regular features but there was something ingratiating and shifting in his blue eyes, an uneasy aggressiveness in his manner. He showed us his hands, the fingers were curled, the skin split in several places. He said he was a bricklayer and it was the cold. 'When it is too cold it is all right, then you not work. Not this weather.' He had been here a little over a year but he didn't like Winnipeg. 'Too many Yous here,' he said. 'We must have another war. Too many Yous.'

A sign on the wall said: UNDESIRABLES MAY BE EJECTED. Another sign on the wall: WARNING. NO PERSON UNDER 21. NO INDIAN. NO INTERDIT.

It took over an hour by bus to get to the address I was given. It was very cold. The slush had frozen in the street and on the sidewalks. And there was that brittle tension of a cold winter night. I had asked a well-bundled-up policeman on Portage what bus to take; but he didn't know. He spoke with a South-East London accent. He said he had come over seven months ago and that I would probably get the right directions from the drugstore that was open on the corner. By the time I arrived the party was well under way.

In one corner a spare young man with a wide ugly mouth, blond straight hair and large glasses was sitting in a chair reading, near-sightedly, *Winnie the Pooh*, and grinning to himself. The father of the host, a thin tall man with a gaunt face, a long thin neck, sat on a settee, by himself, in a corner of the room knitting a pair of socks and occasionally biting from an apple. From a small room by the veranda a gramophone was playing a long-playing record of Scottish Laments; all I could hear was the soft monotonous wail of the bagpipes.

The women sat together on a large chesterfield. They looked washed out, pale, and those who wore 'style' dresses wore them very self-consciously. They talked of their 'winter projects'. One had learned Spanish this winter, another weaving, another pottery. The hostess told me that the first snow fell in October on Hallowe'en and it had stayed right through (now it was mid-April) and every winter the women had some 'project' to see them through. She came from Toronto and all this was treated as an outsider, in the nature of a joke. The men were pleasantly dull, timid, provincial. It was hard to see much outward difference between those in their late twenties and those

G

who were middle-aged. They all had 'solid respectability'
advertised in their entire bearing and with it a passiveness and
deadness.

They fed on academic gossip. They had not made the grade
at either of the large universities in the East or on the West
Coast. Winnipeg was a poor second. But they knew all the details
of what was going on in the campuses across the country: the
scandals, the intrigues, the promotions, the fellowships, the
deaths, the openings. Two stood out from the others. A lecturer
from South Africa who had been to Cambridge and had contri-
buted to critical and literary magazines. He said he didn't like
Winnipeg, but where could he get such pay in England? The
host was a strange little man, not yet thirty, but the external
mould of how he would be as an old man was set: the small
mouse moustache, the high-pitched voice, the glasses, the receding chin, and an impishness continually breaking through with
a laugh, a giggle, or a word. I liked his early poems. They caught
a gay, anarchistic world, zany, nostalgic, absurd. His recent
poems were lifeless, academic, and literary. What had killed the
poet? Was it the university? Growing up? Only in flashes did
one still get the mischievous small-town boy, the Katzenjammer
Kid, kicking against authority. But it was in the person, and not
in his work.

It was a dull evening. After the 'winter project', the talk was
about where they were going in the summer. Those who could
were leaving Winnipeg for the East, the West, the States, or
Europe. One was continually reminded of being cut off. In the
small talk, in the gossip:

Did I know —— at McGill?

I did. How did he get on here?

O, nobody liked him. He wanted to do things his way. And he
didn't like us. He could find no one to go with him to the
wrestling matches.

The old man sat in the corner knitting the sock. The Scottish
Laments continued to play softly and monotonously.

That night, back in the hotel room, I found it difficult to sleep.
I was down to less than three dollars. I wondered from whom I
could borrow. In the end I decided to send a wire to a friend in
Montreal.

SLAUGHTERHOUSE

Next morning I walked from the hotel to Portage and

waited for a bus to take me to St. Boniface. At the bus stop the man beside me kept repeating. 'It's a dirty wind. It's a dirty wind.' It was a cold wind that lifted the loose sand up from the sidewalk and the road and flung it into your face. I asked him how long it would take to get to the stockyards. He said about fifteen or twenty minutes.

'Going to work there?'

'No.'

'Where you from?'

'Ottawa.'

'I haven't been East for eighteen years. We've had a cold winter here. It began with a snowfall on Hallowe'en.'

The bus came and we got on. We crossed over two bridges with muddy water flowing underneath. 'There's going to be floods when they break up,' the man said. Then he kept repeating the French names of the streets in St. Boniface. Had I heard of Louis Riel? I said I had. He was buried here. Then the bus came to flat open country. I saw a large chimney stack behind a railway siding. The man told me to get off here. I walked over the railway tracks towards the stack and the building beside it; the ground was frozen.

What I expected was a smell of some sort, but there wasn't any. A truck stood underneath a long chute that came from a brick building and a man was carefully packing hides. He stood on top of the pile in the back of the truck and carefully put them in their place as if he was packing into a suitcase clothes that he did not want creased.

I was supposed to meet my guide at ten o'clock in the staff-house cafeteria but something had gone wrong with my watch during the night and when I entered the modern, well-lit, clean building, the clock in the wall said 9.15. There was a sign outside the cafeteria: CONDUCTED TOURS EVERY DAY AT 2 P.M. Inside the cafeteria a few men in white overalls were sitting by the small tables. There were silk-screen prints of Canadian landscapes on the wall. A couple of waitresses stood behind the chrome-and-glass counter.

My guide was a short stocky young man in his twenties with curly blond hair and glasses. He called me Norm from the start, I called him Gerry. This show of friendliness is odd until you realize it means nothing, it's a convention. He led me into a room where white coats were hanging. I put one on over my clothes. I asked him who came for these two o'clock conducted tours. 'Lots of all sorts. Mostly out of town. Some farmers who want to see what happens to their animals. And women's auxiliary, Kiwanis, Jaycees . . . '

We walked outside and around the building until we came to wooden pens. There were some pigs in one; in another, calves. I could hear the sound of cows bellowing from inside the building. 'These pigs will be killed at two this afternoon,' Gerry said. 'The pens are not cleaned during the winter, the shit's frozen solid. There's about five feet of shit out there now.' We walked through a large barn. Cows bellowed from the far end of the barn, calves huddled in wooden pens along one side. On the other side, in a large enclosure with bales of hay were two very clean and white goats with two kids. 'Wouldn't they make a good picture?' Gerry said. The scene belonged to something one remembered from a child's illustrated book. 'They lead the sheep up the ramp. The sheep will follow the goats without making a fuss. Then once up, we take the goats away and bring them back here, and they bring the next lot of sheep up the ramp.'

We walked up a steel ramp covered with dry manure. At the top there was a narrow pen with steel gates, room enough for the animal lengthwise. Four cows were goaded into this pen, pressed tight, their heads twisted back over the other cow's back. They were controlled by the jabs from an electric poker which a man used on their rumps. The steel gate behind them closed. Then the man with the electric poker got them into the killing block. A deep wooden rectangular box, enough to take two cows at a time. 'They're scared alright,' Gerry said. 'They can smell blood.' A man stood above them on a steel ramp. He swung a pole-axe above his head, stunned one, then the other. They fell down heavily. Then the floor the cows had been standing on was quickly lowered down to the concrete floor below. They tumbled out on their sides, their legs twitching. A man put a manacle around one of the backlegs, pressed a button with his left hand, and hoisted the animal up to a rail near the ceiling, legs up, head hanging limply down. Then, with his right hand, he carefully, without splashing himself, cut the cow's throat.

Another man put a bucket under the throat to catch the blood. The animal began to move upside down as the small wheel to which its back leg was attached began to travel on the rail by the ceiling at a steady slow pace. As soon as that bucket was full he replaced it with another. And full buckets of blood, with the crimson froth on top like candy floss, were taken away slowly on another rail to another part of the building.

I'm certain one could make a surrealistic film in a slaughterhouse on the killing floor without resort to any trickery. Just recording. A few inches from where I was standing, heads, like in a Cocteau film, severed at the neck, without horns, eyes bulging, tongues hanging out, were going around like the figures of some old medieval clock. Beside it the full buckets of blood were carried on their hooks. Along the walls of the building were the carcasses, spaced a few feet apart, in various stages of being reduced. Some had the hide still on, some without their heads, some with their legs off. Carcasses continually moving slowly to the pace of those small turning wheels on the rails by the ceiling. Away from the walls were separate turn-tables with their own rails and hooks hanging down. Each had either a carcass or a cow's head. Blood was like water on the concrete floor. The men were covered in it. They each had one job to do in dismembering the animal. A machine cut bone, another emptied the stomach, a machine like a saw pulled the hide off, another cut the horns, another cut the animal in two. It went on, around the room, the pulling, the tearing, the cutting, the cage dropping to the floor, the twitching feet, the slash with the knife, the frothy crimson buckets . . . At the end of the room they put the carcasses in shrouds so that the bright yellow fat wouldn't harden and bubble.

Suddenly a pistol shot and everyone on the floor stopped working. The man with the pole-axe stood above us grinning. 'That mocky,' Gerry said. 'He's only supposed to hit the steel to let the men know when he's finished knocking. But he does it when he wants to scare us.' We stood and watched. To Gerry it was a kind of sport. 'Now, I'll show you murder,' he said.

He lead me to the far side of the floor where a tall figure with a thick middle and stooped rounded shoulders, in rubber boots and glasses and wearing a hat, was sharpening a knife very conscientiously on a small stone. The knife was long and thin, and the man wiped it spotlessly clean with a piece of cloth. 'He's a Rabbi,' Gerry said. 'This is where they do the kosher killing. I call it murder.'

Six calves were hanging head down by a back leg from a pulley. They kicked with their remaining free legs. They swung. They bleated. Then the man with the knife stepped up to a small wooden platform and with one stroke cut the throat of each animal. As soon as the six were done another man moved the hanging animals behind a steel partition. The blood splashed down on the tin like rain on a tin roof in a thunderstorm. Some still kicked with their legs. Then the man with the glasses washed the knife and began to sharpen it again. Another six calves were hoisted up.

Gerry took me to another room on this floor. He had to unlock the door. On the floor lay about twenty or thirty skin-enclosed bundles. They looked like bundles of dirty laundry tied together or like huge ears blown up. Some had a small dark head hanging out of the skin, a small calf's head with its tongue fully out. One dark calf lay completely out of the skin bag, its wet fur standing up in tufts. They were the unborn calves taken out of the slaughtered cows. 'You realize, Norm, you're getting things we don't show to others, like this room. I've got two of their skins at home. Their hide is worth more than the whole hide of a cow.' They lay on the concrete floor, blown up skin-bags, a soft green and white and the small dark head sticking out with its tongue. Many of the skin-bags were unbroken and you could see the dark shadow where the dead calf lay inside.

In another room men and women were by tables cleaning the guts to be used for casings. Gerry stopped and became sentimental. 'If I have an hour or so free from my desk I usually go and play with the guts here. I like the feel of them. I worked in a mortuary before coming here and I always wanted to get hold of the guts, but I couldn't. I knew that here was a stiff lying just full of guts that I couldn't get hold of. Have you ever had guts go through your hands? It's a wonderful feeling.'

In another room girls were sitting on chairs by small tables in straight rows like a classroom by conveyor belts which carried sliced pieces of bacon. Their job was to put the bacon slices in cellophane-wrapped packages, in pound weights. A girl would take some bacon that came along the belt. On a clock beside her was a simple scale balance that showed if she was short or over. A snip of the scissors and a quick wrapping up. It was all done quickly and without concentration. They sat there, hands and eyes working mechanically while they talked.

'See them gas away,' Gerry said. 'You know what they're talking about? If they got shagged last night. All of them are easy as anything. A bunch of dopes, doing it for free; they haven't even finished public school. Yesterday I pulled the pants off this one.' He pointed to a young heavily-built girl with blonde close-cropped hair. 'She's got the biggest tits I've seen, but the smallest nipples. If you like, come back to my room and you can see what's going on in the cars in the car-park with my binoculars. I'm going with one in the cafeteria and a friend of mine is going with one in the gut room. They've asked us to take our holidays

with them so we're using their cars. We'll drive down to California.' He grinned. 'It's really a shagging holiday.'

I saw lambs hanging upside down. The man had stopped
knocking cows and was on the other floor sticking pigs and
sheep. I came down the ramp with the dry manure. The two
kids were playing on the bales of hay; a cow was being brought
in by truck . . . After it was over Gerry said, 'Come on to the
cafeteria; you're entitled to a free cup of coffee on the company.'
The waitress who served us was in her late twenties, tall, stout,
fat shapeless legs, a large bosom, and a vacant expression in her
face. She reminded me of a docile cow. 'I'm getting into her for
my holiday,' he said. She waddled around us swishing her
behind slowly and sensually and with a certain contempt.

When I came out it was snowing and the wind was blowing
the snow hard. The truck was still underneath the chute, the
man still carefully packing the hides on top.

It was only later, back in Winnipeg, passing a butcher-shop
and seeing a woman inside haggling over the price for a piece
of meat that the entire morning clicked into place.

I cannot get sentimental over animals.[1] But I did not eat that
day. There was the physical revulsion in seeing the commercial
side of killing, the mass slaughter, the horror, not at the cutting
of the throat or the blood, but in the detachment, the way a
particular cow was quickly lost sight of in the efficiency of those
machines, as other cows kept following on. But though I didn't
feel like eating that day, I knew by tomorrow I would get hungry, the stomach would demand to be filled, and on a hungry
stomach sensitivity is a luxury one cannot afford. And part of
the nausea belonged to something else: to Moo-cows, Baa-lambs,
Chook-Chooks, that were part of one's childhood, that saw them
only in the field, on a farm. And later bringing the chickens to
have their throats cut; it made sense when the next day we had
them for supper. It was this remoteness that allowed one to feel
nauseated watching, and that allowed one to forget. There was
no connection that one could feel personally. The food that one
eats seems so remote from the slaughterhouse. One hates to be

[1] I remember that year in Brighton when we lived in a large house on the
side of a hill. Everyone else in the Close had a large car and a gardener. They
went with the place and with the kind of people who retired here. About
once a month there would be a knock at the front door and an elderly woman,
well-preserved and well-dressed, brought us a sack from a car. Could we fill
it up with our old things or anything that we didn't want? Then they would
sell it. To help look after some dogs. At the time of the Hungarian uprising
we had two sacks left by the door. One was to collect for the Hungarians;
the other for dogs.

reminded, that there is a connection. One would rather not know how much of living is just feeding, for the only time you are reminded is when you are hungry.

The robin in the garden followed me, as I cut the lawn, and snapped up the insects and flies and the small worms. Only after it had its fill, did it fly on to the low branch of the apple tree and begin to sing.

In the late Spring, in Mousehole, our landlord, a kind man with a beard who lived off the land and had geese and ducks, killed a drake for us to eat. He showed me the insides. So much was sex organs and intestines.

You forget why the killing goes on, how one animal lives by devouring another: when your stomach is filled, then you are tricked into all these moralizing sentimental judgments about the taking of life. I'm sure that if I had not eaten that morning, when Gerry offered me those hot dogs and slices of ham from the conveyor belt and those pieces of baloney as we were going through, not only would I have gladly eaten them but I would have stored some away in my pocket for later use. And if one has to kill, to be cruel, I would rather it was to animals than human beings.

FREE SHOW

Walking back to my hotel on Main Street I saw a man, knees bent, weave drunkenly along the sidewalk, then stumble and fall into a dirty puddle of water, mud, and slush. People soon gathered and watched. He tried to get up. He finally pushed himself up, and stood with knees slightly bent and waited with a sick foolish look of complete trust. A man near him went over and gave a sharp kick with his foot on the inside of the man's legs, where they were bent at the knees. He collapsed back into the water and the mud. The man who kicked him laughed. Someone shouted, 'Crawl.' And he began to crawl on his hands and knees through the slush, the mud, the water. People watching; just watched. He began to crawl quickly, then, frightened, he got up and ran down the street. His entire front was soaked black by the water. His trousers and shirt dripping. He didn't look back once.

*

That night I went to see *I am a Camera* the film of Isherwood's Berlin Stories, but mainly about Sally Bowles. It was spoiled by a too neat film ending. And when I came out and walked along Portage, the frozen side-streets with the dirty snow, I thought of myself here, of 'being a camera', the detached observer. Was that enough?

I had walked through a park earlier in the afternoon and saw a sick girl being pushed in a wheelchair. She had a white swollen head, grotesque, like some balloon blown up, the eyes small, slanted, Chinese. A thin mouth, all on a five-year-old body, a fringe raggedly cut across her forehead and straight black hair hung down the sides. I looked at the small thin body, the short legs, but it was the face that pulled my eyes, as if it had a magnifying glass placed in front of it, saying, 'Come, look at me here. This is what makes me different. Forget the other part. That's nothing. That's the same as the others.' And how much of the camera, the eye, is devoted to recording the oddities, the absurdities of life, and letting the continual flow of images, that one sees but does not notice, pass by.

And human relationships had become nothing more than a series of brief encounters. In wartime one accepted that. For a very short while two people were thrown together, reacted violently, parted, and that was that. Now one didn't even have a war to justify one's values or decisions.

How I envied Graham Greene's characters. They rebelled, they were on the run, anarchistic, but they were lucky. They all had behind them an established order of values.

One still clung to a morality but without the faith that ruled it. One was like a chicken running around without its head. All that was left was the personal. One had nothing to fall back on now except the personal. 'Life is there all the time. But a man cannot get at it except through himself.' Nothing, it seemed, could be had secondhand. One was condemned to feed on personal experience.

But you couldn't go around with the eye wide open all the time. You had to put some kind of blinkers on the sides; to exert some sense of one's personality; for without it there wouldn't be any meaning to what the eye sees.

*

A good way I have found to get to know a place is to get lost in it. And for the next few days I walked through the streets, to the outskirts, to the hinterland, the suburbs, along railway tracks, by bridges, to the place where the two muddy rivers meet. My first impression of width, greyness, loose sand blowing, did not change.

I had never before experienced this physical sense of space quite so forcefully. It reminded me of a person I know, a woman, who says very little, who listens to what you say, who says 'Yes' or else encourages you to keep on talking with a slow sleepy smile, or else just sits in the same room and says nothing. But all the time her presence sucks one into inactivity. A heaviness, a tiredness, a limpness, emanates from her that reduces you until you yourself feel tired, heavy and limp. Nothing I saw in Winnipeg had the brittleness of sophistication or of gaiety.

From one of the muddy riverbanks I looked back to the city. The flat melancholy prairie land was still covered in large patches of snow, the same grey colour as the sky. And the flatness the emptiness of land and sky reduced the importance of the jumble of buildings set in it. A string of telephone poles as far as I could see. I remember in Cornwall they had the repeating image of a man on stilts. Here, no sense of movement. Land. Sky. Horizon. Blowing dust. The undecorated buildings. All simple, without complexity, and yet left one exhausted. It just drained away oneself like some indifferent natural blotter.

Next morning the sun was out. And with it more dirty water, mud, slush, on the roads and the sidewalks. On Portage they were having a Tag Day. Young girls and middle-aged women, a tin can with a large slot in one hand, and around the neck a piece of string holding a cardboard tray like a halter. I walked to the C.B.C. and recorded a couple of talks. I met a young TV producer. We agreed to have lunch.

I was to meet him at the entrance to an office building on Portage at 12.30, but I arrived early. While I waited I saw a door in the hall halfway open. Cars drove up and well-dressed men went inside. Occasionally someone came out. I went over and looked in. An enormous waveband, lit up, was projected across the entire centre of the room showing the latest stock-market quotations in Montreal, Toronto, Winnipeg. Against the walls, on wooden platforms, three young girls were writing down figures on the blackboards. There were about a dozen men sitting comfortably in leather easy chairs, smoking, and watching the blown-up waveband (each vertical stroke about six feet high) go by. It had all the casualness of a room in a club. There was hardly any talk or noise. Then the producer arrived, and he drove me in his car to an Italian restaurant in a side-street.

He didn't eat very much. He was eager to talk. Tall, spare, intense, with a nervous face that rarely was still. And as he talked, I remembered how I have talked after being cut off for

several months, not seeing people, then suddenly meeting someone. One talked for hours, senselessly, the talk jumping all over
the place. One didn't want the person to go. And when it's over
you think you feel better, but you don't.

BIOGRAPHY

He said he was an orphan from Budapest, from wealthy parents.
After the war he found himself 'in one of those children's places
where the director's wife was seducing all the boys of thirteen
and fourteen. We looked innocent outside, but we had known
all the filthy things by then, inside. Then we came to Canada.
We came to Montreal and we were met by the wealthy Jews
there, you know the textiles, the whisky people. One of these
wealthy women takes us for a ride to the top of Mount Royal.
We go and look at the city. An airplane flies overhead. She
points up and asks, "Can anyone tell me what that is up there?"
What could we say or do? Did she think just because she came
from some small village that all of us did? Or that we hadn't
been bombed for the last four years? Then she takes us to her
house. She comes over and explains to us. "Now *this* is a lightswitch." They think that we are the same as they were. That we
had never seen a lightswitch in the old country . . .

'The intellectuals that I have met here haven't suffered from
anything. They haven't come to their values from any practical
experience of life. If things come up that require a personal
decision, they back out all the time, and compromise . . .'

We talked about the East: about Ottawa, Toronto, Montreal.
He didn't think much of those he met there. 'They are trying
to make an elite of being provincial. All of them—you know,
the producers, the critics—come from small towns in Canada.
That's the backbone of culture here. "Small-town boy makes
good." And nearly all of them are Anglo-Saxon or Scottish and
they expect newcomers like myself to quickly look up to them
and pack up all the things I have behind me, my roots in Europe,
for what?

'I feel like a Thomas Mann character. Some day I'll have to
make a sentimental journey, like the one you're making, but
back to Europe, to Germany, Budapest, and see where I belong.
Now I'm neither here nor there and you can't be a happy person
feeling you belong to Europe and live in North America . . .'

He spoke enthusiastically of Brecht. He had put on some
plays of Giradoux, now he wanted to put on Brecht's *Mother*

Courage. 'Kazin is all emotion. I saw him in New York. He drags you through the wringer. He's got to get you hanging on to the edge of your seat. But it covers up all the important issues. Brecht is the man.'

I left the producer worrying about being late at the studio. He had to be back for a variety show he was putting on.

'Can I drop you somewhere on the way?'

'Thanks. I think I'll walk.'

'Perhaps we will meet again. In London, Paris, maybe it will be Montreal.' Then he turned up his coat-collar, out of habit, for it wasn't cold, went to his car and drove off.

A NIGHT CRAWL

I was to meet Bobbie, the newspaper reporter, at the Press Club. We had arranged over the telephone that he would show me around the night spots of the city. When I arrived at the club the place was empty. A large room with comfortable leather easy-chairs and chesterfields. I went into a small adjoining room: a few wooden tables and chairs and a bar with a hotplate for snacks. The bartender was sitting on a high stool. We had a drink. He spoke English badly. He was thin, small sharp features, a bald head, thin lips. He said he had come eight months ago from Hamburg, but he didn't like the licensing laws in Manitoba. 'It is ridiculous, hypocritical. You buy bottle in liquor-commission and you go home or to the hotel room and you booze. Drink like civilized people? No.' He had been in London for a visit. He liked the pubs. 'That is proper way to drink; Germany even better.' He judged all countries by their licensing laws. 'It is good money here, true. But . . .' He wiped a glass absent-mindedly. '*Garnichts.* We have plenty of snow, cold, wind and sand in Hamburg, but there is something warm inside when you walk the streets. There is people like yourself, maybe more poorer people like yourself, who make you feel good, important as a person. Not like here. Nobody care here about you. Dog eat dog. You work. Good. Then you drive home. Good. And finished. This is centre of a big city. It should be exciting, *ja.* It is dead, like a cemetery.' But after a few more drinks we stopped discussing Canada, the cold, the licensing laws. And he taught me the German words to *Falling in Love Again.* And I taught him the words to *Ain't We Got Fun.* Then Bobbie arrived with two others.

Bobbie at first looked deceptively young. Then one noticed

that the blond hair was thinning, dandruff on jacket-shoulders, the layers of fat on the back of the neck, the belly pushing out, and the sweat continually appearing on his forehead soon after he wiped it off. He apologized for being late and as he had no car he had asked another person, a New Zealander, to come along. The New Zealander had asked a Nova Scotian who was at a loose end. They were also reporters. The New Zealander went to school in England and spoke a mixture of American with an affected English accent. The Nova Scotian was the dullest person I remember meeting. He looked as if he was ready to fall asleep. A square face, bad skin, a dull brown suit, a scraggy moustache on the top lip, and black hairs sticking out of his nose and ears. He said nothing except 'Yeah, Yeah' to whatever someone else had said. Neither did he contribute towards the drinks. His jaw kept falling open, his shoulders hung down. I wondered if it would be possible to get rid of him quickly.

We got in the New Zealander's car; Bobbie suggested that we drive down Main Street, not far from the hotel where I was staying. We parked the car by the city hall, the large front sign, KEEP WINNIPEG BEAUTIFUL. AND CLEAN. Walked along the side-streets. They were empty, dark and cold. The mud had frozen and it was easier to walk now than in the daytime.

Bobbie said he had been a crime reporter and knew this part of the city well. He wouldn't say where we were going. He crossed over the street, and we all stopped outside a small Chinese laundry. An old wooden shack, a thin opening cut out in the door and the opening was covered by a wire screen. He knocked. A pair of eyes came to the screen then the door opened.

The Chinaman was old, hunched, with a bald head and his face was eaten away in places from some disease. He could hardly speak English. He went behind a curtain in the room and re-appeared by a wooden counter.

'Have you any Rubbee?' Bobbie said.

'Beeg bottle?' The old man said.

'Let's see beeg bottle.'

The old man stooped down behind the counter and brought up a large bottle the size of a milk bottle with a colourless liquid inside.

'One dollar,' the Chinaman said.

Bobbie opened the cork, smelled the liquid and pretended he was interested in buying it. A few bundles of laundry were wrapped in brown paper on a wooden table by a window. The window had the green blind down. There was an opening in the back wall behind the counter leading into a room with a rocking chair by an oil-drum stove.

'Have you anything smaller?' Bobbie said.

The old man became suspicious. He bent down again behind the counter and brought out a small bottle that said 'Rubbing Alcohol'. I recognized it as a standard brand from one of the drugstores.

'Dirty-five cents,' the Chinaman said.

We looked at it. There was certainly more value in the big bottle. A knock on the door. The old man slowly went to the door, looked through the screen-slot, then opened the door. A bum came in, large, unshaven, an old coat, heavy boots and thick woollen socks. He had a paper bag full of empty dollar bottles. The Chinaman took the bag, counted the number of empty bottles and gave the old man one full dollar bottle. The old man put it inside his coat and went out. Bobbie noticed the small bottle was three-quarters full. 'Someone has had a drink out of it,' he said to the old man. The old man appeared not to understand. We went out.

From there Bobbie led us to the next side-street to the Light-house Mission. A large sign said JESUS SAVES. Inside was a long classroom with benches, a stage, and a man in a dapper suit near a microphone. Bobbie said that the man was a politician, but so far he had been unsuccessful. On the benches there were about twenty people. Down-and-outs, panhandlers, bums, un-shaven old men and women, dressed in tattered odds and ends. One Indian woman sat by herself against the wall in a fur coat with large holes in it. Then the slick man said, 'Now let's not cough or make too much noise because we are going to be on the air in three minutes.' The clock on the wall moved to eight. He pointed to a man sitting in the front row who stood up and tiptoed to the microphone. 'Now we will have the blessing by Brother Wolfe.' The man thundered out rapidly. While he was talking two girls crept on to the stage, one carried a guitar. As soon as the blessing ended they immediately began to sing *I Wonder where My Wandering Boy is Tonight*, yodelling at the end of each verse. A woman came next to the stage and, as soon as the duet stopped, she began to read out letters and the answers to them. They were all read in the same hurried over-the-fence-gossip voice, without a pause, as if her entire contribu-tion was one long sentence. The letters enclosed donations and they said how wonderful it was to hear the Lighthouse Mission every Saturday night living out in the prairie. And immediately she went on. 'Thank you Brother MacDonald and for your good news that you can hear us so well we all join you in prayer and hope you will get better soon and we here are praying for your recovery and everyone who is listening to us tonight I want you to pray for Brother MacDonald's recovery and we are all pleased that you will be sending your donation on. Everybody's little bit helps and it is all the same in the eyes of the Lord and the next letter is from Sister Emerick from Dauphin and Sister I'm glad to say is also a regular listener of ours and I know how trying. . . .' So it went on. Then more hymns from the hill-billy duet; another short booming blessing from Brother Wolfe; while the audience waited patiently for it to be over and for the doughnuts and the coffee to be served.

We came out of the Mission. The Nova Scotian had fallen asleep. He woke up in the cold air and said he was thirsty and where were we going to get a drink. It was too late for the beer parlours. A pretty Indian-looking girl with a white streak in her black hair stood in front of a bare window of a small dilapidated house. She beckoned to us to come over. We went across the street.

She was a fortune teller. The small empty front room was curtained off and behind it I could hear children speaking Italian and a man shouting. We haggled about the price. She was firm. 'One dollar. If you are not satisfied, no need to pay.'

She took me to a curtained-off room on the other side of the door. Only a bare wooden table and two chairs. We sat by the table and she looked at my palm. 'You will live a long time. You will make lots of money. Someone loves you, but she is far away. You will be big success, but you must do it yourself. Do not wait for others to do it for you. Only by hard work will you get to your success. And you will have lots of money if you work hard.' Then she asked me to stand up and take out what I had in my left trouser pocket. There were two quarters, a nickle, and a few coppers. She took a quarter and stood facing me and very solemnly she touched one shoulder with the quarter then the other, then opened my left trouser pocket and pretended to throw the quarter inside. All the time chanting in a Welsh accent. 'Bless this pocket, may it always have lots of money.' Then the other pocket. 'Bless this pocket, may it always have lots of money.' She asked me to take out what I had in my back pocket. I brought out my wallet. She asked for some paper-money. I took out a dollar-bill. She did the same with the dollar bill as she did with the quarter, touching both shoulders, then opening my back pocket and pretending to throw it in. 'Bless this wallet, may it always have some money.'

Now she said, 'Have you any questions you want answered?'

I hesitated. What does one say. This was a game and like all games there are certain rules one doesn't break.

'When will my journey end?'

She too hesitated. But not for long, for it was her rules we were using. With the same rhythm that she used in blessing my pockets she said, 'When you make lots of money.'

I paid her the dollar and she put it inside her brassière.

Outside it was cold. In the dark passages, between the houses, tramps sat on newspapers and drank out of those dollar bottles of rubbing alcohol. Some were lying on their side, their hands and the bottle between their legs, as if asleep.

From there Bobbie took us to Moon's café. We all wanted a drink. He knew the woman behind the counter. She gave him the address of two bootleggers. We drove first to an address on Schultz Street. The house was difficult to find. The roads were frozen mud, snow and slush and the residential street was dark, only one street light at the corner. Then we walked along the dark side of the street to where several cars were parked.

It was small like an outdoor toilet away from a wooden house. The snow on the lawn had melted during the day, and the earth in places was muddy, and planks led across the frozen mud to a door. Bobbie knocked several times in the dark. Finally a light flickered through a slot. The door opened. A young boy stood at the door. Behind him a huge fat woman squatted in a chair, a bottle of beer dangled from her hand. 'Never saw you boys. I'm sorry. I don't let anybody in I don't know.'

The second address was easy. Bobbie said it would be easy. He remembered he had come here before and they weren't fussy. Again the slot, the light, and a woman, larger than the other one, opened the door. She was grotesque. She must have been close to seven feet and well over three hundred pounds. Hanging breasts, fat legs, a lot of loose flesh, lifeless, and exaggerated by a torn green sweater that was many sizes too small and a short skirt. She looked deflated as if she had just had a baby.

The first room was dark. A man sat on a chesterfield, and after the woman let us in she went back beside the man on the chesterfield. The next room was dark except for the light that came from a huge jukebox in the corner. It was light enough to see another chesterfield, old and battered, and two chairs. We sat there and waited until there was place in the final room, the kitchen.

An oil stove, two shabby chesterfields against the walls, a door to the toilet, a plain sink with one tap high above it, the pipe to the tap covered in rust. The walls were bare. A single light, very bright, hung down in the middle of the kitchen. A tall young boy with bad teeth was serving the drinks. There was a man in a post-office jacket, an older man in a suede windbreaker and ski-cap, and a short fat man in a suit. The tall young boy was dressed all in black. Black shirt, black trousers. The shirt had white colonel stars on the epaulets. He asked us.

'You all want a nip?'

We said we did.

He asked the others to drink up. He took their small glasses, rinsed them, and gave each of us a brown-coloured liquid that smelled of methylated spirits. I had only taken one sip when he came around. 'O.K., boys, knock it back.' He needed the glasses for the others. There were only two glasses for the entire room, in case of a raid.

Men kept coming in. Some with their lunchpails, others dressed in sport suits, overcoats, windbreakers. A young boy, his face covered with lipstick, brought out a hip-flask. 'A dollar's worth.' A girl came in drunk. She was very thin and wore a light fawn coat, high black shoes. She looked haggard. She drank the alcohol down in one gulp, screwed up her face, then it hit her. She doubled up and quickly went into the toilet where we could hear her vomiting.

Strangers bought each other drinks. They were cheap, twenty-five cents a glass, and after the initial raw burning sensation in the throat, they did not seem to have a great deal of effect. The flavour was that of the Kik that the boy used to colour the alcohol. He kept rinsing and filling the same two glasses and passing them around and collecting his money. He took out a thick bundle of dollar bills and transferred the bundle to his back pocket. His shift was finishing, he said, and someone else was due to come on in five minutes. He said they were open twenty-four hours a day.

The drink had made the Nova Scotian even more morose. He kept on grumbling that he was hungry. We drove to another dark street to a tall undecorated house. There was a light on in a top room. Bobbie was sweating. He went out and knocked loudly on the door. But there was no answer. He knocked several times and still no reply. He threw a snowball up, but couldn't

H

hit a window. He shouted out and threw more snowballs; but no one opened the door. 'I guess the girls are all shacked up for the night,' he said.

And suddenly I became impatient with all this tomfoolery and I wanted the evening to end. Perhaps Bobbie misunderstood me, or perhaps I misunderstood him, or perhaps Winnipeg didn't have 'night spots'; but I had no enjoyment out of this slumming, the kind of pretence that treats poverty as something picturesque. Poverty is always picturesque for those who nip in, have a quick naughty look, then go back to their safe places. Perhaps this evening was for them a kind of joke, an excuse to get away from the wife, the kids, the routine. The New Zealander and the Nova Scotian kept getting more solemn and dull as the evening went on. And Bobbie more of a salesman, selling me the sights of the down-and-outs. He told the New Zealander to stop the car outside a flophouse and in we went. Bobbie went straight to the desk and, confident as anything, asked the attendant for a ficticious Mr. Miller. The attendant looked through the book, to see if Mr. Miller was there for the night. The excuse of this performance was to get us inside to have a look at the husks of men sitting dumbly and patiently around the room by the walls. It was intended as entertainment. And I was fed up and disgusted with them and with myself. I left the three of them and walked back along Main Street. Cold freezing night. Desolate. No dogs, no cats, not a person. The closed cafés, secondhand stores, looked even shabbier in the darkness and the frost. I passed the town hall, KEEP WINNIPEG BEAUTIFUL AND CLEAN, woke the old man who was dozing behind the desk in the hotel to get my room key. The cheap room had the welcome of something familiar; it felt like home. And I slept in until after ten next morning, when the woman came around to make the beds, and to sew a button on my winter coat which she saw was loose.

MENNONITES

At the Press Club, before going on the night crawl, Bobbie introduced me to the editor of *The Winkler Progress*. He was young, short, and heavily built, with the beginnings of a black scraggly beard. 'The beard,' he said in a German accent, 'is just a joke. I'm on the Winkler Chamber of Commerce and we're having a beard-growing contest to celebrate our fiftieth anniversary of incorporation as a town.' I asked him if I could come over to Winkler and look around. He suggested Sunday morning when he would come out and meet the bus at the cross-roads.

I knew that there were several farming communities in Manitoba of Mennonites and Hutterites, and I wanted to visit one. I remembered the film, *The 49th Parallel*, that I saw when I was about fifteen or sixteen during the first years of the last war: when Eric Portman and a few more German U-boat raiders came over by submarine to Canada and made their way to one of these settlements. I didn't know whether it was a Hutterite, Mennonite, or Doukabhor. But I remembered a young girl with flaxen hair; a woman baking bread in an outdoor oven; fields of prairie wheat in the sun; and a cluster of simple farmhouses in the prairie. That brief image of an idyllic community living close to the land somewhere in Western Canada haunted me for a long time.

I had read in a small blue pamphlet, *The Hutterian Brethren and their Beliefs:*

The Hutterite Brethren Church is a community of Protestant Christians—dating from 1528—agriculturalists, a group of Christ's adherents associated together for the purpose of following in the footsteps of Christ and his immediate apostles as described in the New Testament.

We were allowed to come to Canada as welcome settlers in 1918 by the Federal Immigration Department of Ottawa, and in consequence we established seven Hutterite colonies. . . . Now there are twenty-two in Manitoba.

Because of our communal way of life and fellowship in our endeavour to imitate the early Christian Church and because we are considered a 'peculiar people' (Titus 2:14) and because of our nonconformity to the world around us, insofar as we consider things unchristian, unethical and worldly, we are looked upon as undesirable aliens, although our members up to 36 years of age are Canadians by birth and have the same rights as other citizens of Canada, including the civil right to buy, sell, own land, and the free, unhindered right to their religious views without direct or indirect interference and molestations. We find that an attempt is being made to discriminate against the Hutterian Brethren Church by spacing its colonies forty miles apart, so as to drive us out of the province eventually.

It seems unbelievable that such things should happen in Manitoba into which province the Canadian Government in 1874 invited the thrifty God-fearing, peaceful, and humble Mennonites to settle, and guaranteed them unmolested religious freedom and their way of life.

The same privilege brought the Hutterian Brethren to Mani-

toba in 1898 and 1918 as tillers of the soil and they were given the
same rights and privileges.

The Hutterites differ from the Mennonites mainly in their
communal life and they are more conservative. Both are children
of the Reformation, born in the same cradle, so to speak, in
Switzerland. Both were persecuted severely for centuries and
driven relentlessly from country to country . . .

The only other information I had was that they were good
farmers and hard workers. And that possibly the reason for this
threat from the provincial authorities, of segregation and
restricting their buying of land, was due to the pressure brought
by the merchants from the stores in the near towns and villages
around these settlements who saw the Hutterites do their buying
in bulk from Winnipeg, and save money. I wondered why the
Mennonites were not troubled by the provincial authorities.

Winkler was due south of Winnipeg about fifteen miles from
the United States border. On Sunday morning I left the hotel.
It was cold and windy and the sand was blowing in the streets.
I walked towards the bus terminal. Main Street was deserted.
And without people the street looked shabbier and more desolate. Under the dark railway span over the street, past the
window with the large plaster Christ bleeding on its side, the
secondhand stores, the small cafés. . . .

The Blue Goose buses stood washed and shining with both
ends rounded. They continued through to the United States. It
didn't take long to be out of Winnipeg and in flatland. Fields
were flooded, water around the fences. There were large areas of
snow in the fields and in the depressions small lakes where the
snow had melted. The road continued straight. Mile after mile
of tall unpainted telegraph poles and the click-click as the wheels
of the bus passed over the regular intervals of road surface. Then
we turned off the main road and continued going straight on
gravel. If a car came we could see it while it was still a long
distance away; the wake of the dust behind it and the small
speck in front. And after we crossed, we continued for a while
blinded by the dust that we were driving through. Potholes were
in the road, water in the holes. And the flat fields, on either side,
of snow, water, earth, stretched to the horizon. By the time the
bus reached the cross-roads its sides were splattered in mud and
dirty water.

The editor was waiting in a new station-wagon and he drove a
few miles along a muddy road. I could see two small wooden
grain-elevators beside a railway track. And the first street facing

the railway had about six inches of fast-moving dirty water coming from the fields. The water covered parts of the railway and swept by the fronts of the houses. Then we drove through short muddy streets. There were several wooden churches, plain, undecorated, like barns with sloping roofs and in the front, as a centre piece, a small gabled tower: two hands praying. They were painted chalk white and dark blue. A service was over in front of one, and men and women stood outside talking. The clothes were sober: black suits, drab-coloured coats. None of the women I saw wore lipstick. They spoke Platt-deutsch amongst themselves. A few of the younger ones spoke English.

He continued to drive me through the same muddy streets. He was proud of Winkler. He kept on saying that Winkler was the first town to introduce an X-ray unit in Manitoba; that it was first in building an old people's home. . . . Everytime I said something about beliefs, pacifism; he would pass over it. 'Of course we're just the same as other Canadians. Maybe the older people are different. But we're just the same.' Down the short main street. The mud thick. A few stores, a café, a sign waving in the wind, 'Drink Pepsi-Cola', a filling station. He went into the only hotel, a bare room, gloomy, no one at the desk. He went to a back room. Four men sat drinking bottles of beer. They looked as if they were caught doing something they shouldn't. He fixed me up with a room. Then back to the main street. All the stores and houses had sandbags piled up in front. He said this was normal; they expected the floods to come in about a week's time.

He stopped in front of his father's store. Our shoes sank in the thick mud. Besides stationery they sold musical instruments. In glass cabinets were violins, cellos, trumpets. The store was dark with a musty smell like the lair of some animal. I wanted to get out as soon as I could. He gave me an old copy of his newspaper. It was one sheet folded in two so that it had four sides. Across the top: THE WINKLER PROGRESS. PUBLISHED IN WINKLER. THE SHOPPING CENTRE OF SOUTHERN MANITOBA. CIRCULATING IN THE GARDENLAND OF MANITOBA. Then we drove to his house, a small bungalow; mud, ankle-deep, went right up to the steps. His wife came out with two children and they got in the back of the station-wagon. She was a thin, worn-out, blonde girl, lipstick put on badly; it looked odd on the pale face with the white kerchief on the head. She was very quiet. She kept calling me 'sir'.

We drove through the village again, and I wondered if it

would be possible to drive to the Hutterite community which was not far away. We started out, but after a few miles through water and mud the station-wagon kept getting stuck, until finally we couldn't go any more ahead. Instead we went towards the old colony of the Mennonites. We passed fields, all under water. Stalks of last year's sunflowers stood up in some of the fields. 'We grow the sunflowers for the oil,' he said, 'and some sugar-beets.' The wind blew a skin over the water in the fields. The sky was grey.

In the flat land I first saw the poplars. Then, as we came closer, the clearing. The old colony consisted of one short street with a row of poplars on either side. Behind the trees were grey wooden houses spaced wide apart and at regular intervals. Behind the houses, and at both ends of the street, were the fields. Both sides of the street were exactly the same. It was like looking in a mirror. 'It is like the way they lived in Russia, sir,' she said. Cows were grazing by the windows, by the trees, and in the back. The front of the house was connected to the barn in the back. And as soon as you opened the front door there was the warm pungent smell of the barn. It was drier here, and the wind whipped the dust above the dirt road. There was one church: a plain, old barn. There were no lights, nothing on the walls, just wooden benches and chairs. And for the short time I was here I found a silence and a peace that I have, so far, only found in parts of Cornwall.

*

That evening I was invited to dinner at a lumberman's house in Winkler. 'It's a kind of celebration,' the editor said. 'The school hockey coach is leaving after being here two years, and this is his farewell party.' I did not realize then why I was invited nor the sadness of the occasion.

The lumberman looked younger than his age, a sports type. He spoke with a trace of a German accent, but he did not speak very much, he kept on opening bottles of beer and handing them around. We sat and drank from the bottle while more people kept arriving and the introductions were made. Then a young girl came out from a bedroom in an old-fashioned blue woollen dress done up high on the neck. We were introduced.

'What part are you from?' she said.

'Ottawa.'

'But I thought you came from England.'

'No, I come from Ottawa; I have lived in England.'

The others in the room were watching our performance.

'Have you lived in London?' she said.

'Yes. In Muswell Hill, Notting Hill Gate, South Kensington.'

'I'm from Golders Green.'

The room was quiet. It was awkward. Everyone listened and watched expectantly. I realized then that the reason for my being here was that this girl represented England to them and things English; and I was a link with 'home'.

'Have you seen the Lions or the Panthers play?'

'No.'

'But you've heard of Chick Zamik,' her husband said.

I remembered the Gillette advertisements, the man with a hockey stick and skates at an angle as if he had just made a sudden stop.

'He was at our wedding.'

Luckily their child began to cry from the bedroom, and she had to go and feed him, and by the time she came out we were going to the dining-room.

The table was long and narrow and it went the entire length of the room. The children ate in a separate room. There were about twenty of us around the table, mostly business men with their wives. Huge platters of hot wrapped cabbage leaves stuffed with minced meat and rice were brought in and passed around. Then platters with thick sliced pieces of cooked ham. There were large bowls of potatoes, bowls with onions in vinegar, beets in vinegar, slabs of butter, large loaves of white bread. I sat beside the hostess. She was an attractive plump woman with a Main Street look. She was born in a farming village not far from here. She said she wasn't a Mennonite, but it didn't matter. Her two boys were taught German at school, otherwise it was exactly the same as in any other school. Everyone kept repeating, whenever any difference came up, how much they *were* like other Canadians.

They tried hard to be the same as what they believed was 'the outside'. And 'the outside' reached them only through the radio, the cheap film, the advertisements. Whatever was the latest 'gimmick' they accepted and imitated it. It was one way of identification. At the moment it was Liberace with his *Sincerely Yours*. The editor had given me one of his business cards: 'Creative Printing Distinctively Yours.' On Main Street a sign in a window: 'Real Estate—This Home is Exclusively Yours.' Another sign in a photographer's store: 'For the Picture that is Intimately yours' . . .

The English girl was to my left. Across, sat her husband.

'I wouldn't mind going back to England,' he said. 'I had it pretty good there. They treated us right. It's she who doesn't want to go back.'

'But you wouldn't go back to the way things were. That's finished.'

If they were alone they would have quarrelled right there. And the way they looked at each other, they had quarrelled about this before.

The hockey player was a Ukrainian, twenty-eight, blond straight hair, well built, a flat, unintelligent face. He had been playing hockey since he left high school. When he couldn't make a team in the N.H.L., he went over to England and played there.

She was much younger, but far more mature, for she was already beginning to be disillusioned. She had lived hockey since she was a schoolgirl. She read the hockey magazines, followed the teams, knew the players, the gossip, had their pictures and autographs. Then she married one.

'I had it pretty good in England,' he said. 'You should of seen the fuss they made over us in Brighton and Nottingham. Some of the old girls would come regularly and knit us sweaters. . . . At Christmas we'd get presents from people we didn't know.'

When he began to slip down, he still managed to become coach for a Zurich team. But that didn't last long. Then back to Canada; and now this coaching job was over. She said he had no job, no trade, and they had a young child. Tomorrow they were going to Winnipeg. He would try to find some labouring work with a construction gang for the summer and then look around for another coaching job in the winter.

We had ice-cream, and after the ice-cream we drank beer out of the bottles. The men at the table talked about the wonderful job the hockey player had done with the school team. There were no formal speeches.

After the meal the men went back to the sitting-room; the women to wash the dishes and clear up, and then they went into another room. We sat with the young boys and played checkers, performed card tricks, talked about hockey, about the weather.

At the end of the evening the women were called in from the other room and the hockey player was presented with a pair of chisels in a wooden box.

I returned to the hotel around eleven. A gale was blowing. The water, that had flowed by the railway track and the large

flooded patches in the main street, had frozen. I slid down the
street; the wind carried me along the surface. It was dark. No
moon. No stars. No lights. There was no one at the desk in the
hotel. I went up to my room. A bare room, a bed, a dresser,
a Bible. But I could not fall asleep. I wished I had something to
read. All I had was the three-month-old issue of *The Winkler
Progress*. It was strange to pick up a newspaper that didn't have
a murder, that wasn't concerned with other countries, with
politics, or celebrity gossip. On the front page the headlines
were:

ROYALS WIN TWO. PEE-WEES AND JUVENILES ALSO MAKE GOOD.

Three Winkler teams simultaneously scored wins on Tuesday
night of this week which is something unique.

Inside it was all 'social news' about Winkler and the other near
villages: New Reinland, Neuenburg, Blumenfeld, Snowflake,
Friedensruh, Gnadenthal, and Plum Coulee.

SNOWFLAKE: Mr. Albert Siemens has been busy handing out
cigars since New Year's Day. On Monday, the Siemens left for
home, grateful for the many gifts donated by Winkler merchants.
Snowflakers were quite surprised to hear the story of the 24-foot
sausage repeated by Mr. C. E. Greene on 'Neighbourly News'
program Sunday morning. Snowflake was really in the limelight
that day between the radio and the New Year's Baby. There isn't
much going on these days, except shoveling snow and waiting for
more.

GNADENTHAL: Mr. and Mrs. David Peters and family and Mrs.
Margaret Sawatzky did not show up at the turkey dinner held at
J. Fehr's in Winkler. Weather permitting, they will probably
make good their visit, but then there will be no turkey.

BLUMENFELD: Roads were very heavy, some altogether impassable
on Sunday. Very few people were able to attend services. Mr. and
Mrs. Martin Wiebe took the safest way of transportation by
horses and sleigh on Thursday night and made way for Blumenfeld. They visited with the John Elias'. They had a hard time
finding their way back home due to the severe blizzard intervals.
They used a lantern to keep the horses on the right track and
finally reached home safely.

In the room across the hall I could hear people talking, but
only the woman's voice was distinct. In the background there
was some music: it sounded like an old gramophone record.

'You know what I need? I need some loving. I ain't getting it.
I'm at the change of life. You know what I would like to do? I

would like to have one more child. Or take somebody's child. Somebody who can't afford or hasn't got the time. John's going to be sick. Always happens after he has beer. He doesn't have to but he is . . .'

From her voice I began to imagine what the woman was like, but she continually kept changing. First there was a bewildered stout woman with crinkly grey hair, a large mouth set in a plain face, rough hands, overworked. Then she became tall. She lost weight. Her large breasts shrank. She became thin, nervous, unhappy, nagging.

'You've only got one child. Why don't you get more? Do me a favour now, John. Put your sweater on and your coat and go home. There's your coat. Did you have a hat? In the beer parlour? I won't say anything to him. I won't say anything either. Why can't you come over? We got a kid and you haven't. We had a kid once upon a time and we still went out. John, there's your coat behind you. Put that on . . . Dick, you know what I gotta do before I go to bed. In the first place, Dick, how do you know that I'm not pregnant now . . .?'

The music started again. A bottle fell down. The record played, *Red Sails in the Sunset*. It seemed to come from a long way. It brought back those Brunswick records, brown cardboard ones that warped and curled up. And it sounded as if it was coming from the far end of a tunnel, without an echo, a tinny sound, a man's voice, intimate, high, almost like a girl's.

'I married into a family that had two dollars more than we had. But you know what they didn't have? They had no love in that family. They didn't love their mother. They didn't love their father. Your coat is in the beer parlour. This stuff tastes like piss. Don't say that. Don't say that to me . . .'

Then a door opened and I could hear the gramophone playing louder and the sound of footsteps walking away down the hall. The door closed. And the woman began to laugh. Then she stopped. The gramophone stopped playing. And I listened to the wind roar and roar and roar outside the double windows late into the night.

Next morning I woke at seven. I wanted to try again to get to the Hutterite settlement. But as soon as I went out I could see it was worse. The sun had risen on a cold fresh morning with the wind still blowing hard. The road by the railway was a frozen sheet of thick ice glistening in the sun. In the fields, large patches of snow and ice. And the stalks of last year's sunflowers like frozen chicken legs.

I returned to the hotel. A pale middle-aged woman in a man's dressing-gown and slippers was making toast in the kitchen. I paid her for my room and had enough money left for a cup of coffee and two slices of toast. I watched the woman making the toast on an old toaster that she kept opening and closing. She poured me some coffee. Surely I would recognize something of last night in the voice—but there was none.

I borrowed five dollars from the newspaper editor to take the bus back to Winnipeg. And in Winnipeg, walking along Portage, I met a friend whom I last saw at McGill. We had some coffee and he asked me how I was fixed. He lent me thirty dollars. I returned five to the editor. I called up T.C.A., I was lucky, there was room on a flight out to Saskatoon later in the afternoon.

V

SOCIETY IN SASKATOON

I TOOK the first cheap hotel room I could find. I felt tired. There was a shower in the room. I thought I would feel better after taking one, but it was no use. I still felt tired and depressed. I tried to get to sleep but there was a clock outside that chimed every quarter of an hour, and on the hour it played a tinkling tune, like an Austrian music box. At eight in the morning the phone rang from the desk downstairs to tell me it was eight o'clock. I looked out of the window. No snow, no dirt, no slush, no wind. I was on a main street of a small town, clean, orderly, sleepy. There were few cars, few people, and hardly any noise.

I went out for some breakfast and for the first time since I had arrived I was able to go without my winter coat. At the corner of the block, set in the middle of the street-square, stood a small clock-tower like an expensive tombstone with a clock-face set in it. At nine it played that familiar tinkling tune. It was the city's war memorial.

I entered the first cheap restaurant, sat down at the standard horseshoe counter and had black coffee and toast. There was no one in the booths by the wall, a few silent people sat around the horseshoe. Outside hardly any noise, occasionally a person's head went by the window.

Beside me sat a young boy drinking a glass of milk. He was about eighteen or nineteen, freckles, blond crew cut, a white sweat-shirt underneath the leather windbreaker with BRAVES on the front in large blue letters, and jeans. He asked me for a light. We started to talk. He said he was looking for a job. He had failed his first year at university. His parents suggested that he work for a year, 'to get orientated', then try again next fall. He had a weak, innocent face, full of assurance, not a line in it, and a disarming grin. When I told him what I was doing, he began to talk about Saskatoon.

'People are uncomplicated here. There is no night life. No

society. No extremes. You go to a house party or play tennis or go for a drive. It's a healthy place, and the theatres here are as good as you'll get anywhere in Canada.'

Outside I walked along the straight neat, streets. And down each street there was a bit of sky at the end of it. I was invited for lunch by a girl I had known in Montreal.

BIOGRAPHY

She was tall for her age and gawky with pale blue eyes and very blonde straight hair. She grew up in the St. Denis section of Montreal and could speak French fluently. Because the convent did not give her the right qualifications to enter McGill, she could only continue at a Catholic college. She went to Marianapolis and took a commercial course. When her father died, she was twenty, tall, still gawky, and lonely. She decided to take her share of his insurance and go over to London. She spent the money quickly. Then she was forced to take a typing job in the Civil Service. She also had to move into a large ugly building in Camden Town, into a dingy bed-sitting room with a sink and a gas ring and the paint peeling from the walls. The other rooms were let to students, shady tricksters; all without much money. Here she had her first affair with a tennis player from Italy who was over for a few months to learn English. She became pregnant. A medical student from the room next door performed the abortion. She was sentimental and kept the foetus for two days in an empty tin of Nescafé. Then flushed it down the toilet.

In summer her room became too drab and uncomfortable to live in, so she left for Cornwall and got a job as a waitress in one of the large hotels in Newquay. The owner made her his mistress. He had a passion for tall slim youth with light skin and blue eyes and blonde hair. He would go once a year to the slums of the big cities and from the streets pick up several handsome boys and girls and install them as waiters and waitresses in his hotel. He was of the English aristocracy, but he did not belong there. In his early fifties, tall, he might have had a good figure once but he had put on fat, his blond hair was thinning, a flush in his face, a thin mouth. He took rejuvenating pills, tried sexual experiments, and surrounded himself with handsome youth that he rescued from the working-class streets. He loved youth and innocence, and then to corrupt it. It was made all too easy for him. He gave them large sums of money. He let them use his

Rolls. He installed them in luxurious rooms. He splashed good food, champagne, expensive presents, parties. And when he grew tired of them; when he had what he wanted out of them—they still looked handsome and strikingly youthful, but he knew how corrupt they had become—the petty thefts, the jealousies, the lies—he discarded them. They could never go back to where he had picked them up.

For the next two years he took her on his travels in Switzerland, Germany, Sweden, France, and Italy. All she had to do was listen to him talk about himself and be available when he wanted her. Later he used her as bait to bring back young boys for him.

At the end of the two years she had saved up more money than she had had when she came over. She returned to Canada, to Ottawa, married an engineer who worked for the Government. For a few years they lived quietly in Ottawa. And one summer she went over and did a tour of Europe and England in a desperate round-up of memories. Then they settled in Saskatoon, into small-town respectability, as if she had never been away from what she wanted.

They lived in a new house with the front wall all window looking over a lawn and towards the river. They had a Siamese cat, a rabbit, and a Peruvian guineapig who was brought in during lunch and placed on the floor. He didn't move. He just stood there shaking so they had to take him out. After lunch she showed me the children's rooms; the murals of Mexico on the walls done by a local painter; the double bunks; everything was highly varnished and polished. Her husband had to leave with the car to drive down to Regina on some government business. He didn't know if he would be able to get through as there were floods on some of the roads. I decided to get back to my hotel before two o'clock and check out so that they wouldn't charge me for another day. She said she would show me the way, put me on the right road. She came out and as it was so pleasant decided to walk part of the way down. She said this was the first time in four years that she had walked from her house downtown (it took a little over twenty minutes); she kept repeating this as if it was something extraordinary. She had always used the car or a taxi. 'Wait until I tell the girls about this,' she said, 'they won't believe it. Neither will my husband.'

*

I had an introduction to see Mr. M. from a friend in Montreal. He is reputed to have the best private art collection in Canada. When I called up in the morning, Mr. M. was not in but Mrs. M. invited me over for dinner that evening. All I knew about the M.'s was that they came from an old German-Jewish family and when the Nazis came into power they fled from one European capital to another until they came to Canada and settled in Saskatoon. He had inherited a meat-packing empire with branches all over Europe. But since the war, he had pulled out of Europe and opened branches in various parts of the Commonwealth.

I was told to come at 6.15. I asked the reception clerk if he knew where the M.'s lived. He said everyone in Saskatoon knew of the M.'s. They lived across the river. As I had plenty of time, I walked again through Saskatoon, it didn't take very long.

The river was muddy. Large slabs of dirty ice, partly submerged, went by slowly in the brown water. I thought of funerals, coffins, shrouds. Along the sides, the banks sloped to the river. Old bits of dead grass, like tufts of hair, stuck out of the mud. Near the riverline the snow had not melted. There were large bites in the snow where the water sucked out chunks, pulled them down into the water, and carried them away. I crossed the bridge. Looking back to the other side was the Bessborough Hotel. Like the Chateau Laurier, it combined the function of a railway hotel and a civic monument; but the guts were commercial.

By the river the houses stood far apart on top of muddy slopes hidden by trees. But I couldn't find the number. I scrambled up the slope several times and then back to the river. Finally I found the entrance on a residential street. Evergreens on a wide lawn, a horseshoe drive, and at its base a massive square stone building with large windows set in the stone.

I rang the bell. The maid who came to the door spoke English with an accent. She looked Scandinavian. She only opened the door slightly.

'What is it you want?'
'Is Mrs. M. in?'
'What is it you want?'
'I have come to dinner.'
'Is she expecting you?'
'Yes.'
'How are you called?'
'Levine.' .

She went inside and I remained on the stone porch wondering
if my watch was wrong, if it was all a mistake, or had I come on
the wrong day. She returned, her face expressionless.
'Mrs. M. is dressing. You may come this way. She will come
down soon.' Blonde straight hair tied in the back in a bun,
plump young face, about nineteen in a black and white uniform.
She led me into a sitting-room and brought out from a dark
wooden cupboard by the wall a decanter of whisky and a large
glass which she placed on a small table by the window seat.
Beside them was a package of cigarettes and a box of matches.
'Mrs. M. said you should be made comfortable.'
She went out of the room and I was left with the whisky and
the cigarettes. I noticed packages of cigarettes all over the room:
on the small table, on the window seat, on the ledge over the
fireplace, on the arm of another chair, in ashtrays. I put a package into my pocket and had some whisky, smoked a cigarette,
and felt better.
It was a large, long room. A chandelier hung down from the
ceiling and there were several easy-chairs and small tables with
glass tops, a thick maroon carpet covered the entire floor, the far
wall was one large slab of glass. It was still light enough to see
the lawn behind the house and the river with the ice passing
by. Outside everything looked empty, grey, washed out. I could
see no other house. Only the lawn to the muddy river with those
large moving slabs of ice riding down. On the walls were paintings. In the hallway, up the side of the stairs, in every conceiv-
able space there were paintings, as in one of those small art
galleries off Charing Cross which cannot afford the luxury of a
few pictures hung far apart. A few small Emily Carrs; a Chagall;
a Rouault; and the rest were abstract: imitation Mondrian;
imitation Nicholson; imitation Jackson Pollock, and imitation
de Stael. Several were still-lifes. I walked to the glass wall and
looked out at the mud, the river, the floating ice.
The maid came in with three other dinner-guests. And I was
introduced to a Mr. and Mrs. Cowan from New Jersey, and a
Mrs. Patterson from Vancouver. Then Mrs. M. entered the room.
A short, thin, nervous woman in a blue dress, red fluffy hair
swept up, a long Slavic nose, a wide mouth. She reminded me of
Maria Ouspenskaya.
'I am sorry my husband is not here, but he has decided to stay
over for the Rainier–Kelly wedding.'
'I bet he's the only one from Saskatoon,' Mrs. Cowan said.
'Oh, it is not an important wedding,' Mrs. M. spoke slowly in

broken English. 'Black market tickets are only a hundred dollars and I am sure you could get one cheaper. There is so many decayed royalty in the south of France who will sell for less.'

When Mrs. M. speaks her false teeth click. She sits hunched up. No impact of personality. A strangely washed-out person with an interesting face, a Slavic face. A mask that one looks at and is fascinated, but there was nothing coming out behind it. She asked Mrs. Cowan about people in New Jersey and Mrs. Patterson about people they both know in Vancouver. From the conversation I realized that neither were close friends of Mrs. M., mainly the formality of business acquaintances of her husband. Then I was asked what I was doing, where I was from, where I had been, when Mr. Cowan interrupted.

'Carola, did you pay more than seventy-five dollars for that dress?'

'Can't you wait, Joe, until later?' Mrs. Cowan was visibly angry with her husband. She apologized for him. 'He does this all the time. He doesn't have to do it. But he does it. I remember when we began to go steady. Sometimes when we're dancing he'd say, "Did you pay thirty dollars for that dress? If you paid more than ten bucks for that hat you were taken." He even tried to guess how much I paid for my brassière.'

The joke fell flat. Mrs. Patterson quickly began to talk about the fine weather they had in Vancouver and the awful weather it had been since she left. She was on her way to Toronto to attend the twenty-third reunion of her graduating class. The Cowans were motoring back from California to New Jersey. They had come up to Vancouver, picked up Mrs. Patterson, and she was going with them as far as Newark, then taking a train to Toronto.

Mrs. Patterson was the wife of a wealthy insurance man. I remember seeing his picture in the financial pages of *Saturday Night*. She was heavy-boned, shapeless, tall, in her late forties, with a blank expression on her face. She sat silent, bored, neglected. Mrs. Cowan was small, thin, a dark bundle of energy, unsatisfied lively eyes and a habit of making her point in conversation by pressing a finger into your hand. I didn't trust her. Mr. Cowan was over fifty. An ugly squat man, a bald head, glasses. At first he appeared all nose, then you noticed the ears sticking out, the colourless thick lips, the loose skin on his neck, wrinkled. He wore a tight white shirt so that the flesh coming out was forced to spread and hang over in folds. Apparently the Cowans originally came from Saskatoon but had moved

I

to Newark where Mr. Cowan had a woman's clothing store.
Mrs. M. took me around for a tour of the paintings in the
house. 'You're only seeing the worst ones. The good ones are on
show somewhere. I don't know . . . I think it's Ottawa or
Toronto . . .' We entered another large room with paintings on
the wall. The room was more like a gallery, with a few settees
back to back in the middle, tables in the corners and a thick carpet on the floor. They were by unknown painters, mainly by one
who had recently come to Canada from Germany. I did not find
them in any way interesting. They were all abstracts except one
large one, a romantic picture of horses and men in the country.
The men in riding habit beside a stream, grass, trees. 'This
picture is of racing in Budapest. We had our horses there. This
is my husband.' She pointed to a figure three inches high indis-
tinguishable from the others. 'Now we cannot afford horses.'
Then she brought me up to two large bathrooms where more
paintings were hung, and more in the hallway and on the side
of the staircase.

When we returned to the others they were having an argument.

Mrs. Patterson asked me, 'Do you think Mae West is Jewish?'

'No.'

'There, I told you.'

'All I know,' Mr. Cowan said, 'is what this friend of mine in
California tells me. He knows them all personally. Hedy Lamarr,
Clark Gable, John Wayne. He talks to them like I'm talking to
you. And he told me that Mae West's real name is Minnie
Weinstein.'

'I *don't* believe it,' Mrs. Patterson said. 'She doesn't look
Jewish.'

'You don't have to look Jewish. I've got another friend,' Mr.
Cowan quickly changed the subject, 'a doctor, and he says you
can tell a person's character by the kind of funnies he likes. Now
all I'm going to ask you is this. Tell me what funny you like best
and I'll tell you all about yourself. Who's going to be first? Mrs.
Patterson?' Mrs. Patterson looked at Mr. Cowan but said
nothing. 'Just tell me the name of the funny you like best.'

'Tarzan,' she said.

'Tarzan. Interesting.' He began to speak to Mrs. Patterson
deliberately and yet intimately. 'You are straightforward, above-
board, no fuss, no frills. You say few words but what you say you
mean, they come straight from the heart. Your are honest, kind,
generous, and you like to help people. You are sympathetic.

Once you make up your mind, it is not easily changed . . .'

But we were saved from more of this by the maid coming into the room and announcing that dinner was ready.

We began with shrimp cocktail. Mr. Cowan started to tell a dirty story about hunting a moose. So far it was all about a chorus girl and a beer bottle. He was telling it to Mrs. Patterson who kept nodding her head and eating. Mr. Cowan's story now had a French-Canadian trapper, a squaw, and a candle. Meat followed, thick portions done in spices and wine, and with asparagus.

'Mr. Levine, as a writer,' Mr. Cowan said, 'what would you make of this friend of mine? He's always in a hurry. Every time I ask him to stay and have a drink or a cup of coffee, he says no, he's got somewhere to go and he's already late. But you know what I found out recently—it's all bluff. He's got nowhere to go. I've known him for over twenty years and all the time he pretended he had somewhere to go.'

'Maybe he likes to pretend,' Mrs. M. said.

'Is he hurting anyone?' Mrs. Cowan said.

'But to go on for over twenty years kidding himself . . .'

I suddenly felt Mrs. Cowan's finger on my knee. 'See that painter?' She pointed to a couple of dark still-lifes. 'Do you know why he's always got to have food in his pictures; a piece of bread, an apple? Because the guy's hungry. If you gave him a decent meal, the guy wouldn't be painting those awful pictures. He'd be happy. Instead of these dried-up chickens. They look as if they've been dead longer than the rotten apples. Why can't he paint good healthy apples, instead of rotten ones?'

'Maybe he likes them better when they're rotten.' Mr. Cowan was still annoyed at his wife changing the subject.

'I don't know anything that's better because it's rotten,' she said.

'People are sometimes.'

After the meal we returned to the other room. It was dimly lit. The lights from the chandelier looked pretty but did not give much light and there were small lights underneath the pictures on the walls. The far glass wall had now become a glass mirror, and I could see ourselves in this room, in the dark glass, as something remote. Mrs. M. went to a cupboard and brought back vodka, brandy, whisky, liqueurs. Mr. Cowan gave me a large cigar. 'Boy what a meal,' he said. 'You know what I feel like after a meal like that? How about we all go to the theatre? I saw that *Picnic* is on here. I've seen it in Newark, but I don't mind seeing it again. I know the manager.' We all agreed. He

came back from phoning and said it was fixed up, but we did
not have much time. As we drove out from the drive, in his car,
Mrs. M. pointed out a house on the other side of the drive. 'It's
a guest house. There's nobody in it now. Usually it's full. We
have more pictures there. If you could come back a month later,
you would see the house full of people. Now they are in Europe.'
We drove over the bridge; the river was dark; small white lights
were on the far bank. In a few minutes we were in the main
street. We stopped in front of a large bright cinema. It was quite
light inside. A Bugs Bunny cartoon was on.

When we came out Mr. Cowan offered to drive me to my
hotel. I thanked him, but said it wasn't worth it as it was only
across the road. He looked surprised. 'What's wrong with the
"Bessborough"?'

'Nothing. But I'm at the "Western".'

I said goodbye to Mrs. M., to Mrs. Patterson, to Mrs. Cowan,
and when I came to shake hands with Mr. Cowan he gave me a
leer as if I had just told him a dirty joke and he had just got the
point. We could no longer continue the kind of talk that was
going on all evening. I disliked myself for feeling embarrassed.
Crossed over the street and walked towards the Western—where
I had checked out earlier but left my typewriter and bag with
the clerk behind the desk—wondering if people without money
should mix with those who have; and if one deliberately puts
oneself in certain positions inviting to be humiliated.

I picked up my winter coat, typewriter, travelling bag, from
behind the desk and carried them a further three blocks along
the street to a larger hotel where the limousine for the airport
would come to pick me up at 4.20; they wouldn't come to the
cheaper hotels to pick up passengers. I told the clerk at the desk
that I was catching the Edmonton flight, would it be all right
to wait? It was now 11.10. He brought me up to a dark balcony
overlooking the main lobby. There were easy-chairs, small tables,
a carpet, a chesterfield. He put a light on. I sat there and watched
the late-comers come in, going to the desk for their keys, then
waiting for the elevator. Then they stopped coming. The boy
behind the desk began to punch the adding machine. He came
up with a pile of old *Tatlers*. I looked through the glossy pages:
the photographs of one continual ball going; the debutantes 'in
conversation with'; on one page 'They Are Engaged' and on the
other 'Recently Married'. Wealth, money, privilege. Royalty
at Ascot; the Henley Regatta; the Landsdowne Club; racing,
polo, horse-shows; the season. And I remembered that first

autumn and winter in London. Going for weekends to the country houses. The Hunt Balls, the red coats, dancing to *The Harry
Lime Theme*, nothing to drink but champagne; it was all for
some charity, the uncertain young girls excitedly selling raffle
tickets for Christmas turkeys and bottles of liquor, 'So those
Labour people don't get in,' they said. But it was all part of the
game. I had rented my evening clothes from Moss Bros. except
for the shoes; they were my own. My host looked at my laces.
'You know we wouldn't let a man into our club if he did his
laces up the way you do.' The lengthy meals with many courses
and wines and the mothers complaining that England was dull;
that their daughters were not having the times they had. The
eightsome reels, dancing all night; the bust by Epstein by the
stairs in the hall—it belonged to another world. A fat shapeless
woman was on her hands and knees with a brush and a pail
scrubbing the lobby floor. It was only 1.15.

I wrote a couple of air-letters. I went down to the desk and
asked the boy if anything was open at this time. He said the
bus depot, about five blocks away, had a cafeteria that stayed
open all night. I walked out. The street was deserted. At every
intersection lights were going on and off, in a long straight line;
as in those large restaurant mirrors where you see hundreds of
yourself stuck together going into the glass. The lights facing
the street were orange and those facing the avenues red. Orange,
red, orange, red, so many scratches in the black, scratching
silently as far as I could see. It looked like some movie set waiting for something to happen. Then a street-cleaning car came
with a clatter, its huge brush roller in front churning and sweeping the dust towards the sidewalk. I walked in the direction the
boy told me. No sign of frost or snow, but it was bitterly cold.
At the depot a tired waitress with a pasty face was behind the
drugstore counter. I had two cups of coffee and a doughnut,
then returned to the hotel, to the balcony, and fell asleep in a
chair.

I remember being awakened by the boy saying, 'It's 4.20, the
limousine is waiting for you.' Then the drive, half asleep, a
purple film around the city like that around a newborn child
that has just been pushed out. We came to the airport. I don't
know anything quite so lonely as airports, especially in the early
morning, stuck miles from the city, in a flat waste of land. I was
the only passenger and I waited by the glass front wall watching
for the airplane to come from the East and seeing a duck fly
across, and the sun come up.

The centre was white with a round cover, like a shade, not quite steady, trying to cover the sun and jiggling over and again trying to cover it, sometimes giving the effect of three-dimensions, a groove like a diamond-drill bit, deep scooped; then pushed out like the muzzle of a gun; then black as a well. Around this was an area of thin crimson, not very colourful, not as bright as blood. And from that a further area of green, then yellow. /And all the time my eyes were trying to keep on the cover of the sun, trying to cover it, bottle it up. like a garbage can, trying to put the cover on, but it wouldn't fit. No sooner did it appear to go on than it would nervously come off. [Then it seemed that something behind my eyes had started to grow, something very bright and fresh and clear. And what was stale was this modern anonymous airport with its silk-screen poster landscapes on the walls, the clammy taste of air-conditioning and central-heating; the tired faces of the all-night clerks waiting to be relieved; the hot muzzy feeling of tiredness on my face and neck; the mountie standing in the corner posing in profile. There was no barking of dogs. Only something behind my eyes, and I carried it with me as I entered the plane and saw the loose sprawled bodies lying in the seats, eyes closed, asleep.

VI

NOTES IN EDMONTON

I ONLY intended to stop off in Edmonton in order to go North or to the oilfields; but things didn't work out that way.

I took a cheap, noisy hotel near the railway lines about three blocks from the centre of the city. On the first day I wandered around the streets. It was warm, dry, dusty. They badly needed rain. In the paper I read that Ottawa and Montreal were having blizzards.

A year ago I had arranged an exhibition of six painters from Cornwall—Peter Lanyon, Bryan Wynter, Terry Frost, David Haughton, John Wells, Patrick Heron—the National Gallery was sending the exhibition across the country. I finally caught up with it in Edmonton. I went to the University where it was hung. The man in charge was an Englishman, a schoolmaster afraid of his own shadow. He trusted no one. The catalogues, which had reproductions of the painters and their work, he would not allow to be on sale in the same room as the paintings. 'I am responsible for these catalogues,' he said. I knew that they cost around ninepence in England to produce and here they were selling at fifty cents. He finally agreed to put one up on the wall (though he didn't like it; he was sure it would be stolen) and a notice saying that other catalogues could be purchased in the Arts building in another part of the campus. He was like an old woman with the paintings. Three of the larger ones he didn't even bother to hang up, because he thought they might fall down and he would be held responsible. He didn't take to the suggestion of having a stack of catalogues on a table in the room with a box beside them for the money. 'The money and the catalogues would both be gone by the first day . . .'

I remembered the pleasant times with Peter and Bryan driving in the van along the North Coast by Zennor (the gorse-bushes, the orange-yellow flower with the smell of coconuts, the deserted tin-mine chimneys, the sea along one side, the large

135

rolls of earth with the granite mixed with the bracken) to
Marazion to see the printer and making up the catalogue as
we drove. Then Anthony Froshaug, the typographer, coming
over one night to the cottage, the driftwood burning in the fireplace with a salt green flame, his bulky leather jacket sewn together in small strips like the fields of West Penwith, his hair
clipped like a monk, and pulling out the long scroll of paper
with his workings for the catalogue in the neatest writing I have
seen. And when it was over and the exhibition began in Montreal
and we heard that Patrick Heron had sold the first painting, he
sent some money down for us to celebrate. We loaded up with
hard-boiled eggs and began a pub crawl. In St. Ives: the 'Sloop',
the 'Castle', the 'Queens', the 'Western'; then drove over to the
'Engine' at Cripplesease, then over to the 'Tinner's' at Zennor
and then to Mousehole to the 'Ship', then to Newlyn and up the
hill, in Johnny's studio looking down on the harbour and Mount's
Bay; tobacco leaves drying across the ceiling, the bushel of
medlars on the floor, squelchy and tart and soft pulpy flesh; we
drank, we ate, we sang, we dressed up in paper hats, we listened
to records. Marlene Dietrich . . . Bizet's *Pearl Fishers* . . . 'It's the
closest thing to bring back that feeling of the Scillies.'

Then with David in London going along the Thames and
doing a pub crawl by the churches of Eliot's Wasteland, the eels
being cut up in basement cellars, the traders with names like
Burbank and Bleistein, the empty office-buildings, the bombed-
out squares, some music coming from a pub. Then by 'Dirty
Dick's' and London Bridge with the tall giraffe cranes, the smell
of flour from the backs of the warehouses, the pints of beer by
the outside tables besides the Thames, at low tide the bricks
lying together in the mud, the swans preening themselves.

And Terry letting me use one end of his studio, my typewriter
by the window facing the breakers of the Atlantic and those long
sunsets when the sand was flaked with pink, and the hovering
gulls. He was the most excited painter at work I have seen. The
schoolboy joy as he began a new painting, as the colours were
run on to the canvas. The enthusiasm of his talk as he worked.
His boats then were like segments of oranges, with their masts
they looked like musical notes, but set in the blacks and blues
and browns of a walk along the quay. Then back along the Back
Road, the sky twisting as the road turns, to the cottage built
like a lighthouse. The large trapdoor in the floor that you had
to push with your head when you climbed the steps with coal;
sitting by the fireplace and listening to the milk bottles rolling

down the street every time a gale blew; going out late at night to the quay, the public lavatory, the two cats, tails up, running in front on the granite wall, the bollards; listening to the soft sound the sea made as it entered back between the pier.

When I returned to the hotel in the evening I went into the beer parlour and had a couple of draught beers. Round tables with small coloured stones rubbed flat on top: at one table about twenty glasses, all full of beer. Five people sat around it and talked loudly. The man behind the desk in the hotel had given me a copy of *Edmonton Visitors' Guide*:

> Despite more than a century and a half of colorful history, Edmonton is, even for this continent, a comparatively young city. It was only 50 years ago that the little frontier town received its city charter, and it was through those last 50 years that the main growth and development of the city took place. From the beginning, however, the shaping of the city's destiny has been influenced by men of vision and imagination, men who made things happen, who worked and planned for a city that would play a major role in the economical life of their country . . .

A man in a suede windbreaker and a black cowboy hat held up a large magazine with a picture of a nude girl, her legs apart. Then he began to lick her with his tongue. Then he held the magazine up and showed everybody with a foolish grin where he had wet the paper. The others sat drinking. The fawn stetsons; the short boots, shiny leather; the sports shirts . . . the uniform of oil men. And later, when I went into the toilet, there was one of them counting his dollars methodically, putting some in one pocket and some in the other. Then he took a new dollar bill, unzipped his fly, took out his penis, wrapped the dollar bill around it like a sling, and holding his penis in the dollar he went over and urinated.

> The present city of Edmonton had its beginnings in the fierce struggles between two great rival trading companies, the North-West Company and the Hudson's Bay Company, for the rich fur trade of the great Northwest. For the sake of mutual protection from the war-like Indians, and for mutual surveillance, the two companies built their lonely western posts, Fort Augustus and Fort Edmonton, side by side on the banks of the Saskatchewan River. Both forts seem repeatedly to have been destroyed by Indians, re-established on different sites, abandoned and re-occupied . . . In 1821 the two companies united and under the firm guidance of the fiery Chief factor James Rowand, Fort

Edmonton became established as an important post of the vast
Northwest . . .

I wanted to go to Drayton Valley, to the oilfields; but all the
roads to it were blocked. The only way you could get in was by
helicopter, and it was doubtful if there was any kind of accommodation available. I went to the oil company to see if they had
any helicopters flying in, or any kind of transport. The room
was large, women sat pecking away at typewriters and adding-
machines, men were busy stamping and turning over cheques.
And this went on for the entire half-hour I was there. The sound
of the office machines, the mechanical movements. While on
the walls in huge white letters on a blue background were the
words THINK THINK THINK THINK going right around the room
like a frieze.

Today the solitary little outpost of the Northwest Territories
is a great sprawling metropolitan gateway to the north country,
centre of Canada's oil industry, and crossroads of the world.

But in fact it was still a small town, dull and boring.
I had gone into a restaurant for a meal. The fixtures were
standard, the same you find anywhere in Canada and in
America, the chromium plate, the smart look that is not built to
last. The Wurlitzer kept playing a whiny cowboy tune with
yodels at the end. There were Indians, Chinese, and white men,
in cowboy hats and decorated boots. Booths on one side of the
room, a long counter on the other. A woman in a cloth winter
coat, fur around the collar. came in and placed a folded yellow
card at each booth where a person was sitting.

PARDON MY INTRUSION!
I am a deaf mute. I sell this card for a living.
Donate what you wish. Thank you.

There was the alphabet on the other side of the card, like the
shadow game played behind a curtain, making rabbits, giraffes,
ears moving. No sooner did the woman go out, than a young
man came in, crew-cut, and placed green cards saying the same
thing. But he had no luck. My seat cover kept slipping off to the
floor. There was no variety in the food. It was all fried and
thrown up on cold, white thick plates, the fat congealed. The
waitresses were bored. The man in the booth ahead of me kept

opening and closing his mouth like a fish. He blew out a large
bubble of gum, like the skin sack where the dead calves were,
then the bubble burst and he would gather it all up again in his
mouth, chew, and again blow out.

A representative from T.C.A. drove me around the city,
showed me the Legislative Buildings, the river, the airport, and
took me to lunch. Then we went back for some coffee in the
cafeteria of the MacDonald Hotel where a man joined us. His
name was Alberta Cohen, and he was introduced as the tennis
champion of Eritrea and Ethiopia. He told me a strange story
of wandering and exile. He was born in Egypt, then lived in
France, then in Italy. He fought for the Italians against the
British in the last war. After the war he was broke, so he came
to Canada and went up north. 'We were all nationalities and we
make good money.' Eventually he came back, and now he was
the manager for the Arosa Kulm in Edmonton. 'I don't like the
eastern part of Canada. It is too European. I like the West. It is
simple. People are uncomplicated. They are friendly. You will
see for yourself, if you stay here long. Tomorrow I drive to
Calgary. I take you, no cost, we talk, good drive, you tell me
about England and Europe.' I said I would like to go, but I was
trying to get up north.

But I didn't get up north. I was going to Waterways, where
the railway ends and the rest of the transport is done by barge;
but that didn't come off. I was hoping to fly to Whitehorse; but
that didn't come off either. Lack of money. I had arranged for
my letters to be sent c/o the C.B.C. stations across the country
and I was waiting to receive payment for the talks. But though
I called every day at the MacDonald Hotel, they hadn't arrived.
Instead I spent another day and another day in Edmonton waiting for money to come, trying to get a lift up north, but all the
small planes were heavily booked. There was nothing to do but
wait.

*

Whenever I read a travel book and watch how incident after
incident is piled on, I wonder if the author is telling the truth.
Perhaps he is if he is writing about some strange country where
everything is new. Or else he finds the physical details of just
trying to live day by day as a white man out of his element—
like Graham Greene's *Journey Without Maps*—of sufficient
interest to compel him to put it down. But so much of Canada
was just dull and boring.

The days you wake up and you have to give yourself small

destinations or you feel anxious with yourself and end up in some movie or go to the library or just sit in a café, have coffee, smoke, read a paper, watch people.

An old, tall, fat woman rolling from side to side as if one leg was shorter than the other came to the restaurant; the front was completely glass. She began to push the glass wall where she thought the door was, then moved over a bit and pushed again, and then in another place, until she finally found the piece that gave . . .

The girl in the café on Jasper, sitting by herself, smoking nervously, inhaling and sending the smoke out through her nose. Our eyes met and quickly moved away. Then again the search around the room and again our eyes met and again pulled away . . .

By the railway, in a cheap restaurant. No make-up, lips very white, face white, as if she sprayed herself with white chalk powder. And all this whiteness brought out vividly the eyes. They were a very pale blue. A blue I have seen only in the eyes of old fishermen. Around the eyes were black eyelashes, and black lashes on the lower lids. It was another dimension. As if a painter had started a portrait and had painted-in only the eyes; the rest of the face was meaningless . . .

But I was saved from too much of this by being continually short of money.

Food was a problem. On my second day I found a small coffee store that had an Expresso machine. There was always the smell of coffee being ground or roasted. The young boy who was running it was Ukrainian. He wanted to let people know of Expresso, not in order to start a bar himself, but because he had the franchise on all Expresso machines for the city; so that if you bought one cup of coffee, you received a second cup free. And there was always something else that was given free with it: halvah sliced on a plate, ginger biscuits. I would go there every morning for two cups of coffee and biscuits. For lunch I bought some salami at a delicatessen by the hotel, and a loaf of bread, and went back to the hotel room to eat. Then I went down to the beer parlour for a glass of beer; it was very cheap, only ten cents. I went without an evening meal. When I became hungry, I ate some peanuts and went to bed. But I slept badly. The heat of the radiators was too much, and I couldn't do anything to reduce it no matter in what direction I turned the valve. I tried to open the windows, but they were double, and the small slot to the outside was stuck.

And then the money ran out.

There were other times; but how quickly one forgets. Instead, one remembers 'the gesture' of not having money in far more detail. As in Montreal, in the basement room, at McGill; buying two pounds of peanuts every week and deliberately leaving half of the shell intact, but throwing it in with the empty ones into the wastepaper basket. Then on the weekend, towards the end of the month, spreading out a newspaper on the floor and tipping over the wastepaper basket, searching for those nuts in the half-broken shells. It was a game. One talked about it to one's friends, later. Or else C., coming back from the South of France on a Sunday with a penny in his pocket, taking a room in a hotel by Charing Cross, then going across Waterloo Bridge and in the middle throwing the penny into the Thames and saying proudly: 'Now I'm broke.' But on Monday there was the bank in Waterloo Place and the overdraft.

No. No money means going to bed early, doing nothing, daydreaming, walking aimlessly through the streets. Holding the ladder for the man to climb and disconnect the electricity. Finding the wings of the ray hanging outside the door on a hook that the fisherman left, or the farmer from the field above leaving some cauliflower on the doorstep. It means depending on strangers. Going through the streets looking for the stranger, as others go with their head down hoping to find something that someone has lost. It's waste. It makes you bitter. It's boring. It's telling lies. It's going to bed early. It's going to the reading room of the public library. It's just looking at the sea. It's sitting by the desk and daydreaming about the great books that one will some day write. It's having no confidence. It's giving a penny less on a bus for a destination, or trying not to pay. It's using people. It's borrowing; it's taking all the time and giving nothing back. It's the hole burnt in the trousers so that you keep your legs crossed when sitting down. It's telling people you will pay back, you mean it at the time, but by then others have also been promised the same thing. It's quarrels; it's self-pity; it's waste, hunger, isolation, loneliness. One becomes an expensive friend.

A CHURCH CRAWL

Next morning I went to the C.B.C. office; but no letters. I met the T.C.A. representative and he bought me breakfast. He said he would try again to see if he could fix up a flight for me to the North. But at the airport we went into every hangar; the small

private companies with only a few bush planes; there wasn't a
chance for at least another week. He suggested that I go and take
a look at the street with all the churches in it. There was little
else to do.

In the guide-book I read:

UKRAINIAN CATHOLIC CHURCH OF ST. JOSAPHAT. 97th Street and 108th
Avenue. This magnificent church with its temple crosses soaring
into the sky was built entirely through subscriptions from the
congregation. It stands as a testimonial to this good, free country
where these Ukrainian Canadians considered it a privilege to give
their all to build their own temple in which to worship God in
their own way. It was first opened in 1947.

It looked like something that belonged beside the Albert
Memorial. The seven small spires, the seven crosses, the copper
now black on the roofs. And beside it the drab dusty street without trees or grass; Danny's Garage; Summit Drugs; Zar Café.
Inside it had all the gaiety of a badly-done poster. The same
angel was repeated all over the cream walls. No body. Just a head
with blonde curly hair, blue eyes, a tiny mouth, and large
feathery wings hanging down. One wall had a mural of the
Devil, a skeleton of Death with his scythe, and a caricature of
Hitler, while flames and bodies were all around. Everywhere else
the baby faces without bodies, set in between the wings like
enormous feathery ears, stared expressionless from the cream
walls; the smell of incense; a few candles lit in red-coloured
glasses.

I came outside into the harsh sun and asked a girl if she could
tell me where a certain street was. She shook my hand firmly
and said that she was a stranger here too and didn't know. She
was a Mormon. 'I began work today, but I hear he doesn't pay.
I quit on Friday if he doesn't pay me.' The man's trenchcoat.
The blonde straw hair hanging down to the shoulders. The open
face, no lipstick.

Suddenly a truck came with a loudspeaker on its roof blaring.
'Hurry Hurry-On-Down Tonight to the Canadian Legion Bingo-
Bingo-Bang. Sixteen thousand dollars in prizes. Yes, Sir. Yes,
Madam. Sixteen thousand new crisp dollars in prizes for you.
So come on now Hurry Hurry and come win a car, a house, and
hundreds of other valuable prizes that you'll get at the Canadian
Legion Mammoth Bingo tonight.'

She was born in Leamington but left it when she was three.
She said she didn't like Edmonton. 'There's nothing nice here.

No green things growing; just dust.' She waited. I would have suggested coffee, if I had any cash; instead we shook hands again vigorously.

I walked down the street. There was a Greek Catholic church and a French Roman Catholic church on one side, and an English Roman Catholic church on the other. There was an Anglican, a Lutheran, a German and English Baptist, a Dutch Reform, a Presbyterian, a Lighthouse Mission with the neon saying JESUS SAVES. They were all either closed or empty.

THEY

In front of the Lutheran Evengelical a large hoarding advertised a youthful Christ in yellows and oranges and reds and blues. He was blessing a young girl. I walked up the steps, tried the door, but it was locked. I went to the side door. A small spare man with a Hitler moustache was carrying a fern with a plate underneath the pot. There was too much water in the plate and it was overflowing. He put the fern down. I asked him if I could enter the church.

'For how long?' He looked suspicious.

'Only for five minutes.'

I went in from a side door. It was like a lecture room. The benches in a semi-circle were all of walnut and highly polished, as was the floor. I went to the back. The walls were bare, so was the ceiling. Everying was clean, shining, spotless. Three steps led to a platform. There was a picture of Christ flanked on both sides by organ pipes. There was a small undecorated altar with a line of German on the ceiling. The room was sombre, so different from the garish advertisement outside. I asked the man what was the difference between Lutheran and Lutheran Evangelical.

'One when the Pastor says the Creed he shouts. The other says it quiet.'

'Which one is this?'

'They shout loud. You should hear the noise.'

He asked me where I was from and when I told him he looked surprised.

'I got an Uncle in Ottawa. Poldovsky, do you know him? He may have changed his name. Anyway he's dead now. When I came over from the old country, I was to go to Ottawa. I was in the Polish army. My uncle, he was always a smart man. He told me to go into the army, so afterwards I am a free man. He was in the orchestra. And I went in the orchestra. I had it good. In war when it came I didn't get killed, but bullets fly over me, one took my hat off. I go to Canada; for Ottawa. But they lock the train in Ottawa. We try to get out. We cannot. The doors only open when we come out West. I go to a farm in Saskatchewan. Good money, seven dollars a day threshing, no machines. I think I go to see my uncle. Instead I come to Edmonton and become a church janitor. I want my wife to come over. She can, but my daughter cannot. They won't give permission. So my wife don't come over. I wait twenty-five years, without a wife. My uncle die. My aunt die. I save up money, and this summer I'll make a trip to Ottawa. But what will I see, a couple of stones.' While he was talking, we were standing on the porch outside; men and women kept walking by on the sidewalk saying, 'Hello, Felix.' And he would immediately reply: 'Hallo, Hank. Hallo, Lillie. Hallo, Ruth . . . I don't know her name. I think it's Ruth. She's a nice girl anyway. So many come and go here, you're not sure any more. It's a boom-town. Before it was meat and now it's oil. But nothing much happens here, except you get older.'

In the sky the drone of airplanes, all shapes and sizes. Against the horizon the burning waste from a refinery, at night a glow against the sky. There were things here for the business man. And everywhere away from the city, the brown melancholy plain spread out. I walked towards the river. Desolation, waste-land, the sun sucking the mudbanks dry. And above this dark brown were pieces of white, gulls gliding, soaring, chasing one another. It seemed strange to see gulls so far inland. In one's private world they belonged to something else.

Then on Saturday morning a cheque arrived. I was able to pay my hotel bill and have a good meal. I decided to go on to Van-couver. My flight out was early in the morning. But I could not sleep. Pigeons were going between the buildings. It was now 5.45 and had been light for some time. One pigeon kept repeat-ing the same rumble, like the sound of my stomach when I'm hungry. I could see it perched on a dark ledge above. Against the sky, a small head, a fine curve into the rounded shape; it reminded me of a Henry Moore figure. I waited in the room. The smell of burnt milk came from between the buildings. I carried my bags through the empty streets—the secondhand stores; the pawnshops; the fox pelts hanging down in the win-dows—to a larger hotel where the airport limousine arrived to pick me up.

FLIGHT OVER THE ROCKIES

It was a Viscount, with turboprops, and it was much better than the North Stars or the DC.3's. Practically all the seats were taken; it was coming from the East. The young man beside me had also just got on, and no sooner were we airborne than two others in well-cut suits came and joined us. There was room. We were in the front seat. The other two sat with their backs against the lavatory wall on my typewriter and on a gladstone bag. One of them took out a large bottle. It looked like a bottle of expensive perfume. It was kept in a linen-cloth holder. The glass top of the bottle could also be used for a cup. He passed around a shot of rye to everyone. We soon knew each other's first names. One was Eddie, the other Jeff, the third was called Bluenose. They were engineers. Eddie and Bluenose were from McGill; Jeff from Toronto. Again the bottle went around. Bluenose: 'Did you score with yours?' Eddie: 'Yeh. But all she really wanted was to go muff-diving.' Jeff: 'Not mine. We were out in the car necking until four in the morning. Boy, was she hot! A policeman came by, took a look and let us alone.' He took out a neatly folded handkerchief from his back pocket, opened it carefully. Bluenose reached over and pretended to pick up something from the handkerchief. He closed his eyes, and in an affected pose of a connoisseur sniffed the ends of thumb and first finger up each nostril as if it was snuff. Then in a stage French accent, 'A leetle too near de harse hole.' Again the bottle went around. And when it was finished, Jeff brought out a similar full bottle from his bag and passed that around. The stewardess came and asked if we wanted breakfast. Jeff hid the bottle. She took down the small white cushions from the rack above us and placed them on our knees and brought us prepared lunches. Bluenose kept asking her, 'Don't you think I look like Brooke Claxton?' She smiled and said nothing. We had coffee in cardboard cups, and Jeff kept pouring more rye into the coffee, and on the eggs, and soaking the bread. Bluenose got up unsteadily and looked seriously down his glasses. 'Don't you think I look like Brooke Claxton?' Then they began to sing, to the tune of *Auld Lang Syne*, 'We're here because we're here because we're here because we're here . . .'

We were over cloud. Then there was a break and down below were the Rockies. I had looked forward, ever since I was a child, to flying over the Rockies. The real thing was too much like a travelogue. Occasionally one peak stood out by its size from the

K

rest. But it went on and on like giant thick vertebrae. Snow on the tops and the sides, and things again were three-dimensional. What I didn't appreciate before was the width of the mountain range. Even in the half-drunk state, I was conscious of crossing a frontier.

Another break through the clouds, and they all took out movie cameras from their travelling bags and began to take films out of the window. Then one of them dropped the bottle. It didn't break, but the whisky ran out down to the back of the plane. The stewardess came up. 'Now you must not drink here. People are complaining.' Bluenose replied in a deep voice. 'Do you know whom you are addressing? I'm Brooke Claxton.'

They were travelling on their company's expense account. That was the way, they kept repeating to me, to live. 'Those who don't are a bunch of suckers.' The clouds had thinned to a grey mist, and were left behind; and now you could see the peaks, the sides with the blindingly white snow and the dark trees. Bluenose ate some shaving cream out of a tube, then washed it down with the rye that Eddie brought out of his bag. He suddenly got up and staggered to the toilet. He came back looking very pale, with water down his shirt and trousers. He sat down, sprawled, and went off to sleep. Then the others also sprawled and went to sleep.

By the time we approached Vancouver the stewardess woke them up. They washed. They sang again: 'We're here because we're here because . . .' They said together: 'Ray team. Ray team. Fight. Fight. Fight.' Then they went into the toilet and got dressed and you wouldn't have recognized them now. They all wore homburg hats. They were quiet. They assumed poses as if they had practised personality in front of the mirror. Their faces looked the same: young, plump, immature. All their luggage was expensive and new. Each one had three gold initials. They didn't take the bus that was bringing the other passengers into the city, but took a taxi to the Vancouver Hotel. They were all in their twenties.

VII

THE PACIFIC COAST

VANCOUVER

I LIKED it from the beginning. Gulls and the sea and things growing. Green, warm, bright light; no sign of winter. So much for the eyes. And the two mountain peaks with snow and black trees and green grass slopes standing there close like an enormous pair of horse-blinkers, cutting the place off from the slush, the greyness, the dust, the depression of the other side. I bought a local paper. In Ottawa and Montreal they were having snow-flurries. South of Winnipeg the spring floods had started.

I asked a taxi-driver to take me to a small hotel. He brought me to one in Hastings near Main. An old man in a shabby brown suit was behind the desk. When he opened his mouth a wet smile of gold teeth and a bright crimson tongue darted about like a live animal. He was bald and brown skinned. He said I could have a room at $2.50 a night, how long would I stay? I said I didn't know. He took me up in an old elevator to the top floor. The room was at the end of a dark passage, next door to a toilet. A small thin Chinaman, old, came out of another door with a broom and a bundle of dirty linen. He stood and watched as I unlocked the door, and said nothing.

It was a small drab room. An iron bed with a soiled scarlet bedspread. Chocolate paint on the wooden walls. The light: a small naked bulb hung down from the ceiling. One narrow window with a green window-blind that wouldn't go up more than halfway. It looked out on to the backs of dilapidated buildings and unpainted telegraph poles. An enamel sink with a cracked marble top. A thick glass; two small tablets of soap, 'Fragrance'. A rickety wooden table by the bed. A small dressing-table. The only decoration was two calendars on the walls. One was of a young Japanese girl. A close-up of a face, a kimono, a fan held open in a hand, the eyes looking submissive over the fan. The other calendar was American. A pretty girl nude in a pink skin. Her small head thrown back, long blonde hair falling back

behind her. The small mouth open and fine white teeth smiling.
A scarf flowed from around her neck and went in between her
open legs. With one hand she held up a small pointed breast. I
could hear someone going to the toilet. And later, the loud insistent ringing of the elevator bell.

When I woke up it was after four. I went out and walked along
Hastings. A library on the corner. Two Sikhs in light blue tur-
bans were sitting on the steps watching people go by, cars. A
blind man ran a tobacco kiosk by the library. Around the corner
was the heart of Chinatown: restaurants, nightclubs, fruit and
vegetable stores, and a large pin-ball gallery. In the opposite
direction, towards the two mountain peaks, was the waterfront.
I walked along Main Street and saw a small dumpy Chinese
woman being carried out from another small hotel by two large
policemen. She had no shoes or stockings. Her white blouse had
come out of her skirt. Her face was expressionless. They lifted
her up by the elbows across the sidewalk and into the back of a
closed police truck.

I took a bus to Stanley Park. I just wanted to soak in vegetation, in things growing, and the sea. I hadn't realized how much
I disliked the prairies. Weeping willows, spruce, pine, grass.
Drake chasing drake across the park, then coming in to land
with a searing splash beside the female. A muskrat silently swam
across a small lake. There were trails and picnic grounds. I came
out to a pond; frogs sounded. Lily pads lay flat in the water. As
the wind passed, it raised a few leaves slowly up and set them
down again. Movement, I thought, is living. Then along a trail.
The trees so thick that they kept out the light. Last year's dead
leaves hanging as bats from the branches, the colour of ashes.
And by the sea-edge large bleached pieces of wood, split, rotting,
lay on the rocks; enough to have lasted one in Cornwall for
several years. I sat on a large piece of wood and watched the sunset and smelled the wet sand.

'Does it make you think of going down to the beach in the
evening light after a rainy day and gathering the damp firewood
(it will dry on top of the stove) and picking up for a moment
the long branches of seaweed that the waves have tossed and
listening to the gulls who stand reflected in the gleaming sand,
and just fly a little way off as you come and then—settle again?'
I couldn't quite shake off Cornwall.

'When one has had the good luck,' Camus writes, 'to love
intensely, life is spent in trying to recapture that ardour and that
illumination.' And I had returned to Cornwall, to St. Ives, to the

place where one had known it. But there was the inevitable disappointment. It was inadequate to the present. The place looked much the same, but people had moved away, and then one had changed. And yet it remained—for all its absurdities, jealousies, mutual admiration societies, romantic poverty—the place where one had come close to something, felt far more alive than anywhere else, experienced a kind of happiness; but like all happiness it did not last very long.

I remembered the day I left Cornwall. A wet February morning. The tide was out. Some of the boats in the harbour were beached on the sand. I walked by the urinal and along the deserted front. The high water left a line of seaweed, driftwood, the skeleton of a fish. By the slipway three white cards with black letters, black bordered, nailed to the wall of the fishermen's shelter told what funerals would take place this week. Gulls. On the closed café roofs. On the sandbar that lay like an animal across the harbour's mouth. By the open sewer pipe near the Anglican church. Scavengers ready to fly to wherever there was anything to swallow. Eyes. A round black dot of black and a circle of lemon around it. Opened a razor-cut clothes-peg mouth and vomited out her throat. I entered an opening in the wall of the front and walked through a passage up stone steps. This street was also deserted. Washing pushed out by wooden sticks from the sides of the cottages. A gull folded her wings the way an old man folds his hands behind his back, and perched on a garbage can. Past a butcher, the blind down but I could hear him sawing. I saw the Palais de Danse with its green closed doors. The church tower standing higher than the houses. The small hand of the clock looked like a heart as it pointed past the seven. I saw the three funeral cards again in a paper-shop, a baker's window, the Crimson Tours office. I had gone away many times from St. Ives, but I had always come back . . .

That first summer another Canadian and I rented a condemned cottage in Academy Place that needed the light on all the time. The toilet was outside. The water tap was by the toilet. We came here in June not knowing a person and when we threw a party the night before we left in September over sixty people crowded into the two rooms. We both had money, sent regularly, from Canada.

That first summer the whole thing was a continual holiday. A masquerade. A joke. Nothing seemed important. You didn't have to think seriously of money, food, work, or tomorrow. The setting was right. So much of the place was for the senses. And if it rained, we would spend all day cooking some exotic meal that ended with brandy and cigars in a tiny room where the wallpaper was peeling, the walls damp, the light from a gas bracket. We did not bother washing dishes but stacked them until Thursday morning when the landlady came to wash the floor and make the beds. We worked in the morning in the small kitchen and the dining-room until noon, then went for a swim on Porthmoor Beach, by the cemetery; surfed, lay on the sand, dried by the sun. Then back to the typewriter until opening time at the 'Castle'. Then there was always a party going. The best place was at the 'Carn'. We gathered in cars and drove to the 'Tinners', then to the moor and walked across. Candles in milk bottles showed the way. In the path, a head of a cow propped on one side of the fence as if the rest of the body existed on the other. Inside the 'Carn' the phonograph played. A mobile of a fish in the fireplace. From the ceiling shrunken heads, owl faces, of straw. We danced. We drank. Some of the women were pregnant. At another party we counted twenty-three nationalities. Stish, a Polish painter, said, 'Here I'm not a foreigner. In Surrey, Kent, Sussex, I'm a foreigner. Here I'm not. Everybody here is a foreigner.' Then the midnight swims, stripping in the cottage and diving through the window into the harbour, the girls insisting on wearing their brassières . . . the parties on board the French crabbers . . . shooting with a rifle at lit candles in the dark . . . a winter of charades . . . the young girl from London with the horse-tail dancing on the dining-room table in the nude . . . the business men dressing up in berets and jeans coming with their admission ticket—a bottle of whisky or gin . . . It was all wonderfully absurd. But one felt good. Writing was done; pictures were painted. And one didn't care. One was young. And this was new. And it didn't last.

Came to Mousehole two years later to a large house on the side of a hill. We had a high walled garden with bamboo, copper-beech, palms, and roses. And I wrote in a studio the size of a classroom. I could see the roofs of the village below, the sea in between the chimneys. Hear the curlews flying over in the morning. Watch the cows on the hill, large against the sky. The coastline become purple at dusk. And at night the few lights of the pilchard boats and their dans in the bay; the owl from Paul. But this kind of living was pointless. One needed to be involved, not isolated. One had made the mistake of coming down here imagining one's resources were unlimited, when they weren't. Then the money ran out. I 'signed on' at the Labour Exchange in

Penzance and borrowed the landlord's bicycle to ride in twice a week.

St. Ives. Mousehole. The north, the other on the south, in the narrow part of Cornwall about twelve miles apart. They represented the two sides of a coin. On one side it is gay, irresponsible, absurd, and happy. On the other there are depression, quarrels, poverty, and anxiety. Only at the beginning was it ever as clear as that. But as one continued to live here, the coin kept flipping, the images blurred. Sometimes there would be something of that early first summer to break through the other and more permanent face.

But there was still a more subtle face and its appeal was on another level. One had, by choice, turned one's back on a direction that was pulling everywhere else. You kicked against values you refused to inherit. But in the end was it enough? The line separating the retired businessmen who came here with their savings and bought their graves, the divorcees getting older and more desperate, hoping something will turn up, from oneself was very thin. It did not take much to step over and retire oneself and pretend that the gesture of refusing to be involved was in itself a commitment. For this place was a no man's land, let to whoever could pay the rent. And whoever wanted to escape it was made all too easy. The climate was pleasant. I could lie in the sun, swim, go out with the fishermen. There were the friends to talk and to drink with. The walks along the coast or over the moor. It was possible to see good films in the fleapit of a cinema where you could hear the soundtrack outside. Rent was cheap. And the shopkeepers allowed one credit when the money ran out. But it was also a kind of death that got hold of you. The place had become tourist country and the rot had set in. It had become, as Greene said of Taxco, 'a colony for escapists with their twisted sexuality and hopeless freedom'. The stores were full of 'arts and crafts'. And for all the buoyancy, the jazzed-up activity, the gaiety of the outward appearance—there was so much inertia to the place. Men and women in summer lay on the sand and got brown and soaked in the sunshine. You didn't have to do very much—the landscape did it all brilliantly and monotonously. It was made all too easy to pretend. To contract out and live in a hothouse of mutual praise and look forward to every summer's new encounter. A choice had to be made. And the longer one stayed here the more difficult it was.

. . . I walked towards the station. Past the Catholic church, the man dangling from the gallows, 'We Shall Have The Mass'.

The terraced houses with the retired North of England, their fat castrated cats. Stopped at the Malakoff to look at the harbour, someone was taking his dog out for a walk by the slipway; the white-yellow of the sand in the early morning sun; the front with the tightly packed cottages, smoke coming straight up from a few chimneys. One was saying farewell to a whole way of life; without knowing it.

*

I left Stanley Park. It was dark. And went into Murrays to have some coffee. A party of deaf-mutes were waving arms and fingers. They used their hands and fingers like magicians. They wrote what they wanted on small pieces of paper and brought it to the counter. They smiled, they touched each other, they seemed to be having a good time. The only thing that looked wrong was when they waved goodbye. It was done too much like another word. There was something unnatural the way their wrist flapped lifelessly, or perhaps it was their only speech that linked them with everyone else.

On Granville Street the street photographers were flashing their cameras, a large camera attached to their waist, a battery kept in a suitcase on the sidewalk. I returned to the hotel room. For the next few days I just wandered around the place. I tried to economize by not eating in the restaurants but going to the corner Chinese store and buying bread, a half pound of salami, a thin boxful of over-ripe bananas for twenty-five cents, then eating around midnight, getting thirsty, taking the thick glass —it reminded me of the glass with a candle inside that you burn for the dead—letting the water run out of the tap marked C, but the water was warm and tasteless. It didn't take away the thirst and the bananas got stuck in the throat. They gave a smell to the room. Or else I bought some Jutland sardines; they were the only ones that had a key with the box. On the third day I got food poisoning.

I woke up in the morning with a pain, and sweating. I went to the toilet. But no matter how often I went, the pain in the stomach remained. I went to bed; it was no good. I pressed a button on the wall by the bed and the old Chinaman came in. He looked at me. Then pulled back the covers. 'O doity, doity, doity.' He cleaned up the excrement. He bathed me, he changed the sheets, he put a cold towel on my head. He kept coming in all that day and night while I tossed and walked around the room. In the background I could hear another kind of noise going on.

Soon after coming here I noticed that most of the rooms on the floor were occupied by women. They were not attractive, nor young. When I saw them in the daytime downstairs, waiting for the elevator or shopping in the Chinese store, they appeared in a state of stupor, as if they were perpetually drunk. They were Indian, white, Chinese. It wasn't an organized brothel. But the rooms were rented out to these girls who brought men back for the night. Some had steady boy-friends.

I could hear a man's voice speaking English with a foreign accent and a woman shouting back at him. Then the woman came back with a policeman. The policeman asked the man why he wouldn't give the girl back her coat.

'Because the bitch rolled me.'

'You know you are not supposed to have a lady in your room.'

'But she came in, she knocked . . .'

'You know you are not supposed to have a lady in your room.'

'But, Mister Policeman, she came in.'

'Do you understand English?'

'Sure I understand English.'

'I think it's better we forget the whole thing. Here's your coat.'

'Smart policeman, that bitch rolled me and you say forget. What's your number, smart policeman? I'll take you to the court. I'll fix you and that bitch.'

The policeman gave his number and then I could hear foot-steps walk away and the elevator bell ringing.

Then another girl began to yell. Others came to the door, banged on it, and told her to keep quiet. But she wouldn't. They called the man on the elevator. And he came and shouted: 'Rosie, keep quiet or else get out.' She quietened down and giggled. 'Ain't it cute? Ain't it cute?'

I went into the toilet. Empty beer bottles lay on the floor. The floor was wet. In the bowl, in the urine water, was the neck of a tortoise. I watched it; the head swayed silently. Then I pulled the chain. It disappeared with the noise and the swilling water.

I must have fallen asleep, for when I woke up the Chinaman was beside me with a bowl of Chinese soup with shoots of green onion floating on top. He had a Chinese soup spoon, flat white bone with raised sides. I didn't feel like eating but he insisted. Then he went back and stood in the corner of the room and watched. On the window-blind, like a screen, the red and green neon lights were reflected and they continued regularly like a heart beat.

For the next two days I remained in that room. The old Chinaman came in regularly, bringing bowls of soup and crackers and old newspapers and scandal sheets and film magazines that he must have collected when he cleaned the other rooms. He never spoke. Sometimes he giggled when I said something. I don't think he could speak English. On the third morning I felt better and decided to go out.

The sun was out and no breeze and those mountains sticking up there like some candy decoration. Pigeons by the square and the unemployed hanging around watching the pigeons, watching everyone else. People going to work. Across the bridges a sticking-up advertisement for the *Vancouver Sun*. And the newspapers propped up in the wooden holders to the street-lamp-posts repeating on every block the same headlines: DRUG TRAFFICKER ASKS LASH GETS FOURTEEN YEARS. The MacDonald Hotel like all the railway hotels, smoke coming out of the top like a train in a siding. By the station the war memorial, an angel taking up a soldier to heaven. The sun was hot. How easy it cheered one up.

INCIDENT ON GRANVILLE STREET

I was walking down Granville Street when I saw one of the boat passengers who had sat at the same table: the young shy aircraft mechanic. He had just come in, driving a truck from Toronto to Vancouver as a means of getting here. He couldn't get a job in Toronto unless he took a special course. So he came to Vancouver; but it was the same here. We decided to have a cup of coffee in the Hudson Bay caféteria and sat on the seats by a horseshoe counter with the waitress inside and talked about how do you like Canada—and he didn't, he felt homesick and he wasn't finding it easy, and we had another cup of coffee, when a small elderly woman sitting next to him said, 'I can tell you're Scottish. Once a Scot always a Scot . . .'

He mumbled that he was English, but she pretended that she didn't hear.

'I was born next door to Robbie Burns. I taught in Ottawa. My maiden name was Kerr. I graduated from normal school in Adelaide. That's in Australia. What did you say your name was?'

'Wilson,' he said quietly.

'Wilson. That's my mother's name. She's dead. Died in Australia. I went to normal school in Adelaide. That's in Australia.

My husband comes from Bonny Dundee. I was born next door to Robbie Burns. What is it you follow?'

He was blushing and he said very quitely that he was a mechanic.

'That's interesting. I was told in Ottawa where I taught French-Canadian children that they all speak with a delightful Scottish accent. My husband comes from Bonny Dundee. You don't have to worry about my husband, he is retired. What is your name?'

'Wilson, John Wilson.'

'Wilson. That's my mother's name. She's dead. Buried in Australia. My husband comes from Bonny Dundee. I was born in the house next to Robbie Burns. I graduated from Adelaide normal. Well, I must tell my husband. My husband is quite good-looking. I've got him for forty years. He's been with the Jones company. That's a fine company. My husband is retired. And we have no bad dogs. So you'll come up and see us.'

He said he would and took down her address.

'I'm a Scot. And I can see you're a Scot. Once a Scot always a Scot.'

Wilson mumbled that he wasn't a Scot but that he was English.

'You're pulling my leg. What is it you follow?'

He mumbled that he was a mechanic.

'That's interesting . . .' And she continued going on from there. This kept on solidly for over half an hour, Wilson was getting more and more embarrassed. It read like a script. All he had to say was his name, or what he was doing, and she would continue. Finally I suggested that perhaps he had to go to the toilet. He said he did and went away from the horseshoe counter. The woman asked me where I was going. I said eastwards. Did I know Ottawa? Yes, I did. She taught school in Ottawa. And she began to repeat about her maiden name, going to Adelaide normal, that it was in Australia, where her mother died, when a woman of about thirty, who was sitting a few stools away, came and sat down beside me and suggested that perhaps if we talked as if we had known each other, the elderly woman would leave. She was the most beautiful woman I have ever seen in Canada. She was a French-Canadian from Montreal, there was no accent in her English. She had just come back from Mexico. She looked like Michele Morgan. Large grey pensive eyes, very pale, with lots of white and with dark eyelashes. And there was a warmth, a fine woman's body that one was aware of, and a sadness in her face. I tried to detain her with a bribe of another cup of coffee. But the old woman did go. The Englishman came back. She said goodbye. And then to look around the horseshoe counter to see the well-turned-out empty faces of the others and to listen to their comments and their giggles.

I walked down Granville to Hastings to the pier, then retraced my steps. I took in a film. It was *The Third Man*. The zither music; the chase in the sewers; the man saying 'Balloon'; bits of dialogue—all made their impact the first time. What wore well and still moved one were the silent images: the empty swinging doors at the station; the final long shot of the girl walking towards the camera, by the cemetery, sawn-off trees on both sides of the road, the leaves falling. I came out of the film, into the sunlight, and walked back towards the hotel room. I hadn't eaten very much, and for the first time since the food poisoning I was feeling hungry. But I was short of money. And again I began to think from whom I could borrow.

One image kept coming back soon after Sault Ste Marie. It's of a film that's going on. And I see bits and pieces of one's life—not in any ordered sequence, but in a few images with their immediate associations like those pages in *Lilliput* where one page showed an animal and the facing page a human being like that animal. They all hinted as if one's experiences were all part of some grotesque living pun. And this film keeps going on continually and I can see, with a certain amount of detachment, one's self, one's friends, the places one knows. Then on this screen a yellow card with black writing appears like the card that usually comes on to the screen to say: WILL DR. BROWN PLEASE COME TO THE BOX OFFICE URGENTLY WANTED. And that yellow card with the black lettering remains there stationary while behind it the film keeps going on and changing.

My situation was much like that. What I was seeing, what I was doing, what I had done, was all there going ahead at its pace, but along would come these yellow cards, stuck there, with a sign saying YOU MUST GET TWENTY-FIVE DOLLARS RIGHT AWAY. And I would spend energy, time, cunning, anything to get that card out, so that I wouldn't be distracted from watching the film that was going on and trying to make something from it. And when I did remove it, it wasn't really important; it soon turned up in the film itself, as part of the other things passing by, not yellow and black and urgent, but a dull grey . . . but I knew it would reappear.

In the evenings I was invited out for dinners. New spacious

houses on a hill overlooking the city, Burrard Inlet, facing the mountains. Large windows for front walls, the lights of the North Shore twinkled and the passenger boats went by all lit up like a lot of fiery eyes in the dark. It is the most picturesque setting of any city in Canada. I ate, drank, smoked. Everyone was kind and generous. They would drive me around the city, along the scenic drives, to the top of the Mountain. It was freezing cold. At night, snow around us, but below the city spread out like the skeleton of a giant flat fish. And then I would return to Hastings Street, the smell of leather, a hot smell, men in shirt sleeves hanging around the lamp-posts, outside beer-parlours, by the small hotels . . . to my room.

It was a place where you just took somebody to bed with you, made some kind of sex, and then got out. The two calendars on the wall, the pulled-down window-blind with the wind flapping it against the sill, the reflection of the neon sign as in the film *Rope* going on red and green all the time. It was a bare, stuffy, drab room, but after a few days it began to feel like home. I would return to it from the large hotels, from the comfortable houses where I had been invited to dinner or drinks, and it made sense. The three weeks that I spent here were the happiest of the entire trip. There was the brown man with the pink tongue and gold teeth, the beaten man with the Scottish accent who used to be a fisherman, and the small Chinese owner, always dressed in a suit. They took turns, working three shifts, behind the desk and running the elevator. Whenever I wanted to leave anything for safe keeping, they stopped the elevator between the second and third floors. A large hole was cut out of the wall, it was dark and smelled sour. I left my winter coat, my bag, my typewriter. Others had left their possessions: a guitar, a pair of lumberjack boots, a carton with Kotex marked on it tied with rope. Dust gathered. A childish scrawl on the pieces of cardboard, torn cigarette packages, gave the name of the owners. But they were names without addresses.

THE REMITTANCE MAN

One night I was dropped off in a taxi at the corner of Granville and Hastings. I had spent a particularly good evening with a French lecturer at the University. When my first novel came out he had written to me saying that he was also interested in flying and Saint Exupery. He collected advertisements. He showed me hundreds that he had cut out of American and

Canadian magazines and newspapers. 'Look at the horror in this one . . . See how secular values have crept in . . . suffering is reduced to worrying whether the tyres on the car are in good condition or not.' Especially effective were the advertisements for tombstones. They showed a picture of a happy couple in wedding dress, leaving the church, smiling. 'For those you love. For those you want to remember. There's nothing like a good memorial.'

It was a good evening in every way, good drinking, good talk, and we sat in the sitting-room facing the water, the mountains, and watching the lights of North Vancouver. I got a lift back in a taxi with someone who was staying at the MacDonald Hotel, and walking along Hastings, by the cinema that was closed, vomit splattered on the sidewalk, broken whisky bottles, drunks walking as if they had shit in their pants, lights flashing DON'T CROSS, CROSS, when I heard someone singing:

> She's my lady love,
> She is my dove, my baby dove . . .

I saw him standing in the shadow of a building off Hastings doing a song-and-dance act. Then he saw me and stopped. He waited. 'Hello. For a minute I thought by your shadow you were a policeman.' 'No. I like that song.' I think he recognized a fellow-soul, for we were soon walking down the street until we came to an open restaurant run by Chinese near my hotel. We went in and had some coffee. In some of the other booths the poor, the lonely, were huddled asleep.

His name was Henry and he said he was a part-time taxi-driver. He was in his early fifties, going bald, with brown eyes in a sallow face. He spoke a faultless English; at first I thought he was an Englishman. 'I picked up a fare near midnight. They were a couple of nice kids, well dressed and well behaved. He gave me ten dollars and said keep driving. I drove around Stanley Park, Marine Drive, and I could see them in the back hardly moving. I finally stopped and said, "Would you like me to take a walk for fifteen minutes?" They both looked scared. "No," he said. "Just keep driving." I drove on and this went on and I could see that they weren't getting anywhere . . . and they were so desperate about it. I couldn't understand why he didn't get a room. It would have cost him less. Where are you staying?'

I told him the name of my hotel.

'That's not far from here. C'mon back to my place, I have a bottle, it's too early to go to sleep.'

He lived in Chinatown, in a small poky room at the top of the stairs above a fruit store. Stills from stage shows were hanging on the walls, some were piled above a dresser, in glass and gilt frames. They showed long fragile women in long grey sack dresses; they looked as if they belonged to the Pre-Raphaelites. Others showed young men and women with the fixed stage smile, the excitement of youth, and the dress of the 1920's. It was impossible to recognize the young man in those stills—with the slicked-down black hair, the schoolboy face, the self-confidence—with the seedy, stout, beaten man sitting in the room. 'Sometimes looking back at those pictures,' he said, 'you forget it was you, the same you that is here now.' He poured some whisky into a couple of cracked cups. There was a small sink against the wall by the door; a small bronze crucifix above the iron bed; the smell of old clothes; stumps of cigarettes in a saucer; near the bed by the wall was a low bookcase filled with paper-backs, only detectives. And there was the sound of a large fly coming from somewhere in the room, buzzing as if it was caught in a spider's web and couldn't get out.

He said he was from Toronto, but he was sent out here so he wouldn't bring shame to the family, a kind of remittance man. His parents had money, they were in real estate, they sent him to private schools then to university. 'I went up for a Rhodes. The committee who looked after the scholarships were all former Rhodes Scholars. They were now directors of aluminum companies, nickel companies, asbestos, tar, chairmen of banks . . . and all I really wanted then was to get over to England to learn something about acting.' He did not get a Rhodes, but his father gave him some securities so that he had a steady income of fifteen dollars a week. 'It wasn't enough to live grandly, but enough for food and somewhere to sleep, and if you were careful you could do some travelling.'

He worked in Rep, and toured the country. 'The first thing I had to do was lose my Canadian accent. It was a gay time; we did not worry very much about anything. I remember one Christmas Eve in London. There was a party going, then we started pub crawling and ended up at Mooneys on Oxford Street at closing time. I had been to Spain and Mexico and had seen a couple of bullfights. I had on a camel-hair coat that my old man bought me as a sailing present, it was big on me. And when we came out of the pub and the fresh air hit me I suddenly found myself out there in the middle of Oxford Street in the middle of the traffic holding my coat out like a cape and urging on the bonnets of the coming cars. And the drivers played. I was doing veronicas to the left and right. The bonnets of the cars rubbed against me. The crowd shouted Oleh, and applauded. I had about fifteen cars. Then the lights changed, and the cars stopped coming.'

He returned to Canada when the depression came and the money went. He worked for his father in real estate but he didn't like it; he took to the bottle.

'The old man made a lot of money after the war. He became an important civic leader. I guess I was an embarrassment to have around. They were going to send me to Australia, but they decided Vancouver was far enough away.'

He spoke softly, alternating between self-pity and nostalgia, and he began to sweat. I do not know how much he had to drink before I met him, but when we were three-quarters of the way through the bottle his head dropped down to his chest and he fell asleep. I moved him to the bed and took off his shoes and covered him up with a blanket.

I do not know what time it was when I got back to the hotel, but I was quite drunk, and when I came in there was a smell of bananas in the room, there was a half loaf of rye bread on the dressing-table that looked as if the rats had been at it, brown paper, fat-stained where the salami had been wrapped, and a few apples. I wasn't hungry. I dragged the light from the centre of the room over to the bed and tried to read myself to sleep, and fell into a nightmare.

I watched a piece of white jump down from the lookout of the Peace Tower in Ottawa. It looked like a girl's party dress, new, shiny, and very clean. And as it hurtled down—it seemed to take a long time falling—I could see that it had no face, no head, just a human body all covered by this brilliant white. And as it came closer to the ground the white grew larger and more brilliant until I could see nothing but an area of pure white. Then it hit the ground, smashed, and quickly all the white disappeared without leaving a trace. And there was nothing, but a drab empty street.

VIII

FISHING

I WANTED to go out fishing. The only other place that I have been out commercial fishing was with the Cornish boats from St. Ives, Mousehole, Newlyn, in the Atlantic.

Whenever the writing was not going; whenever I became rest-less and wanted to be off somewhere; when I felt cut off and sat for hours by the typewriter facing the window doing nothing just looking out at the roof-tops and the bit of sky in between, watch-ing the cats blot out the light as they went from roof to roof and looked in at the window—I would go down to the granite quay with the moss growing in the cracks and steps hacked out of the side and ask Willie Care or Jack Worth or Norman Wallis or Uncle Oss if I could come along. I would be out a day, a night, sometimes a couple of nights, long-lining, pilchard driving, or crabbing. That was after I had lived there a few years. The first time was different.

It was my second summer in St. Ives. The place was over-run with tourists. It rained nearly every day and they were made to leave their bed-and-breakfast places in the morning after break-fast and they were not allowed to return until evening. They crowded into the two cinemas, in the reading-room of the public library, or else you could see them huddled in their rain coats on the beach or standing by the rails, or in the narrow doorways, looking miserable like a lot of wet birds. Perhaps it was because the writing was not going and I had already realized when that happened there was nothing one could do except something physical. In any case I was tired of just watching those small plain boats, the dark mizzen back of the wheelhouse, the plain blue, black, grey colours, the straight bows, the tension in the wood tightened-up at the stern and the bow; at low tide beached high on the sand, or riding out a gale tied to the bridles that were cemented into the side of the harbour. I had watched the men go out before it was light in two rowboats with a net, in the bay, dragging for sand eels at daybreak, then having the very

L

old men bait them up on the hooks and curl the line with the
baited hooks neatly in the large wicker baskets all that morning
and afternoon. I had watched them go out, come back, unload
. . . the fish auction at the slipway in the morning . . . the black
nets laid out on the grass of the Island to dry . . . the men pacing
up and down by their harbour-shelters when the weather was
too rough to go out. . . .

So I asked Michael behind the bar in The Castle, and he told
me to go and see a fishmonger who took me to a wholesale fish-
yard in the Back Road where I was introduced to Uncle Oss, a
short wiry man in his early fifties. He brought me, that night,
to a cottage in the Back Road where the rest of the family and
their wives were sitting around the Cornish grate in a half-
circle. The father, white hair curling out from his captain's cap,
a handsome gentle face, the black sweater underneath the dark
suit. The mother, over eighty, grey hair parted in the middle
and pulled tight in a bun behind her head, unable to move from
the wicker chair, the mouth set crooked in the face, the head
shaking. And the three brothers with their wives, in their forties
and fifties, all dressed in black, suspicious.

The room was dark and neat. The brass on the grate was
polished. Old family pictures were on the dark walls. The cottage
smelled and looked as if people had lived in it a long time. They
began to ask questions. Where was I from? Why did I want to
go out? What did I do? What did my father do? Did I have
any brothers or sisters? 'If you're sick we don't turn back.' After
two hours of questioning the old man said I could go out in the
boat. Later that night, walking with Uncle Oss along the front,
the moon lighting up the road, the walls of the cottages; everything else, silent. 'We do everything in front of father,' he said,
'to keep him interested.' The old man had the boat built on the
sand by the side of the harbour. They all had shares in it. Later
I understand the suspicion of 'the stranger.' It fitted in with the
Wesleyan chapel, the Salvation Army, the work, the cottage, the
isolation, and the poverty. One had entered into 'a way of
life.'

Here it was a question of ringing up people on the telephone.
The public relations officer of one cannery passed me on to the
public relations officer of the next. I could have gone whaling
if I had the sixty dollars to fly to the northern end of Vancouver
Island; next month I could go with the salmon boats. Finally a
voice at the end of a telephone said I could go out on Friday
with a dragger.

Friday morning it looked like rain. I put on my old trousers, sports shirt and heavy blue woollen sweater and took my jacket, went across to the Zenith Café and had a couple of fried eggs and coffee. Then went out and began to walk towards the fish dock. You couldn't see 'The Lions' nor the trees and the grass on their slopes. And the houses, the street, in the dull light, looked different. By the time I reached the fish dock the mist had begun to lift and there was that pleasant early morning feeling of a hot day.

There were hundreds of small boats packed tight in the wharf's U; long poles standing upright beside the mast, and two other poles in front of the small wheelhouse. Women were gutting fish on wooden boards inside a warehouse and there was the smell of fish being smoked. A truck rolled by and picked up some fish and ice from a boat. I saw a sign 'Independent Co-Op Fisheries', and wooden steps. I went up the steps. The man who greeted me was tall, large, easy-going, a generous face like a St. Bernard. He wore canvas shoes, a green sports shirt. Behind the desk was a short man with a windbreaker and a turtle-neck sweater. The tall man was Jim. He was the skipper of the *Willow Point*. We talked a bit. He wanted to know if I had been out before. I said I had, with the Cornish boats. Then they discussed the price of various fish, decided that mink feed and dogfish livers were fetching the best price. Jim had brought some blankets and sheets for me, and he lowered them down to the boat by a bucket. Then I went with him to his car, a long yellow De Soto with chromium rings on the side like small portholes.

He drove first to a beer-parlour and we had a couple of drinks. There were other fishermen there. One was being ribbed because he fell asleep at the wheel and ran his boat on to the rocks. Then Jim drove down to a liquor store, and he came out with a cardboard case of beer. From there he brought me to a drinking club. The walls right around the room were of glass. They were so arranged that you had the illusion of seeing palm trees inside the glass. We sat on large highly varnished barrels and had a few brandies. Then he drove down to Chinatown and parked the car in a derelict garage and we took a taxi back to the fish dock. The case of beer was put in the bucket and lowered. I followed Jim down the broken iron ladder by the wooden piles of the wharf. I met Harry and Les, the others of the crew. Another fisherman came down the iron ladder, slightly drunk, and we all sat on the side of the boat by the slimy log booms, in the hot sun, drinking bottles of beer, joking. Finally Jim said it was time to go. There was the final gesture of tipping back the beer bottles and throwing them over the side. Then the small boat started to move.

Past the waterfront, the small wharves bitten-in, choked with seine boats, salmon boats, draggers, the sun bleaching, one against the other, masts, lines, wooden poles, so many straight pieces sticking upright. In Coal Harbour an Esso barge refuelled us. On one side North Vancouver: neat houses terraced with trees rising up to the slopes, green hills, behind the hills the mountains with snow and dark trees. And on the other side Vancouver looking majestic from the water, no sign of Hastings Street, Main, the waterfront, only skyscrapers, the MacDonald Hotel, Stanley Park, the Lions Gate bridge. In the gulf the water became a dirty brown, and it was choppy.

I spent most of the time in the wheelhouse. It was now Jim's shift. The three of them had eight-hour shifts at the wheel. But they were all feeling rough. Harry had a hangover. He had been off drink for six months, then he went back onto it the night before. Les was also drunk the day before. So drunk that he said his wife would not take him to a wedding that they were invited to. Jim, although he did not show it, said he was also feeling a party they had the night before where six bottles of rye were consumed in the evening. For most of that first day I was the only one who made ham and baloney sandwiches and ate, the others drank beer until all the bottles were gone. Then we took swigs from the rye bottle that Jim kept in the wheelhouse underneath the charts. I became sleepy and went down to the cabin, by the engine, and went to sleep in the top bunk.

When I woke up the air was stale, the engine going loud. I climbed the wooden ladder to the deck, it was late afternoon, the sun still bright, the sea like a mirror. We were surrounded by islands. Dozens of them. All shapes and sizes. They were right beside us, thick with fir trees forming a hunched back. The water was flat, dark blue and shiny and the trees were very sharp in the water. We slipped quietly through. Jim said, 'Over there is the United States.' It was just another group of islands. I thought of Hart Crane's image, 'adagios of Islands'; it hadn't made sense until now. They were all around us and they went backwards at different speeds, the close ones slightly blurred. Cormorants flew by low and black. Harry called me into the wheelhouse. 'Listen. This is London.' I listened to the static, to the words and the applause coming over in waves. Bulganin and Kruschev were leaving London after their visit. Beside us the flat shiny water, the slow moving boat, and fir trees, as island after island went slowly backward . . . Europe never seemed further away.

The sun was down when we passed Victoria and into the Straits of Juan de Fuca. A swell started, also a wind, and the boat began to shudder as she hit the rough water. Every time she bucked Jim talked to the boat. 'Now, Sarah, you old sow. C'mon, girl.' We talked about Cornwall. His first wife, who had died four years ago, came from Penzance. We talked about fishing, about life, taking swigs from the bottle.

I became hungry again and went to the kitchen. There were several pounds of ham, baloney, cake, tins of various things, fruit, steaks, chops, all neatly packed, the perishables kept on ice. There was an oil stove and coffee was always brewing.

We passed Cape Flattery just before midnight and I went back to the bunk. But I couldn't fall asleep. I was too cold. Then Jim came down and went into his sleeping-bag. They all had sleeping-bags. There were a lot of magazines: *Police Gazette*, *Man*, *Picture Post*, a magazine called *Swank* with a lurid description of Maxwell Bodenheimer's 'last days' and a shortened version of James Cain's *Serenade* that I had read before.

Next morning I slept-in, Jim woke me up at eight. I felt rotten. Whether it was the beer or the whisky or the smell of the diesel engine going just in front of the bunk. The hatch was closed. The air stale. I had just time to get dressed and come up for air before I felt sick. But nothing came up. I thought the fresh air would help; but it didn't. I had a thick throat, it was difficult to swallow the hot coffee. The sun was shining, the sea very blue, very empty, silent, and the slow continual heave. I tried an orange but that soon came up. No sooner would I settle down for half an hour than I would have to go to the rail.

They started to drag. They lowered the stabilizers out from the sides and put out the net with its mesh that made it look like a hula skirt, then the lines, and the otter doors apart, keeping the front of the net open in the water as the boat moved slowly along, the net dragging on the bottom.

When it was pulled up the mesh was jammed with fish. Harry swung it over the boat. Les divided the net into portions by using a steel chain as a belt and releasing a portion at a time so that the fish could be handled on the deck. Then they began to sort the fish. They threw back small fish, shark, skate, halibut (which they were not allowed to catch by dragging), ray, and bass. Ling, cod and dogfish they kept. Also grey cod and sole. Jim used the echo meter to find out exactly where he was, to see if there was any feed there, and to tell him about the bottom. If feed was there, there would be fish.

Around us were sea birds. The largest were the goony birds, coffee brown, large as geese, and awkward. Their wings folded twice as they came into land beside the boat (the seagull only once) the first portion folded back, the second ahead, and the third back. In flight the wing was straight but they still looked ungainly. They hung around the boat eating the offal that Les threw over the side as he gutted the fish. He threw the livers of the dogfish into a large tin can and threw the rest of the dogfish over the side. There were gulls. There were thousands of small birds; when they rose in the distance, it looked like rain. Jim called them sea-swallows. Some of the goony birds were pecking away at the small birds, pecking at their eyes, as they floated on the water. After the fish were packed in one of the holds with crushed ice, the second drag began.

But after four drags, Jim decided there wasn't much point going on that day. The fish had got less and less. It was getting late. The first drag was near noon, and now it was after five. He decided to spend the night at Ucluelet. I told him that I would return from Ucluelet, as I wanted to go back to Vancouver and head into the Cariboo. I had planned to go out for a couple of days, meet another boat which was returning, and transfer from the *Willow Point* to the boat. As I didn't feel too good, he agreed. I steered towards Ucluelet. And having something to do I immediately felt better. I kept the bow against a high wooded hill that rose out of the water, and started to sing. As we got nearer to the hill I could see a small inlet. But distances on the water are deceptive. What looked like half-an-hour's ride took us over two, to get to the entrance. Then Jim took the wheel, there were sunken rocks and reefs. And we left the sea and came into the calm of a fjord.

The land was very near on both sides. Everything again was silent and still. Jim pointed out, on the far shore, a cluster of huts as being an Indian reservation. They were wooden huts, unpainted, built on poles like stilts. We went further in. Dusk Not a ripple on the water. Salmon boats huddled by small wharves. We tied up beside a wooden wharf and climbed up a long slimy ladder.

Les and Harry were too tired, only Jim and myself went into Ucluelet. A wooden sidewalk, the road unpaved, it was a short street with a restaurant and a hotel. Inside the beer-parlour, the place was crowded and noisy. Some Indians, some young boys, a few old men. There was a lumber camp not far away and this explained Saturday night. We had a couple of draught beers that tasted awful, the place smelled of lavatories and spilled beer. Then we went outside in the dark to find out if there was an airplane leaving the next day. Dogs were barking, no lights, a few houses in the clusters of trees. We found one that Jim knew was where the women looked after the plane passengers. But she was out. We knocked on another. A dog barked. A light went on. No one could help until tomorrow.

We returned to the wharf, to the boat, down the long ladder with the slime and the broken rungs. Large logs were by the ladder, floating in the water. Jim told me to walk sideways so I would not slip.

In the morning we were up while it was still dark. Les made breakfast and we drank several cups of coffee and as a last gesture, at daybreak, we stood together and urinated over the side. The water was dirty, two fish came up to the surface. They looked like perch.

I climbed back to the jetty, a fine frost on the wood, and watched the boat go away. It was a clear cold morning, not a wind. Everything seemed still as a lake. On the far shore the plain stilt wooden houses, the thick trees, the small groups of salmon boats by a jetty, and behind were the hills thick with trees.

Everything was still except for some blackbirds and the sun coming out. Two cats sunned themselves in a window box. I could hear the gulls. A rooster crowed. I walked along the gravel road, by the hotel, the restaurant—everything was closed. The loudest sounds were my steps on the gravel.

It was one of those times you don't forget, when everything for a while seems right. The silence, the freshness of the air, and everyone else asleep. I walked along a road that had recently been cut through the bush. Huge roots with the stumps turned on their sides lay above the ground, while a few yards from the roots the green and the very straight fir and cedar stood, and the sunlight came in patches on the road. Some of the thick roots were cut many years back, for they were the colour of ashes. Between the trees I could see smoke rising thin and straight.

The place was pock-marked with clearings in the forest. I took a trail. It was wooden, three planks wide. Skunk cabbages on both sides, then bush and trees. Skunk cabbage: two green lettuce leaves and a yellow leaf with a hard candle in the middle.

I could hear the sea breaking on some rocks as I passed more tree roots, upturned stumps, and skunk cabbage bogs. The ground was rarely level, a few houses in another clearing, the dogs behind the houses sunning themselves, an old car lay rusting on its side.

I walked back to the jetty. There was no one about. I sat down on a step. A loon's clear sound came from somewhere in the distance. Cormorants were sitting on rocks a few yards from the shore, their hanging wings stretched out. Then I could hear the static of a radio-telephone from one of the boats further down the jetty. 'What did you get off the Cape? Nothing. I'm going for the cabbage patch. I haven't had any luck this morning. I've got three little ones but there's nothing much doing. I've a few but they're so goddam small it's hardly worth it. Nice-looking water down here but that's about all you can say about it.' I scrambled down the slope to the boat. There was a short old man in his undershirt, a shiny bald head. He was in the cabin boiling a salmon in a pressure cooker. He showed me several small glass jars with the light pink-colour slices of fish. The boat was neat, spotless. He was a Finn and he could hardly talk English. He said he worked by himself. He liked it that way. He had caught a couple of little salmon, it was still too early, so he decided to can them. He had painted the boat, he was going across to the opposite shore so the sun could get at it.

The place didn't wake up quickly. Around nine a few more dogs were on the dirt road. I went into the hotel; there was no one about. I went up the stairs to a washroom and washed my face in cold water and felt fresher. Then I returned to the jetty and waited for the plane.

It was a small seaplane and I was lucky, one Air Force passenger did not show up. I sat in front with the pilot, he was a schoolboy, eighteen; he packed seven in behind, three sat on their baggage by the tail. He flew at a thousand feet. The hills on either side slanted higher than we were. He followed the valley over the islands and the canal system to Alberni. I could see the slopes bare of trees, hacked down, to look like a field after it has been harvested and the stalks not cleared away. All along the water there were log booms.

At Alberni I got on a bus to Nanaimo. The woman beside me was also in the puddle-jumper from Uclulet. She was excited. She kept on saying how pleased she was to get away, as if she didn't believe it. This was her annual holiday to Vancouver then to San Francisco.

The bus kept climbing, then going down through thick forest. The woman kept on saying: 'These are nothing . . . wait until you see the big ones . . .' There were firs and some old beeches with their roots above the ground and in a few places young birches. The sunlight came through the leaves in patches on to the undergrowth and the grass. The trees were big and the foliage was thick, but it was not gloomy. And we drove mostly out of the sun in the shade of these grey, rust trees.

The woman said she probably made a mistake, the big ones were up island. She said Ucluelet was all right for a man, good fishing, and he had his work. But for a woman, nothing to do. 'Everybody knows you. We all belong to the same church clubs.' She would be gone, she said, for three weeks. She looked happy.

From Nanaimo the boat back to Vancouver. And it was good to be back, to walk along Hastings Street, to go up the old elevator to the storeroom in between the second and third floors and pick out in the dark one's bag and typewriter, then back to the familiar room. I shaved, changed, went out and cashed the five-dollar cheque that Jim gave me with a Chinese grocer. Had a couple of hamburgers in a cheap café, walked by a playing-field and watched a baseball game between a Japanese-Canadian team and an industrial team from Vancouver. It was the first game of the season and there was a crowd standing around the playing field, mainly old Chinese and Japanese, unshaven, old clothes; it was free. Later two men came around with tin cans shaking the coins inside and everyone began to walk away, and returned as soon as the men with the tin cans had passed. The Japanese were easily the better team; their pitcher had more control, and they could hit.

I left the sand-lot and walked back towards Hastings. A large Salvation Army band was playing in the middle of the street and men were walking behind it. Then they stopped, turned inwards facing each other, and in twos began to walk through the path made by the others. There were women dressed as cheer leaders in white uniforms, bright purple capes and yellow caps; some of the men carried swords which they pulled out and made a guard of honour, while the civilian-clothed ones walked underneath the arched swords and into the Salvation Army Temple. Then the men with the swords and the women with the capes followed in twos into the Temple.

I thought of the Sundays in St. Ives: the girl from the news-papers' with her bonnet tied squarely on her head; the boy in the fruit store; the red-faced fat man who delivered bread and who carried the Salvation Army standard in a leather holder that was tied to a belt around his waist . . . standing by the slipway every Sunday at four, or coming around through the Back streets, stopping in the square by the garbage cans, singing a hymn, reading out a bit, then the knocking on the doors with the tin cans. And when it was cold in winter the jazzy rhythm that started every service: 'I'm happy in the service of the Lord. Boom. Boom. Boom . . .' The feet stamping, the arms flapping and crossing and slapping the sides.

SCHOOLDAYS

I was tired of the local literary figures and tried to get hold of Jim, but he was not at home. So I returned to the hotel and there was a message from Jim saying that he would ring back in half an hour. I waited downstairs. The hotel had its own beer-parlour (like all the cheap hotels in down-town cities) attached to the lobby of the hotel. I sat in the lobby, a bare empty room facing the street. A few wooden chairs against the side wall. Old men sat in the chairs. There was the 'regular'. He looked like a rough W. C. Fields with a bulbous red nose, blown up by some disease, smoking a pipe. He sat there, like myself, by the brass pots filled with spit, broken cigarette butts, the floating tobacco making the liquid the colour of urine, and watched those who came in, and those outside. There was the desk and the elevator and the public telephone booth. I waited for Jim to ring. Went into the beerparlour. It was crowded and noisy. A man came along and said he was rolled of eighty bucks, could I buy him a couple of beers? I said no, but gave him a cigarette. He went around the room with no luck. I returned to the lobby. I picked up a local paper. A Sir had a column, and another Sir looked after the bookpage. He wrote as if it was still the officers' mess in England; the other the country squire. The Sir in the bookpage said of a girl, 'She was a "tart", I can think of no other word.' Two men stood on the sidewalk by the door holding hands, they were singing, they were drunk, they kissed, and walked down the slope of the street holding hands. Young boys stood in groups watching the girls walk by. Some of the girls went upstairs with men. But still no call from Jim. Neon signs: Coin City, Games, Movies, Billiards, A Gym, A Fortune-teller, 'Smilin' Budha', and The White Lunch Cafeteria, a cup lit up with moving serving figures, a butler, a waitress, all in black, going around the cup like an old church clock. It was now after nine. The Scotchman behind the

desk arrived to take over from the dapper Chinese owner. The
Scot told me: did I get a message to call up C.N.R. telegrams?
I rang up. They said that there was a wire for fifty dollars from
my Canadian publisher. I had, in desperation, wired a request
for money to be sent, but that was a couple of days ago. I had
less than two dollars in my pocket. On the strength of the
advance, I went around the corner to Pender Street, passed the
store where I bought my salami and bananas and sardines and
bread; Chinese ideograms on the windows, Chinese names in
English. A record playing in a store where very crudely drawn
postcards were on display; health magazines with breasty
women on the covers, practical jokes, and the soft high whine of
a Chinese song coming from a top window above a fruit store.
Old men walking in drab-coloured suits, slippers, crumpled
collar buttoned at the neck, no tie. There was one bare room
with a stove in the centre, an oil drum with a pipe going out
from it and then at right angles straight across the ceiling. Men
sat around the table, all reading Chinese newspapers, some
played cards. Past the fruit stores with fruit in neat pyramids,
Chinese labels and English ones. An amusement arcade. I went
into the restaurant, long, booths on both sides, most of those
eating were Chinese. I had a good meal, the plates were chipped
and cracked; the food was delicious. I went the whole hog, had
sweet and sour spare ribs, noodles, chicken with almonds, egg
rolls. I returned to the hotel, but no phone call. I tried his home,
but still no reply. So I returned to the arcade and was soon
wrapped up in the noise of guns firing at climbing monkeys, at
the nude pictures, what the butler saw, the flick-flick-flick over
like a strip-tease, each picture removing an article of clothing,
and the pin-ball machines. I played them all. I enjoy the colours,
the balls moving, things lighting up, the sput-sput-sput noises.
Once you set a ball going there is something inevitable about it.

When I came back it was nearly midnight. I bought a piece
of watermelon from the store at the corner, and returned to my
room. I had just about finished eating the watermelon when I
heard young girls' voices singing in the passageway.

> Schooldays. Schooldays.
> All those golden rule days;
> Writing and reading and arithmetic
> All to the tune of a hickory stick.

I looked out. There were four women in bare feet and loose
dresses, some in kimonos, holding hands going around a tall

gangling young boy who was in the centre. He was drunk and had a fixed grin all the time. He wore jeans and a U.B.C. sweater. They held hands and continued walking around him:

> She was my girl in calico,
> I was her handsome bashful beau . . .

They sang in small, thin, children's voices. It seemed strange at first to see and hear these large women singing in such small children's voices, and the university student lifting his legs as if the floor was moving, leaning backwards, grinning. Then one of the women, a stocky Chinese, left the others and took out a large flabby breast from her gown, cupped it, and with a minimum of movement she drew the boy's head down while with the other hand she stuck her nipple deep into his mouth. His knees immediately bent and he went down to her height. And in this way she led him slowly into her room. His arms dangling loosely by his side. She looked as if she was entrusted with something very fragile as she closed the door.

*

I only got to know one girl in the hotel. Although got to know is an exaggeration. I never saw her sober. I would meet her in the Chinese fruit and vegetable and grocery store on the corner late at night, standing there in a stupor as if she was drugged, the other customers looking at her, she not caring. Or else coming back with someone in the elevator, a shapeless sullen body. There was something untidy about her, a carelessness that I remembered from the start. We used to greet each other 'Hi.' 'Hi.' 'How's life?' One night it was misty outside, the room was too sticky to sleep, and I was writing down some of the things that happened during the last few days, when she came and knocked on the door holding a bottle of rye and a thick glass. Would I mind if she came in and we had a drink together? I took my thick glass from the cracked sink and we sat on the bed and she poured generously. Neither of us said very much. She looked unhappy. It was the first time I had seen her for more than just in passing. She had a pretty face until she opened her mouth. Her teeth were bad. I tried to make conversation. She only grunted back. 'Hot night. Yeh. Room's stuffy. It's worse in August.' Then she closed her eyes and lowered her head; I thought she was going to sleep. But she began to weep. What could one do? Sit here, glass in hand, and watch. The red-green-red-green light kept flashing on the window-blind. She did not cry for very long. She opened her eyes. They looked helpless, like the eyes of a person who always wears glasses and suddenly takes them off. 'The best part of the day,' she said blurring her words, 'is about ten seconds in the morning when I begin to wake . . . when I don't know who I am, where I am, or what it's about. And then, I wake up. And I think how nice it would be just to wake up in the morning and not feel that here's another day that has to be got through.'

VICTORIA

The farthest west my air-pass allowed me to fly was to Victoria. And no sooner did the airplane leave Vancouver than we were over the mouth of the muddy Fraser river, into the gulf, over those islands that I had passed through a week ago; then Victoria, very green, at their end. In less time than it took the bus to take us out to the airport we had crossed the gulf.

It was Cheltenham with sea air. And not the Cheltenham that I knew but the Cheltenham of music-hall jokes: a comfortable old people's home; women on bicycles; English tweed and woollens; quiet, retired, residential. But that was a first impression. Later one realized how much it belonged to the Coast. The heat, the slowness, the thick foliage, the bungalows with the nice drives, blossoms on the trees and blossoms on the sidewalk and roads, the large gardens, the blue mountains with snow on top across the water.

It was provincial middle-class English in exile. But they had none of the ruthlessness of those I met in Montreal and Ottawa after the war who had come over because Labour had come in. They were continually running down England, the Socialists, the 'bad conditions' they left behind, though they kept in touch with 'home', with their friends who had gone to Kenya, Rhodesia, and regularly received *Punch*, *The Times* Calendar, the *Illustrated London News*, the *Tatler*. They took jobs as 'companions' with the wealthy families in Westmount, Outremont, and Rockcliffe. They wrote letters, they answered the telephone, they cooked, they read to the grandmother, they went on errands. Then they returned to England to the house falling in decay in one of the horseshoe Gardens off the Gloucester Road and South Kensington; to Sussex, Surrey, Bucks. 'London has become full of foreigners.' In Canada they charmingly accepted hospitality, but as soon as they were back in England amongst their own kind they ran down Canada, the Canadians, and entertained their friends by telling jokes in a Canadian accent.

Victoria had none of that ruthlessness that I have found so characteristic of the English middle-class in exile. It was placid; it was easy. It had not changed much since Emily Carr's time. 'Victoria was like a lying-down cow, chewing. She had made one enormous effort of upheaval. She had hoisted herself from a Hudson's Bay Fort into a little town and there she paused, chewing the cud of imported fodder, afraid to crop the pastures of the new world for fear she might lose the good flavour of the old to which she was so deeply loyal. Her jaws went on rolling on and on, long after there was nothing left to chew.'

I stayed in a hotel that was a converted private house, very quiet, very clean. Above my bed was an illuminated scroll of Kipling's 'If.' I walked about the streets. How warm it was. Men and women in light summer dresses and suits. The streets were clean, not very much traffic; it looked wealthy.

For something to do I went to a public school on the outskirts. There was the cricket pitch, the wide grass lawns, the grey stone building with ivy and Virginia creeper, the prefects, the cadet corps. The headmaster was from Oxford, very English, precise, a mathematician. All the masters were from England. I sat in on a scripture class given by a minister who talked about Isaiah, on passive resistance. But he might as well have been alone. The boys sat in uncomfortable chairs and worn desks and openly read comic books, talked to each other. He had no control of the class. He continued talking in a precise sermon-tone while all the time there was a continual movement as one boy left the room and another one came in. The headmaster drove me back to town in his convertible Cadillac. He said proudly that he had spent a thousand dollars on getting a midwife to come out from England to deliver his second child.

I went and had some tea in the Empress Hotel. It was difficult to believe that one wasn't back in a hotel in Bideford or another one I remember in Harrogate. The Edwardian high-backed sofas, settees, tall chairs; the elderly ladies with kind faces, the thick carpets, the pillars, the piano and the cello playing in one corner of the room. Oil paintings of four generations of the Royal Family on the walls, above the fireplaces, flowers on the tables. Old men with canes. The small lights from the candelabra. Candlesticks over the fireplace. Ferns in vases. Wealth and the retired and good manners talking quietly, while the cello and the piano continued to make a noise in the corner.

Signs in the street: 'Old British Fish and Chips. Take some

home.' 'English Crumpets Served Here.' 'English Sweet Shop.'
At a fifteen-cents store: 'We will cash your Family Allowance
Cheque. Ask any salesgirl.' A card in the window:

LADY WRESTLERS

Main Event

ORGN ZEPEDAR   VS.   MILLIE STAFFORD
Mexican Champion   Minneapolis, Minnesota

Or else it was phoney for commercial reasons.

A warm and cheery welcome awaits you at
"OLDE ENGLAND INN"
by your Host and Hostess
Squadron Leader Lane (ex-R.A.F.) and Mrs. Lane
Late of Yorkshire, England.

TUDOR ENGLAND IN CANADA
Half-timbered, gabled, reminiscent of Tudor England, set in
the midst of three acres of lovely grounds, with vistas of Sea
and Mountains all combine to ensure perfect relaxation.

EXACT REPLICA OF WILLIAM SHAKESPEARE'S BIRTHPLACE
This quaint residence of your host and Hostess enhances the
charm of the lovely surroundings of Olde England Inn. You
are invited to photograph this unique place.

Real English Tea
Real English Trifle a Speciality
Also Roast Beef and Yorkshire Pudding
and Toasted English Crumpets

A stay in "Olde England Inn"
has all the charm of a visit to
England itself.

In Thunderbird Park they had a couple of Indians doing
imitation totem poles, copying them from the originals that were
in decay in the sheds. Two were working on 'The Tallest Totem
Pole In The World' and on Yates Street there was a sign in a
photographer's shop offering prizes for those who sent in the
best picture of 'The Tallest Totem Pole In The World'. The two
Indians had done imitation totem poles all over the park, they
were standing there brightly painted. I saw the original poles
lying on the floor in the shed. The wood was cracked, all the dye

had come off, they were worn and bleached by the elements. But they had a vitality about them, the large lidless eyes, that none of the imitation poles for all their gaudiness could simulate.

At night the Parliament Buildings were lit up, a harness of lights, a cake decoration, with a fountain in front changing colours. One could be in the Old Steine in Brighton with some of the lights of the Palace Pier. Except here there were neon-lit pictures of the Queen over a garage, and more pictures in the restaurants, in the stores, in the hotels. In the other cities the Queen had to compete with Hollywood starlets. There was no reverence, she was just another postcard. Here she was 'Number One'.

INDIAN RESERVATION

I had a letter of introduction from the Indian superintendent in Vancouver to Councillor Louis of the North Vancouver Mission. The superintendent told me not to get there before noon. 'The place is dead in the morning; they're all asleep.' I took the ferry across to the North Shore. On the slopes of the mountain was a residential suburb: new wooden houses with lots of green between them, and the straight streets, neat, clean, going up like steps. The light green changed to dark green, to the black trees, to the large patches of snow on the peaks.

I found the reservation not far from the pier. A wooden gate going across a narrow dirt road with thick overgrown grass on both sides. The road was uneven, the earth hard. The main highway ran around the far side of the reservation. The houses, set back from the road in the overgrown grass, were all made of wood, unpainted, spaced apart, the windows stuffed with black. There was no one outside. It looked like a ghost-town. I went up to the first house and knocked.

The man who opened the door was short, bow-legged, in his fifties. He wore a heavy Indian woollen sweater and when he smiled or talked he showed badly fitting false teeth.

It was Councillor Louis. I showed him my letter. He invited me inside the house and introduced me to an elderly man and woman sitting quietly in worn-out leather chairs; they were visitors from the reserve at Point Grey. He introduced me to his wife. She was an untidy woman, short and fat, wearing a brown print dress. A flat nose, prominent cheekbones, black hair parted carelessly in the middle. She waddled across the room and sat down again and continued knitting a heavy woollen sweater like the one Councillor Louis was wearing. The room was seedy, squalid, and run down. The few pieces of furniture looked as if they had never been new. Rags and clothes were thrown haphazardly about. The wallpaper was peeling, the bottom half of the walls were painted a chocolate brown and the paint was chipped. Bits of crockery, a small phonograph with a large horn, old brown Brunswick records, mixed with the black, were in a sliding heap on the floor, a dog lay stretched out near the woman. She had taken her feet out of her slippers; her feet were very small. On the walls were a few photographs of Indian hockey and baseball teams. It seemed as if everything one possessed in the house was exposed, nothing was hidden away in drawers or cupboards.

We walked outside. The place was silent. A tall Catholic church by the dirt road. No sign of life from any of the houses. Occasionally I could hear the sound of a car as it went by on the main highway. We walked along the dirt road, some of the houses were falling in decay. The wood was black. They seemed to be sinking into the high green grass around them. Beside another house a few chickens in a coop, a dog, a solitary apple tree.

A tall figure came walking slowly towards us leaning on a stick. 'Here comes Chief Andy Paul,' Councillor Louis said. The figure looked like a character out of Damon Runyon, a caricature of a bookie. He had a battered homburg hat, set rakishly on the head, a blue winter coat with the collar turned up, cream gloves, and a stick. The coat collar hugged the neck as if he was trying to hide that he was wearing a shirt without a tie and that he had not shaved for several days. Chief Andy Paul suggested that we go over to his house. It wasn't very far, we walked slowly, the chief had difficulty with his breathing.

It was a much neater house than Councillor Louis's (Chief Andy Paul was a bachelor). But it was bare. All it had was an oil stove in the middle of the room, two chairs, and a desk by the wall with a telephone. On the wall he had framed various pieces of paper: the articles of association, saying that he was the editor and the owner of an Indian newspaper in English. Another piece of paper said he was invited to the Coronation of Elizabeth II; and others said that he attended various Indian conventions in Canada and the United States. He spoke with difficulty. No sooner did we get in than he sprawled in a chair and desperately sucked in air. He said he had asthma. The Chief said he wanted to be a lawyer but he did not go to university.

M

'You should hear him argue,' Councillor Louis said with pride.

They both insisted that the Indians had money of their own. When they sold land, it was land that belonged to them. There was no charity. But they had to have it all done through the Government. They were unable to make any decisions, any transactions, without government approval. I asked a few questions. Why does an Indian stay on a reservation? He doesn't have to pay income tax. He gets a yearly grant of food and money. He has security, though he does not have a vote.

Then Councillor Louis asked if I would like to meet Chief Moses, the Chief of the Mission. I said I would. He went to the telephone and spoke first in English. 'Hello Chief.' The rest were guttural sounds of Indian dialect. Yes, the Chief would see me. I said goodbye to Chief Andy Paul. He had taken off his homburg, but he lay stretched out in his chair, one leg over the side, his wintercoat on, trying desperately to breathe.

Outside we passed an old man working on a long canoe. It was the length of a full-grown tree. The old man shaping it had hollowed it out of a cedar log. 'He's the last one here who knows how to do this,' said Councillor Louis. Young boys in sweatshirts and shorts were running alongside the highway. 'They're getting into shape for the canoe race against another Mission. I think we'll win. That's one of mine running.' He pointed to a small brown boy in white shorts and a canary yellow sweatshirt, jogging with the others around the highway's edge.

We walked to a plain undecorated wooden house. A small grass lawn in front; two dogs were copulating on it. Councillor Louis knocked on the door. A girl opened it. 'Is the Chief in?' We went into a dark bare room and I was introduced to Chief Moses, a solid fine-looking man. He had great dignity. He said he was a longshoreman and worked at the docks. He spoke in a low husky voice. But he did not talk much. He sat on the brown settee—the well-defined handsome features, the prominent cheekbones, short white hair, body erect—as if his bearing alone was enough, and that there was no need for much talk.

Though the room had more possessions than the other houses —an old radio, an old piano—it still looked empty and poor. The walls were painted that dull chocolate brown. Washing hung in the kitchen on a line from the ceiling. There wasn't much light. He called to his wife and she came in from the kitchen. A shapeless fat body in a brown print dress. She could not speak a word of English. We shook hands and she returned to the kitchen.

The Chief said he thought it was best for the Indian to remain on the reservation where he belonged. Chiefs were hereditary, and for a while they both talked about their ancestors. Then Councillor Louis brought out a folded piece of paper from his jeans. Someone on the reserve was applying for assistance. They spoke in English for my benefit. How long was it since she had it last time? The paper needed the Chief's signature. 'It is our money,' he said as he signed it. 'We get it from the sale of our land, and it is kept for us, but we cannot touch it. It has to pass through the Department of Indian Affairs.' A young child with white skin, black hair, kept running in and out from the kitchen. Chief Moses finally caught the child and jogged it on his knee. He laughed, he said he had many grandchildren. We got on to sport. He was much more interested in that than anything else. He proudly showed me photographs of himself, as a young man, with various lacrosse teams of the district. They were propped on the piano and on the walls.

From the Chief's house Councillor Louis brought me to see Annie. She had a kerchief over her head, a plaid shawl around her shoulders, a full skirt down to the ankles. She was the oldest person on the reservation. A large black stove was burning wood, several large kettles were on the stove. Her face was long, brown, and creased with wrinkles. She would throw back her head, open a toothless mouth, and laugh at herself. 'Oh, I'm old; I die plitty soon. I got good girl Mary she look aftly me.' Mary was a girl who would not marry, she was in her fifties, and was ironing when we came in. One of the kettles began to boil; the steam rose quickly to the ceiling. The room was bare, spotless, and poor. There were no doors to the few other rooms. They faced this main room like the few spokes of a wheel. In one room was a black iron bed, a small crucifix on the wall, beads on a wooden dressing-table, and the picture of the Pope underneath the crucifix.

I left Councillor Louis with an undertaker who had come over from Vancouver to arrange a funeral for the next day. An old woman had died away from the Mission. She had no money. They were going to bury her here where she once had lived.

I felt depressed. This was the first time I had been on a reservation. Later I went to others; in the Interior and on Vancouver Island. Amongst trees, hills, bracken, water, a reservation with its gloom, its silence, its poverty, somehow belonged closer to the landscape. Here, at the foot of a slope with the neat residential streets above it and the backdrop of the mountains, while

across was Vancouver, the skyline of skyscrapers and hotels—
you were in some other country.

I can understand Fenimore Cooper romanticizing the Indians.
They were the most relaxed people I have met. What did hurry,
rush, mean to an Indian? The Catholic priest in Williams Lake
said it was because they had no sense of original sin. 'They don't
realize that one has to work by the sweat of one's brow. That it
is only by work that one gets ahead. The Indian does not really
care whether he gets ahead or not.'

And the small overgrown cemetery fenced off from the reservation by wood and wire. I saw the black iron crosses stuck in
the earth with the fleur-de-lis in fretwork. Some had tin plates in
the middle of the cross. All they had was a name and 1900 after
it. To record the century of one's death was enough. Most of
the plates were missing. That didn't seem to matter either. The
place was overgrown with grass, brambles, and weeds. A fresh
grave was there, the earth neatly heaped above the ground. But
it wouldn't be long before it was swamped by the grass, the
brambles, the nettles.

Of course the white man did not like something he could not
understand, so he tried to destroy it. There were the 'do-gooders',
especially in Victoria, the rich women who had nothing to do,
frustrated, lonely, ambitious; they found the Indians 'a good
cause'. There were the business men, the Chambers of Commerce, the Jaycees; Indians were a tourist attraction. 'Come and
photograph the Largest Totem Pole In The World.' The trinkets
sold as souvenirs in the tobacconist and arts and craft stores
right across the country. There were the 'culture departments';
the advertising agencies using Indian and Eskimo 'poems' for
the right client. In the Vancouver Art Gallery they had a large
display of *Potlach* (the feasts the Indians once gave in order to
show off one's wealth and rank). A great fuss was made over this.
While their descendants were herded into a grass ghetto . . . the
chiefs going through the gestures of a dumb-show.

I spent all afternoon and early evening in the Mission.
The silence. The gloom. The inertia that one was beginning to
understand; how one behaves when one has lost hope.

THE COURT ROOM

Next morning I went to the courthouse as I wanted to hear
the case between the policeman and the man who stayed across
from my room and had his wallet stolen. He had told me to

come to the courtroom as he might need me for a witness.
The police building was on Main Street about two minutes
walk from my hotel. Old Chinese and Japanese and Indians
and whites were hanging around the streets, leaning against
buildings. The morning was hot. Shirts, sleeves rolled up, except
the old Chinese who went around with their shirts buttoned up
at the neck. Bums and panhandlers asked for handouts. The
pawnbrokers, the overcrowded newsagent with the sexy tabloids,
the wooden shacks, cheap cafés and cheap hotels. But the police
building was new, and the police court brand new.

The courtroom was about the size of a university lecture room.
Several benches sloped down to the front of the room. Old age,
the unemployed, the downandouts sat on the benches. As I came
in a policeman gave me a mimeographed sheet with all the cases
that were going to be tried. I could see no sign of the man who
had his wallet stolen.

Panelled wood painted light green on the walls, air-conditioned
ceiling with fluorescent lights. A clock on the wall by the
prisoner's dock. The judge entered in a dark business suit, a
spare elderly man, and sat behind a desk in a leather chair with
a tall straight wooden back, and underneath a small coloured
photograph of the Queen. Policemen were standing at the back
of the room.

It was entertainment. Two men were charged with stealing
swing-taps in a house. A man was caught sleeping on the C.P.R.
railway tracks. All the rest were charges of being drunk. Their
names were called out. A door in the front wall opened, and they
entered the room hesitantly, blinking in the strong light, nervous,
hair uncombed, unshaven, their clothes looked as if they had
slept in them. Those who tried them sat in front of the benches,
well-dressed, they talked and joked amongst themselves, they
watched the men come in, stay a few minutes, then return the
way they came. A young boy stood up and read the charge in a
monotonous voice as if he was mechanically describing a travel-
logue. The judge gave justice. So much money or so many days
in jail. But there was no choice. Only in one case: a short aggressive man with a sallow face who went to the dock from the spectators' benches was fined fifty dollars or two weeks in jail. He
was so pleased when he heard this that he took out a thick roll
of dollar bills and wanted to pay the judge, but he was told to
go to another room for that. But for the others it was the same
routine. 'Can you raise twenty-five dollars?' The man in the
dock remains silent. 'Seven days.' One man asked if he could use

the phone. 'If you think that will help,' the judge said in-differently.

The next one was a middle-aged man with a small round face and wearing a blue sports shirt, a creased chocolate-brown suit. He was caught sleeping on the railway track by the docks. 'What do you plead?' 'Not guilty. I had my ticket for the boat and I still had two hours to kill so I lay down and had a rest.' Then a tall, well-groomed man, in a grey summer suit came up from the front bench. He was a manager from the C.P.R. and gave his evidence. 'The accused was found sleeping with a newspaper over his head, with his shoes off, and I think he was drunk. He certainly smelled it.' The judge, after a lecture, decided to let him off this time if he took the next boat away from Vancouver. The man agreed to do so. Then a lawyer stood up and suggested, 'Perhaps we should keep him in jail until twenty minutes before the boat sails so we make sure he gets on it this time.' The judge agreed. The schoolboy voice read on haltingly. A policeman gave evidence. A Sihk in a light blue turban and grey scraggly beard had to have an interpreter. A detective gave evidence. It was all rehearsed. You could see the manner they were taught to give it with hands behind the back, with 'your worshipping' continually. The judge was a professional. The policeman was a professional. Only the victim, if he was poor, was the amateur.

IX

THE CARIBOO

IT WAS George Woodcock and his wife Inge who told me about the Cariboo. I was staying the night with them, on the North Shore, in their flat on the slope of the mountain, having a delicious meal of Polish meat balls that Inge had cooked, and they told me of a journey they made a few years ago through cowtowns, reservations, across a semi-desert. I decided to go as soon as I could.

On Saturday morning I checked out of my room, left my belongings in the storage hole and walked along Hastings towards the bus station. It was a hot sticky morning. Fog had come in from the sea. It looked like rain. You could not see the mountains or the trees. I had slept in and went without breakfast. I knew there was only one bus and that went at seven. But when I came to the bus station a few minutes before seven there was the bus marked 'Prince George', the door was closed and three men were waiting by the door on the cement platform. Two were in jeans, T-shirts and leather windbreakers, and with army knapsacks. The other wore new hunting clothes and carried fishing gear.

I had bought a return ticket to Clinton (I was left with ten dollars and some change) that would get me far enough north. From there I would hitch-hike further north, then hitch-hike back to Clinton where I would get the bus to Vancouver.

The two men in jeans asked me if I could buy them a cup of coffee as they hadn't had any breakfast and they were broke. They had not shaved for several days and they looked as if they did not have much sleep either. We had coffee standing by the soda-counter in the station. They were French-Canadian from New Brunswick. They were going to Lac la Hache to work in a lumber camp.

By the time we came to Chilliwack the sun was out and there were broken grey clouds around the mountain tops. Lilacs and apple and cherry blossoms were out, white and pink petals on the sidewalks and on the trees. The valley was flat and fertile. Cows in the fields. Shiny green grass. And beside us the mountains, the peaks covered in snow.

At Hope we were let off to have lunch. I had a hamburger and coffee. The food was expensive and I was trying to economize. Two boys were sitting at the horseshoe counter. White T-shirts and jeans. 'This soup smells rotten. You could have saved thirty-five cents. It smells like sewer water.' And he smashed the bowl on the floor and they both walked out. The woman at the cashier's desk watched and did not move. She was middle-aged and placid. She came from Eastbourne. She said she had been over here for four years and was returning in a year's time to settle down with a boarding house. She said she had had enough of this kind of life. Above her head, on a ledge, propped up like a photograph, was a tray with a badly painted picture of the Queen in its middle.

At the next bus-stop three elderly Indian women climbed in, their luggage small cardboard boxes with string around them. A cluster of wooden shacks. A few horses tethered to the trunks of trees. Indians standing against the wall of the beer-parlour. A large poster advertised a coming Stampede on the front of the general store. Hidden among the trees a clearing with black wooden houses of an Indian reservation. It was like the beginning of a cowboy film with the location and the extras ready; and everyone silent, hanging around, waiting for something to happen.

Then we entered a dense forest: the dark bark of the thick fir; the burnt-black, thin, of the jackpine; the light-rust, split, of the pine; was close and thick on both sides of the road. Sometimes the sun came through and showed how lush was the undergrowth, and the size of the tree-roots above the earth. The bus climbed steadily. Up horseshoe bends, levelled out, and then a further rise; while the drop down to the muddy Fraser river became more sheer and deep. Sometimes there would be a gap in the trees or else the road swung out and went along the edge of the slope and you could see the opposite side of the canyon, thickly covered with pine and fir, and the sheerness of the drop to the river. There was no barrier between the edge of the road and the drop. At the more dangerous bends felled trees were placed, like matchsticks, by the edge. The mountains were now dark blue and black, and behind us.

Then the trees began to come further apart. The road dusty

and more level. And when we stopped to let people off our dust blew past us. Then the rocks. Mounds like a series of graves with yellow flowers. The Indian woman behind me called the flowers Blackeyed Susans. They were larger than daisies, orange petals with a deep wine centre. She said they used to boil them and eat the roots. The man with the fishing gear was drinking beer out of a bottle and singing a bawdy song about a man who had no hips. The driver stopped the bus, went to the back, took the beer bottle away and threw it so that it smashed on the rocks. 'We don't have no drinking here.' Apart from the two French-Canadians, the fisherman, myself, and an American from California who was going to work in a lumber camp—the rest of the passengers were Indians, mainly women in cheap cotton dresses clenching a fist with their money inside.

After the rocks came the sagebush. Small fistfuls of short gorse, purple and green and coated with dust. The change from the thick growth to this semi-desert was sudden; even from the bus. Occasionally, in the hollows of the dry land, there would be a shallow pool and cattle grazing.

Then we arrived at Clinton. I left the bus and walked along the main highway, unpaved, which was the main street, and went into a hotel.

*

Saturday Night. After cleaning up I went down to the hotel's beer-parlour. Men sat in cowboy hats by round tables with several glasses of beer by them. On the walls were huge steer horns, old wagon wheels. The inside of the room was made up of wooden logs, highly varnished. As I entered a voice said:

'Hey, fellah, got a cigarette?'

I began to take out my package.

'It's O.K.,' he said. He brought out a package from his sports shirt pocket and showed it to me. 'I've got my own cigarettes. I just wanted to see if you're a good guy. Come and sit down and I'll buy you a beer.'

He raised his hand, showed four fingers to the beer waiter standing by the small bar cut out of the wall.

The man's name was Leo. He was in his thirties, sparely built, blond reddish hair, going bald. His face was flushed. When he smiled he showed white false teeth. He pretended he had a guitar and began to sing *Jingle Bells*. The man sitting beside him was slumped over asleep, his chin touching his chest. He was thick and shapeless, like some candle which has burnt too long and the wax has run down and hardened. The other person

at the table looked like a caricature of the small-town Justice of
the Peace. A cheap dark suit with a gold chain running into his
vest watchpocket. He had on a black cowboy hat that was too
large on his head. He was drunk and sullen.

'Where you from?'

'Ottawa.'

'The East. That's where I come from. I come from Hamilton.
Stopping here?'

'No. Just passing through.'

'Don't listen to buggernuts,' Leo said. 'He'll soon tell you his
story; how he was a Bible-thumper down East.'

'Well, what's your story?' The man said.

Leo again pretended he had a guitar and began to sing:

> Tell me your stor—ee.
> Tell me your stor—ee.
> Tell me your stor—ee.
> Then I'll go to bed.

A fight started in the middle of the room. No one interfered.
They threw a few wild punches. Then they stood there, calling
each other names, banging chairs for emphasis.

'I'm old,' the man said hesitantly. 'I'm seventy . . . been here
thirty years . . . I'm going to tell you all about life . . . but I
don't want to talk about it . . .' We ordered another round.

Then the beer-parlour closed and we had an hour and a half
before it opened again. Leo suggested that we go over the dirt
road to Les's Café.

As we entered, a man in jeans, cowboy hat and boots was
standing in the room talking loudly and earnestly. 'I wish I was
somebody. I wish I was somebody. I wish I was a girl. Then I'd
have lots of clothes.' His jeans were torn and you could see the
white skin. He talked to no one in particular. And no one paid
him any attention.

In the centre of the room was a horseshoe counter. Wooden
booths were along both walls. One waitress was inside the horseshoe. The other served the booths. The proprietress, the waitress
inside, was a dark Italian-looking girl, thin and suspicious. The
other girl was placid and looked worn out. She had a vacant face
with a bad eye. The iris was almost colourless and it lay half
under the top lid. From a distance the eye looked completely
white. She had a small child in a high chair by the door to the
kitchen.

Leo and I sat down at a booth and ordered a couple of hamburgers and coffee. Then he pretended he had a guitar and began to sing *Jingle Bells*. The proprietress told him to behave or else she would throw him out.

He stood up, unsteadily.

'I can lick any woman in the house.'

'Sit down, Leo.'

He sat down.

He got up. '

'Sit down, Leo.'

He sat down grinning.

A voice from another booth called out, 'What happened to your friend, Leo? The French-Canadian.'

'He beat me out of sixty dollars. Sixty bananas. That's a pretty good friend.'

A young boy came to the booth and asked Leo for the money he owed him. Carelessly Leo brought out a handful of bills and put them on the table. The boy picked out a five-dollar bill. 'I'd better hold on to some of your roll or you won't have any left.'

'O.K., Mother.'

The boy stuffed a few bills back into Leo's pocket and then carefully counted the rest and put them in his wallet. Suddenly Leo left the booth and staggered towards the nickelodeon in the corner by the door.

'It's Saturday night. Why no music?' he called out to the room.

No one replied.

Around the horseshoe counter, on the fixed round stools, were boys, a few Indians, with long side-burns, wearing skin-tight jeans, sports shirts underneath leather windbreakers, cowboy hats and pointed cowboy boots, some black, some red and some pale yellow. All of the boots had scalloped tops and very high heels; dust covered the gaudiness.

'It's Saturday night,' Leo called out again.

Still no one replied.

An Indian went to pay his bill. The Italian-looking girl said it was eighty-five cents.

'Why that?'

'You had sausages.'

He tried to flirt with her, but she wouldn't have any of it.

'Dig,' she said contemptuously.

'No money?' Leo taunted the room. 'No money, no funny.'

He went around the room repeating 'No money no funny, No

money no funny' as if it was a private joke. 'I'll toss anybody, double or nothing,' he shouted.

Still no one replied.

'Toss you,' he said to the proprietress.

She did not answer.

'Chicken.'

'Yeh, I'm chicken,' she said.

For a few moments the café was silent, then Leo shoved a coin into the nickelodeon. A record began to blare. *The Poor People of Paris*. Leo grinned and made as if he was playing a guitar and began to shake his hips. A man entered the café. Leo shouted out above the music: 'Hey, Saturday, goin' to buy me a beer?'

I left Leo in the café and walked outside. The air was fresh and cold. Though the sun had gone down there was still some light. A couple more hotels (chichi hunting-lodges for American tourists), a small church, a shack that said it was a bank, a general store. You did not have to walk very far along the main highway before you came to one end of the place, and a few minutes in the opposite direction was the other end. I turned off on to a narrow side-road, passed some wooden shacks, unpainted, with fields behind them and the snake fences. An Indian child was playing with a dog on the road. I continued for another quarter of a mile and ended back where I had started. I had walked in a circle.

Back in the hotel two old-timers were talking about 'the good old days' when they were drivers on the ox-wagons going through here. They repeated the same story to everyone who bought them a beer. The proprietor told me about the ghost towns in the Cariboo. They mushroomed in the gold rush. 'Barkerville in 1867 was the second largest town west of Chicago; it had thirty-four thousand people. Now there's only a handful. Everything in the place is overgrown. In a few more years you won't know anyone had ever lived there at all.' He spoke nostalgically of the past; it was far more adequate than the present. I was tired from the bus ride, and the beer made me sleepy. I decided to have an early night. But once in my room I could not sleep. The room was too warm. Down the hall someone was playing a guitar and singing cowboy songs. I tossed for a while and then went down to the lobby.

Leo had passed out and was asleep on a chesterfield, a blanket wrapped around him. Several others had also passed out and they lay in various positions on the floor, in the deep leather chairs. I

went back to the room and listened to a dog barking, to steps
going to the toilet, and people being sick.

Next morning the place was deserted. At breakfast I asked the
proprietor where everyone was. 'They're gone back to camp.
They're only Saturday-night men,' he said.

An elderly man, tall, slightly stooped, came to the table where
I was sitting and had his breakfast. He asked me where I was
going. I said I was hitch-hiking northwards. He said he was
going as far as Williams Lake after breakfast, and would give
me a lift.

Outside, the place looked asleep. A few black mongrel dogs
were out in the middle of the road sunning themselves.

*

He was an insurance man and he made two trips a year. He
would leave Vancouver for two weeks and drive through the
Interior calling at the logging camps, the cow-towns, and at any
odd house on the way.

We passed wrecks of cars off the road lying upside down and
on their sides without wheels or engines, stripped of anything
usable, rusting away. Further in the fields, at the mileposts, were
the old stage coach stops: derelict buildings, black, disintegrating in the sun. The trees began to reappear. A sparrow hawk
flew over and sometimes a few crows.

He spoke about the small farm he had north of Vancouver, of
his apple-trees, his chickens, how he did all his own work. Then
he tried to sell me insurance, unsuccessfully.

My job was to keep a lookout, on my side of the road, for any
house between the trees. He was looking on his side. He found
the first one, a log cabin, unpainted, about thirty yards away
from the highway in a small clearing. On one side of the cabin
stood a large new car; on the other a pyramid of opened tin cans.
We got out and started to walk towards it. And as he walked he
began to snap his fingers and wave his arms as if he was ex-
plaining something to himself. He worked himself up to such
a pitch that as soon as the door of the cabin opened, the words
immediately started to flow. He spoke confidently, friendly, and
convincingly. But it was a waste. A rough, unshaven youth, bad
teeth, opened the door. Hair-dishevelled, bare-footed, holding
up his trousers. He looked as if he just got out of bed. He
listened while the insurance man went on. Then a woman's voice
called out from inside the cabin. 'What's he selling?' 'Insurance.'
'What company?' 'Crown.' She said she already had insurance.

He tried three other isolated shacks. It was a bad day, Sunday, and though it was after eleven, they all had to be woken up. Each time, as soon as he left the car, he went into the routine of snapping his fingers and waving his arms, working himself up, so that when the door finally did open the same patter, repeated, sounded each time amazingly fresh and convincing.

The trees became thicker, the land more rolling. Cattle were grazing in the open spaces and BEWARE OF CATTLE signs were tacked on to trees by the road. Snake fences. None of them had nails or wire. They supported each other by the ends of the logs interlocking at slight angles.

At Lac la Hache several men were putting up boards for a baseball diamond, fencing off the area. The insurance man stopped to get some gas and tried to sell some insurance to the man filling up the tank. He said he had no money. They lost a lot of time through bad weather and everyone around here was pretty hard up at this time, perhaps at the end of the summer.

I left him at the crossroads before we got to Williams Lake as I wanted to get further north, today, if I could. A car soon stopped. The driver said he was only going for a few miles. He was a French-Canadian looking for a logging camp; but he could not find it. He drove a few miles further than he intended to, then decided to go back to Williams Lake.

I was let off by a small stream which had expanded because of the melting snow coming down from a gentle slope. Saplings floated in the water. And beside them a cluster of young poplars, not in leaf. It was a straight stretch of road. The snow had not completely melted and you could see it in the dark between the trees, shrinking back like some skin.

A rattle of sound came from the water. The sun was hot. Jackpines (burnt black bark, short green needles) swayed like mobiles in the wind. You could hear a car a long way away. And after it went by, it would become quiet again except for the rattle from the water. It sounded like frogs.

Finally a gasoline tanker picked me up. The sign in the windshield said NO LIFTS. The driver was a young, husky man from a small town in Alberta. He was working at Williams Lake ferrying gasoline to Quesnel. He had been here for two months. We did not talk much. He was watching the road and had to double-clutch every time he changed gears. After going a few miles, the silencer on the exhaust came off, it was right under the cabin floor. For the rest of the journey across gravel roads, potholes, dirt, dust, and stretches that were being paved, there was this monotonous banging like rifle shots going on under-neath us.

A deer lay dead by the side of the road. Further on a cat with its entrails out. I caught a glimpse of a couple of deer among the trees, then they rapidly disappeared into the forest. Crows and two magpies. Away from the highway, further into the forest, in the dark, the vivid white of snow on the ground. Some-times a clearing and a cluster of shacks. And a small wooden white church, with a tall cross made out of two logs painted white standing in front of the church on a grass lawn with one gravestone.

At Quesnel the driver said he had to go on a few miles to empty his load. He said he would pick me up in an hour's time by the bridge if I wanted to go back to Williams Lake. I walked around the small place. For something to do, people came to see bulldozers and tractors working on the excavation of a new site. In a store window, baby carriages beside rifles and fishing rods : civilization and the bush met in the general store. The same thing in another store. A large picture of Horowitz was beside that of a grinning cowboy, 'The Lone Pine.' I went into a restaurant and had a cup of coffee. It was owned and run by Chinese. The nickelodeon played cowboy songs. The usual horse-shoe counter and booths along the walls. I went out and walked through the empty streets. The only other people out were watching the bulldozer and the tractors. A side-road led to Barkerville. I made a half-hearted attempt to get to it. But there was no bus going that day. I tried hitch-hiking; there was no traffic. I asked someone with a car if he knew anyone driving in that direction—how much would he charge me? He said ten dollars. I walked back to the bridge and watched the fast-moving river until the tanker came along.

WILLIAMS LAKE

The dust was blowing down the Main Street, a short street a few blocks long, from the highway to the railway tracks. An old Indian with his woman behind him went to a garage and took a drink from a rubber hose that was on the ground. Wooden sidewalks. Cars parked by them. A cowboy on a horse rode slowly down the middle of the street.

I went to the Lakeview Hotel right opposite the railway tracks and asked for a cheap room. The woman behind the desk said she had one for five dollars. I asked her if she had anything cheaper. She said I could share a room with a Mr. McKay for two dollars seventy-five.

To get to it we had to go through the kitchen where a Chinese cook, stripped to the waist, was working by the stove. Mr. McKay opened the door after the woman had knocked several times. He was timid, unshaven, grey hair, going bald. He told me that he had been here for the last four days, meeting the bus twice a day, to see if his missing gear was on it. He had left his gear on the bus coming down and he could not get on with his work on the railway without his gear. He warned me that this was an expensive place. All he had was a hamburger once a day, and that cost fifty cents, and toast and coffee in the morning. While I washed and shaved he returned back into his bed and went underneath the sheets fully dressed.

The room was small, narrow, and dark. Two iron beds by the wall. A cracked enamel sink. The door consisted of various bits of wood nailed crudely together; it ended several inches short from the floor. The wall was a thin partition. Behind it was a waterpipe and every time I turned on the tap in the sink the pipe made a wailing noise. There were no windows. The naked bulb from the ceiling was on all the time. The only bright spot in the room was an old pin-up that was stuck to the wall. A girl with large thighs dressed in a black bathing suit sat in a swing with her knees apart. Mr. McKay asked me what time it was. I told him it was almost seven. He thought he would get ready to go down and meet the bus and see if his kit was on it.

I was hungry and went into the nearest restaurant. It was the same as the others. You were not allowed to sit in a booth unless you ordered a minimum of thirty-five cents. But that was not difficult. The further you went into the Interior the more expensive food became.

Outside dust was blowing. I saw the driver of the gasoline tanker. He drove up in a new green Buick. He had also changed into flashy sports clothes. Unlike the other cars in the street, his was shiny. He said he only bought it last week. He was very proud of it.

I had an introduction to the Indian Superintendent at Williams Lake. I asked several people on the Main Street if they knew where Mr. Christie lived. But they all said they were strangers to the place or else they had not long come here. I went to the drug store. The man spoke with a European accent. He said he was closed. I said I only wanted to know where Mr. Christie lived. He told me to go up to the end of the block then turn right. It was the last house on the right, a stone house.

When I knocked an elderly woman answered. She called her husband. Tall, white-haired. I showed him my letter. He asked me in. His wife sat in a chair listening to the radio. An English thriller was on. And for the next ten or fifteen minutes the three of us sat there not saying anything, listening to doors creaking, young girls being left alone, a thunderstorm, a man trapped in a basement room, a shot. And it was over. Who was the murderer? Was it the lodger? They didn't seem to know. Then the local Catholic priest came in from the kitchen entrance and the radio was switched off.

Christie told me something of Williams Lake. 'It's a transient place. Most of those who are here, are here only for a few years. That's why you will see the shack and the new car. The shack is only for a short time, it's expendable; but the car goes with him. It used to be a cow-town. Now there is a boom in lumber, and cattle is second. But it is not what it should be. The small lumber companies who were forced by the big lumber companies to leave the coast have come inland. They won't last long. They will stay here while the demand is on and while they can compete with the larger mills. It is only a matter of time before they will be pushed further and further into the bush until it won't pay them to cut trees. The ones that stay here are the ones that go broke. The others make a stake and move on.'

We talked about Indians.

The priest said the Indians did not like the white man. 'They have only met the poor white who is only interested in making money out of the Indians. He cheats them, sells them bootleg whisky. I can tell you a story about two Scotchmen. It is a true one, my father told it to me. It happened up north from here. The Indians were dying of smallpox. From three thousand they were down to a couple of hundred. And these two Scotchmen went around picking up the blankets that were covering the dead Indians and then selling them . . .'

Then we got on to writing.

The priest said he liked Mauriac.

I asked him if he liked Graham Greene.

No, he did not.

I asked him why.

'Because I met Graham Greene, at an officers' mess in England during the war. He had just given a talk . . .' And here he imitated a very fruity Englishman's way of talking. 'That fellow obviously can't do a thing himself and yet he proposes to tell others what to do.'

N

I asked the priest if that wasn't a frontier attitude where it was necessary to be one of the boys before anyone would listen. I remembered my first summer at Wawa. How the priest there had to first be seen working with a pick and shovel around his church, levelling the ground, before the men decided that he was all right, and would come to church.

He agreed. But he did not see anything wrong with it.

There was an awkward silence. The priest took out his package of cigarettes and tossed a cigarette across the diagonal of the room into my lap. There were other awkward silences when we seemed to have run out of conversation. Then he would take out another cigarette and throw it across the room like a baseball pitcher.

We talked about Riel. His father knew Riel well, he said. 'He was a quiet man and could play the violin. I know he was being used as a tool. The fur traders were trying to take a last dig at the Government. The Hudson Bay Company were having a monopoly on the fur trade and the fur traders didn't like it. So they used Riel. But he should have gone free. You know the first two times they tried to hang him; it didn't work.'

That led to an argument on capital punishment. He was in favour of it. 'I couldn't care less how long or how short a man lives; it's what he does with his life that matters.'

Mrs. Christie came in with some coffee and ham sandwiches and pickles. The priest said that he went to see a Pole this morning—that both he and Christie knew—he had missed Mass. The Pole was in his house with some friends of his and they were having a party. So the priest joined in, drank out of the bottle . . . 'You have to be one of the boys here. Not too much city idealism. You have to see and forgive . . .'

On the wall was a small bronze crucifix. And over the piano, on the wall, a large picture of the Pope. There were a few photographs of Indians on horseback, a boy in army uniform, children, and a sunset over a lake.

At midnight the priest left. Christie gave me a note to go to the Indian reservation about seven miles from here.

I went outside. It was pitch black and cold. No moon, no stars, no lights. The only sounds were some dogs howling not far away and my steps on the wooden sidewalk.

Back in the hotel room the air was stale. Mr. McKay was awake, fully dressed, in bed. Only his boots were on the floor. He said he had no luck today but perhaps his gear would be on tomorrow's bus. He hadn't shaved for the past four days and the stubble was dirty. I asked him what would he do when the money ran out. He said he did not know.

*

Next morning we went out to have some breakfast. We were both economizing. I was down to two dollars and eighty cents, after paying for the room. I intended to hitch-hike back to Clinton and from there take the bus to Vancouver with my return ticket.

We went to the corner restaurant, horseshoe counter, booths on both sides, and we both had coffee and toast with jam. We ate slowly and did not talk. Outside, the dust was blowing across the railway tracks. Beside the line, in a wasteland, were large sections of pipe that were going to be used for the gas line east.

Then a bus stopped outside the restaurant and around twenty women came in. They all looked amazingly well fed. The bus had a large sign painted across the side: WOMEN OF THE MOOSE. I asked Mr. McKay who they were.

'They're a charity organization.'

'What do they do?'

'Oh, they just go around doin' good.'

They filled the booths and the rest of the stools around the counter and began to place their breakfast orders with the young Chinese boys who were frantically bringing back bacon and eggs, ham and eggs, omelettes, from the kitchen. The women took over the restaurant, talking loudly to each other across the room. 'Is that a fact . . . Not a bad dump . . . It's a hundred and one per cent horse-town . . . Hi . . . That's for sure . . .' Then they tucked into the food. They enjoyed eating. Two of them sent their orders back: they wanted their eggs done differently. We watched them, and had another cup of coffee. Most of the women wore rimless glasses. You could see the way they ordered the Chinese waiters around that they were used to have men get them things. I thought of their husbands who had to make money for these women; and how they translated it into various layers of fat on their arms, around their chins, their rumps.

I asked Mr. McKay what would he do when the money ran out. He did not know. But he still felt sure that the bus company would provide him with new gear if he did not get the old one. He looked beaten, staying in bed all day, going out to meet the bus from Vancouver, then the one going south from Prince George, returning to the room and back to bed. I did not know what would be better: this defeat, or clinging to this ridiculous hope that somehow his gear would turn up.

*

I was supposed to meet an agent at the Department of Indian Affairs at eleven and drive down with him to the Reservation. But he wasn't there. I waited on a bench in a bare waiting-room. The place reminded me of the M.O.'s room during the war. There were the terror-posters saying what venereal disease could do; what T.B.; that the Indians must not have dogs in the house; that the fly is a killer. There were pamphlets giving photographs about sickness and disease. Indians came in, cowboy hats, jeans, cowboy boots, and discussed their 'problems' with one of the men in the building. Then the agent came and he drove up the slope to the end of the Main Street, to the cross-roads and along the highway. I could see the cattle-pens by the railway tracks and the still blue lake. He left the highway and drove down a bumpy dirt road.

The schoolhouse stood by itself in an uneven field of overgrown grass near the rough dirt road. A small, new, wooden square with coloured paper flowers pasted in the windows. He rang the bell-button. The woman who opened the door wore glasses and had a book open in her hands. She was plump; the belly stuck out; grey hair cut in a fringe. She wore a pink blouse, a very short dark green skirt and running shoes with white ankle socks. We were introduced. She spoke English badly with a thick French accent. The agent asked if it would be all right to look around.

'You govrenment h'inspector?'

'No.'

'Okay. Come in.'

We went up the stairs and into the one classroom.

She went to the front. We remained at the back. She clapped her hands.

'Everybody stand h'up, smile, look 'appy.'

The children stood up, smiled, looked very shy.

'Now say: Good morning, Meester Odell.'

A sing-song chorus: 'Good morning, Meester Odell.'

'Now say: Good morning, Meester Laveen.'

Again the chorus: 'Good morning, Meester Laveen.'

'Okay. Sid-down.'

The chairs in which they sat were attached to their desks. They were unmarked, and highly varnished. The room was spotless. The floor polished. Not a thing looked out of place, or in any way used. The first two rows had the youngest children. Each row was a different grade. The row by the window was the last grade in the school. She told the first three rows to go on with their work and began to read with the fourth and the fifth the story of Jack the Giant-killer.

But her reading was difficult to follow. Her French accent made it sound as if it was full of jokes. She would read a couple of sentences, then the two rows chanted back exactly what she had read; then she would ask a single boy or girl to read it back again. At the end of a paragraph she asked them questions.

'What is 'ero, Jimmy?'

''Ero is brave man, many medals.'

'Dat's right, Jimmy. And what you tink 'ero is, Doris?'

'Brave man, no afraid of nothin'.'

'Dat is also right.'

They would take glances to the back. They didn't fidget or make a noise. The blackboard had the alphabet, large letters in a clear commercial script. There were coloured pictures on the walls of animals and trees. Down the stairs the teacher lived in two neat little rooms, spotlessly clean.

The agent drove from the school on the dirt road a few hundred yards further away from the main highway, to the Reservation.

It was warm, silent, gloomy. Not a person was out. The houses were all made out of wood, logs, which had turned black, and they were spaced around the perimeter of a green eye. It was noon. But nothing stirred on the perimeter. The sun was warm. Dogs slept in the back of some of the houses, on wooden planks, over wooden bunkers. No smoke. No light. The houses were all the same. Dark, squat. A gabled roof, a door, small windows. And ladders nailed to the side of the houses and others on the sides of the roof.

At the first one we called, the agent addressed her as Sophie. He never called an Indian by a second name. She was sweeping. It was a bare room. A bare wooden table, unpainted by the wall. In one corner was an iron bed and something was huddled underneath the blankets. The agent went up and pulled the blanket back. An Indian was lying there in his dark shirt and jeans. He did not move. Sophie said, 'Joe was out on a party last night.' The agent threw the blanket down over the huddled shape. The figure did not move. They discussed business. Sophie rented a couple of beds to Indians who came from other reservations to work in Williams Lake. She was thin, dark and friendly. The agent said he would come around again next month.

In the next house, the agent knocked and went in. 'Hello, Emily. How's the leg?' She was an old crone. Full of age and pain in her deep wrinkled face. Her leg was broken and it was done up in a cast. The cast was dirty. The room looked as if no one had ever swept it or had ever put things away. A thick rope went across the diagonal of the room from the ceiling, and on it was thrown every kind of clothing. The stove was a large black oil-drum, with a piece of pipe going to the roof. Bits of firewood were by the stove and scattered in the corner against the wall. There was a large pot on the stove. But no smell in the room. Only gloom. The old woman sat by the stove, hunched over. She sat there like some Greek chorus in the darkness. When we went out, her husband was coming back with two pails of water.

From the Reservation I went on to the main highway and started to hitch-hike. The first car that came along picked me up. They were a young couple from a small town in Alberta. He was an oil-operator, and they had been living near his work in a caravan for the past two years. They were driving down to Seattle and San Francisco for their holiday. He had a couple of fingers missing on his right hand.

At Clinton we stopped for something to eat. The street was deserted. We went into Les's Café, that also was empty; only the waitress with the bad eye was serving. A truck full of Indians drove up and they came in. A pregnant woman with a baby carriage went by the window. Outside: only the dogs.

The landscape continued to go backwards. There were the derelict houses disintegrating in the sun at the mileposts; the cars rusting on their sides, the sage bush growing through them. The mounds of rocks, low hills, trees, and back through the Fraser Canyon. By the time we came to Chilliwack it was dark and the driver was too tired to go further. They decided to stay at a motel for the night. I took the bus to Vancouver.

I refunded the return half of my ticket and walked along Hastings to the hotel. A warm night. Patrol cars. People walking. Men hanging around the corners, by the street lights, outside beer-parlours. The Scotchman was on duty. He asked me how it was and gave me several letters. He stopped the elevator in between the floors and I entered the hole and picked up my stuff and took them up to the room. One returned to the shabby

stale room, the two calendars, the green blind, the cracked
enamel sink, the iron bed, and felt happy.

One of the letters had a cheque for thirty-five dollars. On the
strength of that, I went around the corner to the Chinese
restaurant and had a large meal. And from there I went into
the Arcade and spent what change was left on playing the
machines. Then walked in the streets. It was a warm night.
There were many others, mainly Chinese, walking the streets as
well.

*

I was reluctant to leave Vancouver, Hastings Street, this room.
I felt I could go on writing about it a long time. I had discovered
a good bookshop in Murrays. There was the public library on
the corner. Next to the hotel a newspaper store with foreign
papers hanging from the walls and lying on the floor,
Confidential, Movie Screen, paper-backs, funnies. Whenever I
could afford it I went around the block to Pender and had a
Chinese meal. Or a piece of smoked Alaska cod, white butter
flesh, or grilled herrings with a slice of lemon, in a café on
Hastings that stayed open most of the night. I bought cheap
fruit (watermelon, grapes, apples, bananas) from the Chinese
store on the corner, and salami, rye-bread, sardines and cheese.
And sometimes, the same things in the indoor market further
down Hastings, and ate them back in my room. On Main Street
there was Harry Harra's fish store. The first time I bought some
barbecued salmon-bits. Later when I walked by, I would stop for
a while and we talked about fish, about baseball, about the
absurdities of war, by the large counter of crushed ice with a
sloping enamel side and the two taps. He was Japanese and was
transported inland during the war. He came back and had to
start over again. 'No Junk Here.' Spring salmon, light grey skin,
spotted, and the smoked pink-red flesh. Prawns in a yellow bowl,
shrimps touching their whiskers on a plate. Smoked salmon,
mahogany, lying like two book ends. Rock cod, herring, smelts,
sturgeon. For someone like myself who likes fish Vancouver was
a good place.

It was also a good place to be alone in. I walked down to the
C.P.R. docks and watched the gulls, the boats, the water in Burrard Inlet, the ferry-boats to the North Shore, the houses on the
slopes, and the mountains. There were days when the sun was
out when they appeared very close and thick like oil paintings.
Water. Trees. Mountains. Everything happened for the eyes.
Wherever one walked—no matter how drab the human in the

street—Nature appeared so brilliantly polished. And on other mornings when it was misty, a fog from the sea, or rain, they disappeared. Even the streets, the houses, looked different in the grey light without the handsome backdrop. Or to Stanley Park. Or walking through the streets. One kept meeting strangers. All it seemed one had to do was just be around and not have any particular destination. And you would cross and bump into other people's lives. One heard the strangest confessions, humiliations, absurdities, foolishness, and suffering. 'And, to balance them, amazing endurance.'

But I decided to start back while I was still in funds.

CHINAMAN

He never had a name for me. Neither did I have one for him. Whenever I wanted him I pressed the button. We rarely spoke; neither knew the other's language. I had just about finished packing when he said. 'Comeback. Comeback. Comeback.' He sounded like a guinea-fowl croaking. I shrugged and said maybe. I wanted to give him something. I had an old blue Harris tweed jacket. I took it out of the bag and gave it to him. He took it. I went to the elevator shaft and rang the bell. He stood there, by the pile of soiled linen, old newspapers, film magazines, in the dim passage, holding the jacket and a broom.

X

STOP OVERS

FLYING EASTWARD

THE BOREDOM of commercial flying. It was too detached. There
was nothing more violent than a rate one turn. It wasn't the
physical part of flying that tired one so much as the boredom
of what the eye saw, there was nothing it could get hold of.
From this height the third dimension disappeared. You could
see the shadow of the tree better than the tree itself. And then
a small town appeared. And with it man's rage for order. Then
over trees again and no reference except for a few scars, lumber
camps mowed down the side of a hill. How clear from the air
can one see the way man hacks into Nature. Here are the raw
shapes: the bush, the hills, the trees; one vast sprawling repetition. And then the neat mathematics of a small town. The roads;
straight, curved, and straight; the rectangles with houses and
streets like a parking lot, each house the size of a car. While
around it this massive hide of trees and snow and rivers and
lakes rolled out. Occasionally a village burned into the hide like
a brand on a steer. Clouds. And coffee and biscuits and magazines and sleep.

Then the clouds thinned and I saw the land without green,
without mountains; but square fields: and, scattered, were clusters of isolated trees, the colour of dust, like sores in the fields.
The change was sudden and startling. As if something had flattened everything out, rolled it to the horizon. Some of the fields
were freshly ploughed, the turned earth, the colour of mud and
beside them were the yellow-brown patches of last year's stubble.
You could see the contour-ploughing of the wheatfields better in
the fields with last year's stubble. They stood out like the rings
of a cut tree. And they repeated, in every direction, to the
horizon. Patches of water where the snow had melted in the
hollows of the fields. Ice still on the lakes. The only movement
in a thin river that jigsawed two pieces of land together. Our
shadow on the ground the size of a thumb went rapidly over the

ploughed fields, the lakes, the long thin roads, and a few isolated farm houses.

Then a large white cloud passed underneath us and the sun lit it up in rainbow colours and suddenly we were fixed: black with a ring of white in the cloud; the wings, the four engines; then the cloud went backward and we were back as a shadow, not distinct, just a moving black rectangle going over the fields and the water melting to form lakes. We were going down. There was turbulence.

The highway became wider, the farmhouses had sides, the clouds were above us, the pattern of the ploughed fields spread, our shadow became the shape of an airplane. I could see telegraph poles, the intense white-black of cows, a yellow tractor in a field, fence posts, then the city: Edmonton, the roofs of the houses shining like new cars. Gulls over the river. Washing waved in the wind, its shadow behind. The wheels were lowered, we dipped, and the streets rose. We didn't stay long at Edmonton and it was a quick trip to Calgary. The landscape near Calgary, like the hide of an elephant only sand-coloured.

The stewardess on the plane asked me what did I do. I told her. She said she wouldn't marry a writer. 'You know how things are today. I'd be a little more practical.' But she was bored with this milk run and she fell asleep on the trip, her shoes off, her mouth open, the make-up stale and thick: under the nostrils it looked like a separate skin. Gone was that glossy finish, that smile with the coffee and biscuits. But the coat hangers, dangling behind her, woke her up and she disappeared in the toilet. When she came out she looked ready to face anything. The automatic grin. Her sing-song, 'Bye, Bye.' Everyone that went down that gangplank had a smile and a 'Bye' from her.

CALGARY

Calgary was dust, wind, and the streets being torn up. After the freshness of the Coast, the rich vegetation, one was back to the prairie dust and wind and depression. Potholes, cars splattered with mud, puddles. And that limpness that I felt first in Winnipeg. Faces in the street, the bad complexions, less colourful, although there was the occasional cream-coloured Stetson in a large car.

The hotel where I stayed was dark and gloomy, with dark leather furniture and middle-aged salesmen full of hearty goodwill and confidence. They sat in the leather chairs in cheap suits, frayed cuffs and talked 'big deals'.

Along the main street they were pulling up the road. At noon the men in overalls and ski-caps sat on the sidewalk eating their lunches while the dust blew by. One walked with face screwed up, turned sideways, dust particles blew into one's eyes.

In a secondhand bookshop two elderly Jews, looking as if they came straight from the Old Country, and a genial middle-aged woman carrying too much flesh, breathing heavily and audibly, were watching the few customers looking over their tables heaped with thousands of secondhand soiled paper-backs. A man drove up in a fine-looking, two-tone car. He came in and at random picked up three dozen paper-backs. He told one of the brothers to wrap them up and package them and then send them airmail to a Yukon address. He said it was his year's reading. If he did not come in next year, he would send them some money for another three dozen. Then he gave them a five-dollar bill and drove away. I picked up for a quarter: *A Farewell to Arms, Reflections in a Golden Eye,* and *The Man Within.*

In nearly every store window, in the advertisements in the paper, you were reminded that this Sunday was Mother's Day. 'Mother Loves Flowers' . . . 'Sunday is Her Day : Say It With A Gift' . . . 'Especially for Mom, real cool panties'; and watches and washing machines and photographs and chocolates . . . 'Because She's Extra Special Mother Will Love A Gift of Shoes' . . . In the social column, between the paragraphs: 'Remember Mother with a Gift From——'.

I remembered Murray Street on Mother's Day. How punctually every May on a Sunday morning the cars drove up with all the boys from the A.Z.A. (later they joined the Optimists; the Kinsmen; the Rotarians; the different brotherhoods and lodges). They piled out of the cars and ran up the veranda steps, and the son whose mother opened the door called out, 'Greetings to the best Mother in all the world.' And he would give her a red rose. They all sang a verse of a sentimental song about Mother that was on the hit parade, they all kissed her, made a fuss about her, then on to the next veranda, the next block, and then the black cars drove away the horns blowing . . .

I wandered through the hot dusty streets. It was difficult to get lost. Streets ran north and south on either side of Centre Street; and the Avenues east and west; the railway tracks ran through the middle. From the air it looked like a car-park. I decided to go and see a film; then back to the hotel; the optimistic salesmen, then lying in bed reading. After three days here I had enough and went out to the airport.

The glass front wall. Charlie Kunz played softly before you opened the glass doors. A girl in uniform smiled. Silkscreen prints of Canadian poster landscape on the walls. It was the newest airport I had seen; yet I don't know anything quite as lonely.

Railway stations are different. They belong to the city. When the railways pushed west, where they stopped a town grew up. They marked a social division. You lived on one side of the tracks or the other. (The wrong side was the east where the smoke drifted.) But airports belong to something else, something anonymous. You go from one airfield to another; the buildings look very much the same. After a flight the physical change from one place to another is sudden, but you only notice this after the drive into the city. At the airport one is still suspended; you move your watch an hour forward or back.

They are still a novelty, a cheap form of entertainment. I remember in Ottawa, and later in Montreal, driving out to Uplands or Dorval with one's girl, parking the car and watching the planes land, watching the passengers come out. And the hundreds of other cars parked around the airport doing the same. It was cheaper than a drive-in theatre. The small ones still have the old Air Force shacks, the dull green and red huts. But the new ones belong to the glossy fashion magazines, or a funeral parlour: glass, chrome, clean, hygienic, recorded music continually playing softly in the background. It is the air-conditioned nightmare of Henry Miller; the difference between the drabness and the dreariness of the city and the sterilized smartness of this lonely empty place set in a wasteland of flat land with some kind of excavation continually going on around the perimeter.

MEDICINE HAT

I decided to go to Medicine Hat because I liked the sound of the name.

Flying eastwards out of Calgary, not a tree anywhere, a few foothills; maybe in the hollow, a small lake, or a thin twisting river; the rest of the time the land looked like some unimaginative pastry. The rectangles of the fields were as regular as zebra crossings: this year's growth, last year's, this year's, dark, sandy, dark, yellow-brown. The whole land's surface as far as one could see was one continuous pattern of these yellow and dark fields, a flat ladder that stretched out below towards the horizon.

I was the only one to get off at Medicine Hat. A cluster of R.C.A.F. training huts, small bit of grass in front, and a strong wind blowing, the windsock was right out. The taxi-driver began to boast about the place. 'It's the cheapest place in Canada to live in.' I heard it from about six people that day. 'A good place to retire . . . You know you can live here on your old-age pension.' It was the natural gas. 'We're in a crater and heating is very cheap.'

In the stores, in the hotels, there was a continuous slow burning jet on. It was still cold and the heaters were on all day.

The railway cut the place in two; not that it was a large place to cut. The Main Street was short. There were five-and-ten-cent stores, the library, a few hotels, a few fruit, hardware, and grocery stores. But the streets were so much the same. I knew the prairie small towns from my wartime flying training. You could interchange them. The same dreariness. Ladies coming in for a milk-shake, gossip, and then going away, nothing seemed urgent, no one rushed. In the restaurant the men were in overalls, they worked on the railroad, a diesel engine stood very large not far from the restaurant window. The waitress spoke with a heavy accent; she said she was Lithuanian. She was saving up her money to move to Toronto or Montreal. In another restaurant there were three young men sitting at the counter. They came from Holland. They had been here for three years and they already had a car, a Dodge, but they wanted a better one to go for a tour to Banff. They intended to spend another two years in Medicine Hat, then return to Holland. 'Yukon mak eet dees Sommer.' 'Issy.' To get their speech one would have to write it phonetically. 'You need money to start some business at home,' the most talkative one explained. 'You need capital. You come to Canada. You make the money. Then go home and start the business.' But there was nothing to do except the film or the restaurant, sometimes a dance. Another bus had come that afternoon, they said, with more immigrants from Europe. 'It is a good place to save money.' And they returned to discuss the virtues of the Daimler and the Mercédès-Benz.

I went to the newspaper office. It was a large building near the river. I asked the editor whether he ever reviewed books. 'That's culture,' he said. I thought he was making a joke, but he wasn't. He went to a green filing cabinet and brought out three books: two war-stories and a detective, and with it a syndicated review from the publisher in the States.

From there I walked back on to Main Street. Dust was blowing. There was no one outside. I crossed over to the other side
and was passing a woman's beauty parlour when I saw a picture
of Sophie, in the window, advertising a new hair style.

It happens all the time. It seems, almost in spite of oneself, all
the worlds we ever inhabit are somewhere to be found in our
personal orbits, and at the oddest and least expected moments
they whirl into our consciousness. Sophie was a Swedish model
I knew for a short time in London some six years ago. And with
it came back that strange autumn and winter of cocktail parties,
weekends in the country, fast open cars, the crowd in Campden
Hill and Holland Park. A kind of wealthy Bohemia. A tall
blond handsome Spaniard, who wanted to be a poet; he played
the horses, he said he averaged winnings of £15 a week. He
rarely got up before the first racing edition was out. His father
was a well-known Spanish journalist. The doctor with the twisted
mouth; he wanted to be a painter. He had painted in Brittany,
in Provence, in Cornwall, and in his smart studio-flat he walked
about in a black beret, blue sailcloth windcheater. His father was
a General. The advertising man who, after every art exhibition
that he went to, came back and did imitation Calders, Nichol-
sons, and Francis Bacons. He wore fancy waistcoats, grew a
beard; he walked with a stick that was the sheath of a sword.
His father was an internationally known architect. And there
were many others. None of them was talented, but they all had
inherited money, good manners, taste, lucidity. How they loved
to talk. They talked out every emotion, so that there was no need
to get it down on paper. It was a comfortable, well-fed, but pointless existence.The trouble was that nothing ever really bit them
deeply. They were not failures; they would not allow themselves
to be involved that much. They remained spectators kept down,
yet supported by the achievements of their parents, depending
on money and strangers to keep them going. They liked the
stranger immensely at first. Then they had to find someone new
to like immensely.

And here was Sophie who had passed through them on the
way somewhere else, small mouth, good teeth, smiling, the hair
blown backwards, the black sweater, looking very much the outdoor girl. And here was the dreary main street, the dust blowing,
the dullness of a small town.

Flying eastwards across the prairie you could see the desolation, the vastness, and the emptiness, better at dusk. The few
lights spread out far apart. Puddles of water in the fields, thou-

sands and thousands of them, the size of small lakes; melted snow gathered in the depressions of the ground. They were shiny; they were like mirrors, set in the black.

And then after Winnipeg one was back to forests and lakes.

LAKEHEAD

There is no mid-west in Canada as in the United States. Between Winnipeg and Ottawa there are no large cities. There is rock, lake, bush.

I was the only one to get off at the airport. I asked the driver to take me to a cheap hotel. He suggested the 'Adanac'. I asked him to repeat the name. 'It's Canada spelled backwards.'

The hotel was small and the room dreary without being comfortable. They had not bothered to remake the bed from the person who had checked out in the morning. I washed and walked out through Fort William.

There was hardly anyone out. The closed movies advertised a Sunday midnight show at 1201. A few people were walking to church. A cool wind blew from the lake, which I could not see, there was a long freight train in between the street and the lake. I got on a bus that took me to the outskirts of Fort William where another bus from Port Arthur was waiting. A young crewcut sat down beside me. We talked about sport, about the strike that was going on with the seamen of the lake boats against the owners for higher wages. He said he had worked on a lake boat for over three years. The conditions were good, but not the pay. He was sure that the men would win.

I could now see the lake and the boats, idle by the sides, like a lot of tied dachshunds. We passed several grain elevators, large blocks of concrete with the smaller, houselike building on top where the machinery for running and loading the elevator was. There was a glut in wheat, and the wheat in the elevators could not be sold, not at the 'world price'. The farmers were not allowed to sell more than three hundred bushels a year into these grain boards. The farmers were not happy with the politicians; the 'world price' was being undercut by the United States in the way of aid to foreign countries. There were two elevators that belonged to private companies and others that were provincially owned; Saskatchewan and Manitoba had theirs.

In the lake a peninsula. It was flat, until near the end of it the land rose, was hacked, to form the figure of some effigy, like

those lying on top of tombs in cathedrals. The boy, who was a
sports reporter for the local paper, said, 'That's our sleeping
giant. In summer when the pulp and paper mill blows its smell
over the place, we know the sleeping giant has farted.' We passed
men, Slavic-looking, walking around, sitting on door steps, hanging around street corners. He said most were Finns, like himself,
the others were mainly Ukrainians.

The bus came to the main corner and I got off and walked
down the slope towards the water's edge. Small trunks of trees
were piled so close together that I was only able to see the water
in a few spaces. I walked along the railway tracks by the front,
parallel with the main street which I could see up the short
slope. And there were the signs: the windbreakers in the streets,
the heavy lumberjack jackets, the black lunchpails, not much
English spoken, the physical deformities; the bush was not far
from here. I walked back towards the main street. Old women
dressed in black sat in front of their houses on the wooden steps.
Secondhand stores. A sign said 'The Finnish Book Store', a sign
in a grocery advertised 'The Canadian Finnish Film Society'.
A few Indians better dressed than the ones I saw in the interior
of British Columbia. Sunday was quiet. Men stood in groups on
the sidewalks, spitting by a sign that said fifty dollars fine for
anyone spitting on the streets. One was back to the general store;
the old European women with dark shawls over their heads
watching the empty street from behind the glass window, cats
beside them.

I went into a small café and had a hamburger with chips and
a coffee. The same fixtures, the same small town worship of
home-made signs. There were the advertisements for Cokes,
Pepsi-Cola, 7-Up, and various cigarettes. And a sign tacked
on the wall: IF YOU'RE SO SMART WHY AIN'T YOU RICH? On the
stools; the men one had seen in Sault Ste Marie and at the
Mine.

I took a bus back to Fort William and returned to my room.
The bed had been made and beside the Bible on the dressing-
table were two glasses enclosed by blown-up paper bags. 'For
your personal use this glass has been sterilized and carefully
wrapped to keep it clean—an individual service.' While around
the dreary room dust and dirt were carefully hidden away:
underneath the bed, in the cupboards, on the windows. There
was a phonetic alphabet card propped up by the glasses in case
one wanted to send a telegram. In wartime we were taught that
B stood for Baker; now it was B for Bank. What was once D for

Dog had become D for Dollar. And L for Love had changed to
L for London.

*

I had run out of money again and telegraphed a friend in
Montreal. He sent me fifty dollars. I spent another three days at
the Lakehead.

Every morning I went out, walked by the lake, through the
streets, took the bus, passed the new shopping centre in between
Fort William and Port Arthur—the houses of each city were
already stretching out to meet it. It was the only bit of colour:
the flashy chain-store fronts, the self-service, rides for the kiddies,
a parking lot. The same suburban shopping centre that has
sprouted in every city across the country. It looked incongrous
in the flat wasteland, facing the railway tracks, and the drabness
of the houses and the streets.

It started to rain. I went into the small library and read some
of Emily Carr. There is a good feeling of the Coast; an accept-
ance of the Indians without trying to make something personal
out of them. I much prefer her in her writing than in her painting. Like other painters she writes simple, vivid, and exact,
as long as she is describing some external action, or recording
something that the eye sees. When it comes to express feeling
the language changes; she becomes 'poetic' and rhetorical. 'Roof,
walls, floor can pinch to hurting while they are homing you, or
they can hang and enfold. Hurt enclosed is hurting doubled; to
spread misery thins it. That is why pain is easier to endure out
in the open. Space draws it from you. Enclosure squeezes it
close.'

I prefer her when she is simply describing things.

'The man and the woman got out and dragged the canoe high
on to the beach. There was a baby tucked into the woman's
shawl; the shawl bound the child close to her body. She waddled
slowly across the beach, her bare feet settling in the sand with
every step, her fleshy body squared down on to her feet. All the
movements of the man and the woman were slow and steady;
their springless feet padded flatly; their backs and shoulders
were straight. The few words they said to each other were guttural and low-pitched . . .

'The man gathered a handful of sticks and lit a fire. They
took a big iron pot and their food out of the canoe, and set
them by the fire. The woman sat among the things with her
baby—she managed the shawl and the baby so that she had her
arms free, and her hands moved among the kettles and food . . .'

o

I asked the librarian if I could see *The Times Literary Supplement*. She brought me a thick plastic folder with the latest copy. It was April 1955. I said that this was over a year old. She went back and then returned and said that it was the last issue of the paper. I assured her that it was still being published and she was just as certain that it had stopped. She began to make up a story. She made it up as she spoke, saying how the newspaper had to cease publication because of the shortage of newsprint in England and that it would restart when times were easier. I decided to go into a beer-parlour.

There are beer-parlours in Canada that are like tombs. No one talks. You just sit, drink beer, and watch television. In winter they are draughty and depressing. In summer they have a stale sour smell. Some have become like restaurants and you can have beans on toast, hotdogs, ham sandwiches with your beer. You sit by the round table with the salt-shaker and pepper, put up a couple of fingers, and the waiter brings you two beers on a round tray, and you give him a quarter. I prefer the noisy, crowded ones in the poor end of town, by the railway tracks.

'—— you, sir. Think by twisting my arm you twist the world?' And he gestured wildly. The man was fat with a ski-cap on his bald head, pushed back so that the peak pointed upwards. His sports shirt was open to show black hair on his chest. He kept dancing up from the table, pretending that the air near him was someone elusive that he was trying to hit. 'The old double cross; one-two; one-two.' The only decoration on the wall was a picture of last year's National Hockey League champions. Two came and sat down by my table. One in a suede windbreaker, the other in a leather one. The air was full of smoke and people talking. The fat man who was shadow-boxing said, out loud, to no one in particular, 'You don't mind if I go and —— myself to death.' He went towards the toilet. Then the suede said he had a game last night to see who could drink eight beers without using hands. He bent down and put his nose inside the glass, sucked some of the beer into his mouth, then gripped the glass with his teeth, and began to slowly tilt the glass until nearly all the beer was drunk, then he put the glass back down on to the table; he said the glass began to slip. He took out his top plate and ran his tongue around his mouth, then put the teeth back in. 'I'm getting $1.90 an hour, sometimes two bucks, with the new machine I'll get almost three. That's pretty good jack, three bucks an hour. I'm only twenty-two, started work from Grade 8 . . . And you should see those ginks with their college educa-

tions. Hell, I've passed them all. Last week I went fishing and
drank skunk beer. Have you ever tried that stuff? And yesterday
at the paper mills someone brought a dead muskrat and put it
through the wringer, then put it down Rollo's back. We were all
sick. And today I threw an orange peel by the steampipe and
then I pissed on the steampipe and you know what it stinks like?
Then I told Ellefson to get that orange peel. You should've seen
his face. Later the shift boss came. I had the water hose. He takes
and puts his hand on the water hose and I get soaked. So I hit
him. He tells the Superintendent. But the Superintendent is a
good shit.'

A heavy man in a ski-cap with a large nose, red face, at the
next table was drinking by himself muttering all the time in a
monotone: '——ing right . . . ——ing right.' The boy in the
leather windbreaker said, 'I'll be makin' pretty good jack in a
year or two.' He took out his wallet. It was overstuffed with
dollar bills and papers. He brought out some pictures of young
girls. 'You know her? Hot piece. This one's pregnant and she
doesn't know who knocked her up. This one is a good kid, went
to Winnipeg to have her baby. I picked her up in the stadium.
She was sitting higher up. I turned around and I could see she
had no panties on.' The man at the next table kept on in his
monotone as if he was a record with the needle stuck. The other
man came back from the toilet, had a couple more glasses of
beer, got up, and did some more shadow-boxing. There was
cigarette smoke, loud talk, someone shouted. While these two at
my table continued to boast about money, about girls, about
what they had done.

I walked out of the beer-parlour. The rain had stopped. The
air was cool. The sun was still strong though it was late afternoon. Sparrows were making a noise, chasing each other down
the street like a whirlpool. I walked to the waterfront, across the
railway tracks, the sun on my neck, the sound of a train shunting. Two cargo boats had smoke coming out of their stacks.
Cars were parked. It wasn't much different from the other small
towns on the border of the bush, except for the lake, and the
cool air coming from the lake.

That night I couldn't fall asleep. I decided to go out and get
some fresh air. The place was deserted. In a side-street a couple
of drunks were lying on their stomachs across the sidewalk
having a game of pull wrist.

XI

IN MONTREAL

I RETURNED to the top room in Mrs. R.'s rooming-house, undressed, and went to bed. But cats in the back yard kept snarling and whining, the street cars kept rumbling by, so did the trains. It was a full orange moon. I thought of Montreal. How does one tell about it? Where does one begin . . . ?

One can begin anywhere. Like now. I'm lying in a bed in a room just off Dorchester. And I remembered the room in Dorchester when I was at McGill. It was down wooden steps in the basement by the boiler. A narrow room, large enough for the plain iron bed and a chair. A tiny window by the ceiling just cleared the level of the ground and let in fresh air, the smoke from the passing trains, grit on the pillow, the walls, the skin. The small light was on all the time. One enjoyed this gesture of protest, for you knew you had control over it and could end it whenever you wanted. One's friends were invited down. They drove up in their father's cars and had a good look.

Or the absurdity of waking up in the morning, half asleep, with that untidy feeling of grit on the skin, in one's nose, on the tongue; rushing out late for a nine o'clock lecture, no time for coffee or toast at the café on Green Avenue, waiting for a taxi, while the silent Jehovah Witness stood on the sidewalk pushing a copy of *Awake* towards me . . .

I switch the knob on the small radio in the room on a chair by the bed. CJAD. 'Make Believe Ball Room Time The Hour Of Sweet Romance.' And I remembered that year in the rooming-house on Prince Arthur; all the rooms were let to students. The year the Biro came in, it stood on the dresser like a trophy, in its chrome pedestal. Upstairs Sy was in bed with his physiotherapist second year. Next room fat Edith worried again about her periods, looking around for a rich husband. In bed at the far end of the room Percy, daydreaming about the

time he was in command of a corvette and in the end running
her aground. Going to the 'Brother Andre', 'The Nitecap', 'The
Samovar', 'Ben's' and four a.m.'s . . .

I had made a list one time in Cornwall of the eating places I
knew in Montreal. How each one brought back bits and pieces.
'The Chicken Hut': the plate full of whole chicken livers with
French fries and a cup of coffee for sixty cents. The pregnant
waitresses shuffling on flat shoes. There was another regular
besides myself. A French-Canadian with bad teeth and a sallow
face in his early twenties. He worked in the government. He was
neat, and spare, and withdrawn. For the short time I saw him
he wore the same clothes every day: the chocolate-brown sports
jacket and the grey flannels, the green tie with the silver tie-clip
and cufflinks to match. Two waves set in brown hair. I thought
he was a homosexual. After a week we began to sit at the same
booth and have our plates of chicken livers. One noon he said
he was homesick. He came from a small town in Manitoba. His
father died when he was eighteen and he had been sleeping with
his mother. 'She said she was too frightened to sleep alone.' But
it worried him; he felt it was wrong, so he left home and came
to Montreal. 'Now, I know I cannot marry. I can be faithful only
to my mother. I tried. About a dozen different girls. It's no use.
It's humiliating. . . .'

'Au Lutin qui Bouffe': this was reserved for something special
because it was expensive. The drive in the taxi through the
French slums and then entering the foyer-like theatre, the signed
pictures on the walls: movie stars, hockey players, the principal
of McGill, the politicians. Select your piece of meat from a
counter then go and sit down in the dim room, a large pond in
the floor with huge yellow green frogs squatting on the waterlily
pads. The piano beside the pool and the blind pianist playing
the popular classics. Then a girl in a brief skirt, black fishnet
stockings, came with a camera. Her assistant carried a small
suckling pig and a baby's bottle of milk. The piglet was placed
on top of your table and one held the bottle while it went
greedily for the nipple, slobbering the milk. The flash-bulb exploded. The night before going overseas; the end of an affair;
the beginning of another . . .

And there were others: 'Mother Martin', 'Slitkin and Slotkin',
'Pauzes', 'The Bucharest', 'Aux Delice', 'Dinty Moore's', 'Horns',
'Ferns', 'The Windsor Steak House', 'Chinatown', the drive-in's,
'F.D.R.'s', the 'Honey Dews'. There was no chronological order
about the experiences and the images they brought back. Nor

did one, at the time, understand their meaning. But later the pieces began to fit.

*

And then I climbed the wooden steps up the side of Mount Royal to the lookout and looked down on Montreal. But the view was all wrong.

I remember looking at St. Ives—from the height of the bus stop at the Malakoff and further up from Tregenna Steps—it was the perfect picture-postcard. A piece of land flung out like a small bent finger into the Atlantic; the C of the harbour; the waves coming in like horizons in reverse; a few fishing boats; gulls; the lighthouse in the bay; the island criss-crossed like a hot cross bun; and the pretty little sand beaches. But in the back streets, in condemned cottages with the water tap outside and soapy water stagnant in the gutter, they were living on national assistance. Damp funeral cards. 'Bed and Breakfast' signs. The retired middle class on the terraces who came here with their savings and bought their graves. And the careless people who come to places like St. Ives anxious for the new holiday encounter because they need for their existence—to feed their pretence of being 'a painter', 'a writer'—a lot of strangers passing through. Then shot through the poverty, the squalor, the boredom (like those fantastic balloon shapes that the wind makes blowing through the spokes of a wheel which has passed through fish slime) were the lyrical absurdities of the summer. When the stenographers and the typists and the art students came down. 'The Yellow Peril', 'The Black Tulip', 'The White Goddess', 'Sin on Stilts'; that fitted. Where Gladys Jenkins, Jean Middleton, Sheila O'Connor, Thelma Elkin would not. And swimming at night in the nude in the harbour, 'The Black Tulip' marching through Fore Street, her white panties at the end of a broomstick; the all-night parties in cottages on the moors; the homosexuals down from London; the rats squeezing at night down the drains; the tiny rooms with the walls damp, the light from the gas bracket . . .

But from a height how could one see this or guess it?

I left the tourists taking their pictures (they were brought up here by calèches and cars) and returned down the wooden steps, down the side of the mountain, came out opposite Fletcher's Field, and walked towards Park Avenue.

THE GHETTO

At first there were only a few signs. A delicatessen store. A doctor
and a dentist with Jewish names on the front of a house. The
houses with outside staircases and mazuzas nailed by the door.
This could just as well be repeated in several other parts of
Montreal. But then the images piled on. Y.M.H.A. Hebrew
signs on gravestones. Men and boys in skull caps. Priests and
rabbis waiting for street cars. Kosher Meat Markets. Rocking-
chairs on the verandas. Old women with shawls staring from
windows. Old men on the outside steps reading *The Forwards*.
Jewish signs saying 'Room To Let,' advertising a summer cottage
in St. Agathe. The warm smell outside a house making baigel.
Synagogues and Catholic churches . . .

I walked down L'Esplanade. Children, no place to play, played
on the road or the sidewalk, scattered when a car went by. They
tied one end of the rope to the stair and skipped. Underneath
the space that was made by the staircase they ran, rocking-chairs
sat, rubbish dumped. No gardens. At the most a tree growing
out of the cement. Men sat on the steps by open doors. The food
smells, the disorder of the corner-store: barrels of schmaltz
herring, salamis sweating in the window, cheese, chalah, bags of
peas, Kik, beans, onions . . .

I crossed Villeneuve. Laundry hung from balconies. The winding staircase went up, then branched like a river leading to two
or three separate doors and flats and iron balconies. Inside the
door, at the bottom, was a long rope by the wall attached to the
latch. You rang. They pulled the rope upstairs, the door opened.
So that on entering, the first thing you saw was a person standing at the far end of a telescope at the top of the stairs holding
on to a rope . . .

I came to St. Joseph. A boulevard, trees in the centre. In the
midst of squalor, trees, grass, new buses. The wind had blown
down the yellow green blooms of the maple. They lay on the
sidewalk and on the road. As I walked through them they
squashed and squelched like thousands of caterpillars. I crossed
over Laurier. French was spoken by the garage mechanic.
Laurier Strictly Kosher Meat Market. In a rusty tank huge carp
hugged the bottom, their brown scales like small open fans;
sawdust on the floor. On a brick wall posters of the local Union
Nationale candidate ·in the coming provincial elections. An
advertisement for Rock n' Roll at the Forum. An old sign for a

Jewish play at the Monument Nationale. In chalk across the brick: 'I love Angela'; 'Jenny is a Bum'. On the road, potholes, manure and dust piles, broken milk bottles, used toilet rolls, old newspapers. From a backyard someone was sawing wood, the saw wailed through the wood and a woman's voice on a veranda called 'Motel, Motel', and a dog barked from the entrance of a yard . . .

Crossed over Fairmont. Passed a synagogue. Kids shouted in Yiddish and English. Hopscotch on the sidewalk and the road. Tip the ice-box against a wall. How sure. Very very sure. How far. Up to the corner and back. . . . On St. Viateur two old women met and talked.

'Shaindel, how are you?'

'How should I be.'

'Shaindel, where are you going?'

'Where should I go.'

'And how is your daughter?'

'Like my daughter.'

Young boys went by carrying their prayer shawls in small velvet bags. An ice-truck with wooden sides went slowly along the street and men delivered blocks of ice to the doors. A block away, against the sky, the round dome, the large cross, of a Catholic church.

Down Van Horne. There was another road that ran between the backs of these houses. It stank of garbage. In wet battered pails, in bins, in wooden crates; the flies all over them. Wooden poles carried electricity and washing lines. Unpainted wooden fences, bleached and cracked by the sun, snow, rain. An old silk stocking lay in the middle of the road by a drain; a *True Romance*; a box of Kotex. The backs of these houses were a jumble. Some had tin on the outside, but the tin had curled. It looked like a large tin-can that had not opened neatly, or that, having opened and taken the contents out, one tried to force back the tin to cover up whatever was no longer inside. They were run down, from too much living.

Things came in sections. There would be a clothing block, 'wholesale only', then poultry and meat, fruit and vegetables, and food stores of all sorts. The delicatessens with hanging salami, smoked meat, tongue, the large glass jars with pickled green peppers looking like preserved intestinal organs; the brilliant red cherry peppers. By Rachel Market live chickens in steel cages. A man bent their wings and laid them on the scale. On the window-ledge, on the floor, hundreds of loose yellow chicken legs. The faces of the fowls like those of the old Jews standing in the doorways, walking the streets.

On St. Lawrence a ginger cat had been run over. The head was crushed, but it was still alive. Its convulsions jerked it into the air. Someone stopped a car and asked the driver to run the cat over again. He did. But he had to do it several times before it died. The poverty, the squalor, had not changed. Only, as I discovered later, some of its inhabitants.

*

I was having a hot smoked-meat sandwich in a delicatessen on Park Avenue with Usher D. He looks like an athlete who has gone soft. The smartly cut suit, the bow tie, the short greying hair, were constantly betrayed by the dead weight of his bulk; the slightly bloated face; and the uncertainty in his eyes. He is the owner of a large catering service in the city and his job is to sell 'personality'; to arrange, with whoever is giving a wedding or a reception, 'the details'. He is suspicious of most things but remains completely in awe of anyone who has 'education'. He left school at thirteen to go to work. His belief is that everyone who matters today is a specialist of some kind, as he is of the catering service, and you can buy the specialist's services with money. I have rarely seen him angry. But when I asked him why he was moving away from here, he suddenly became annoyed. 'Because those lousy immigrants have buggered up the street. They're dirty. They go around howling to the moon at night and dress up like a bunch of freaks. It got so bad that we had to get our councillor, a Frenchman, to tell them to stop.' Then his tone changed. 'I think it will do you good to see them while you're here.'

So he drove me in his large sky-blue car down Jeanne Mance, L'Esplanade, and stopped in front of houses where young boys in skull caps and payasan (long fine strands of hair flapping in front of the ears, like spaniels) were standing and playing. Many of them were blond, but they all had a solemn self-conscious look like the old Dutch paintings of children with grown-up faces. We saw a small woman standing in a doorway. 'That's their women,' Usher said with contempt. 'You can tell their women by the way they wear their kerchiefs.' The woman in the doorway had a white kerchief tucked in and tied on top so that the ears were covered and her hair kept in. It was tied the same way as I had seen Indian women wear theirs on the reservations in British Columbia. While we drove slowly through these

streets with French names—a Yiddish soap opera was on the car
radio—Usher kept pointing out the men. Long beards, black
silk coats, large black Jesuit hats; but you could see by the face
they were not very old. Usher dismissed them. 'Who wants to
live with those good-for-nothings? They don't like us any more
than we like them. They think we haven't suffered; as if they
have a monopoly on suffering.' Down another street and he
stopped in front of a dingy wooden house. It looked the same
as the other houses around it. 'And this is where they worship.'

*

As this was Friday I decided to go to the Temple Emmanuel
in Westmount, not far from where I was staying. Large cars with
rakish back fins were parked in the side street. Inside the men
and the women sat together on comfortable wooden seats. It was
a half-circle, sloped like a theatre, rising sharply towards the
back, and everyone was smartly dressed. Very few, especially of
the women, looked Jewish. A raised wooden platform was in
front, and a small pulpit on it. It was brightly lit up. A heavenly
choir came from somewhere near the ceiling, also an organ.
Tonight was a special occasion, a *bas-mitzvah* (confirmation) for
two thirteen-year-old girls, twins, dressed in bright green dresses.
This was something quite new and nothing to do with religion.
It is one of the innovations brought in from the United States.
The two girls stood on the platform and recited their lines. The
father and the mother were also up there, a little more nervous.
The whole service was a parody.

Gone was the richness of the Hebrew chants, the loudness,
the cantor stammering over the ritual 'as if it was crammed
full of jokes.' One could believe in that. There was something
human about the man snuffing up a thumbful and then passing
it around, the drinking of the red wine after the blessing, the
schoolboy games and tricks that were played by those participa-
ting, and the complete unpredictability of the way the service
was going to go. But what could one make of this solemn, dull,
castration, in an English translation that was flat and boring
and not helped by having it hesitantly chanted in a colourless
monotone. It sounded like a very self-conscious elementary class
learning how to read. Then the cantor went to the pulpit and
gave a sermon. What he said was of no importance—a schoolboy
lesson, a biographical sketch of an insignificant Hebrew prophet
—but his manner hypnotized the congregation. He was a ham
actor, posing, pausing, scowling, using every kind of obvious

dramatic trick. Then there was the blessing, and that too was from the States; the prayer books were published there and where it said 'Bless President Eisenhower', the congregation chanted 'Bless Prime Minister St. Laurent'. Then more from the heavenly choir, the organ played, and it was over. Everyone stood up and congratulated each other and then hurried to their cars.

I felt disgusted with the whole performance. Why all this hypocrisy? Either you make the break and that's that, or else you believe; not in this watered-down, diluted, trying-to-ape-a-church service so that really we're not different you know . . . They thought that with money they could change anything that was uncomfortable. And they did. They were able to run away from the messes they made in the slums, in the ghettos; to places like Westmount, Outremont, Notre Dame de Grace, Town of Mount Royal, Snowdown. Now that they found it necessary to have a religion, there was no point in having an uncomfortable one.

I walked out into the cold night and went to the nearest bus stop and took a bus, then a street-car, back to Park Avenue. I wanted to get back to failure.

I entered a small store, newspapers, comics, magazines, a few booths, a soda-counter, and had some coffee. A couple of taxi-drivers were watching a Hopalong Cassidy film. A boy and girl sat beside me talking about movie stars; and in the back room, behind a curtain, a card game was going on, with a young boy running in and out carrying sandwiches and Cokes. Behind the counter was a boy, about eighteen, wavy blond hair, pimples on his forehead and on his chin, glasses. He had a white apron on and a green-and-yellow polka-dot bow tie. As he was working behind the counter he kept on chanting. 'Makin' lots of money. Makin' lots of money. Hi, hi, hi, I'm makin' lots of money.' And he kept this going while his hands squirted flavouring into the milkshake cans, cut bread, made sandwiches, poured coffee, hit the cash register. The nasal accent, a thin sound off key. Hi, hi, hi, the voice coming out of the huge horn of an early phono-graph. 'Makin' lots of money, Makin' lots of money, I'm makin' lots of money . . .' The taxi-drivers smoked cigars and stared at Hopalong Cassidy; the boy and girl kept talking about movie stars.

From there I went further along the street, into a larger restaurant, to have a meal. Halfway through, someone arrived and sat in the booth behind me. I could not see him, but I could hear his slow quiet voice say in broken English, 'A T-bone steak, well done, with French fried, please.' When the waitress came with his order he began to plead quietly, 'Do I look good to you? Do I look good to you? Tell me? If I look good to you, I've got a car.' She said she had a date later on. He was insistent. 'If I look good to you, there's ten dollars in it for you.' But she wouldn't have any of it. She was in her early twenties, getting stout, but there was an immediate perceptible vitality about her. She had large breasts. You could see her brassière through the faded green uniform. Her round face, a baby face with vacant blue eyes, stared as if she was really thinking about something else all the time. He tried again when the dessert came and the coffee. 'Do I look good to you? Do I look good to you? Tell me. I'll make it fifteen dollars.' At twenty she gave him a slow smile and said, 'Well, we'll see.' When I went out to pay my bill, I passed where he was sitting. He was short, bald, in his forties, with rimless glasses and sad bulging eyes, a well-fed face. He was sweating. It was obvious he had been refused too many times.

All next morning it haunted me. 'Do I look good to you, tell me?' I saw it wherever I looked.

McGILL

There is (as Scott Fitzgerald has said about a New England education) in Canada that respect for 'a McGill education' which is the ruin of all provincial places, which drains them yearly of their most promising young men and women. They came from the small towns in the Maritimes, Quebec, Ontario, and from as far west as British Columbia.

The tents were being put up for the garden party underneath the trees on the one side of the straight main drive that was like a park. The other side of the drive was a wide grass lawn that had chairs placed neatly in tight rows like a flower-bed with grass borders. In front of the chairs—the lawn continued then sloped abruptly upwards to a branch of the main drive— men were building a wooden platform at the bottom of the slope, decorating it, fixing loudspeakers. Convocation prelimina-ries had not changed.

I was tired from walking and sat down on the steps of the Arts building. The doors were closed. A mailbag lay beside the red mailbox by the doors. A mound of grass. A red fire hydrant.

The stone tomb of James McGill. And the ghinko tree. Spacious-
ness. Peace. Silence. And then a sudden sound of car horns
going on and off and several black cars flashed along Sherbrooke
Street by the Roddick Gates, white streamers from bonnet to
windshield; it looked like a wedding. And then back to silence,
to trees, grass, pigeons, squirrels, 'Please Keep Off', young children with their nannies. It was this incongruity that always
struck me about McGill. A piece of country stuck right in the
centre of Montreal. A sanctuary. I remembered being told, in
my first year, that McGill had its own police; that if you committed a crime and entered these grounds the city police could
not touch you.

A calèche enters the campus from McTavish Street, the horse's
hooves sound distinct along the drive. Clop, clop, clop, by
the library, the Redpath Museum and up the slope to the Arts
building. An airman and airwoman in uniform (it is part of the
tourist route) look unsteadily out from the black collapsed hood.
Then it disappears towards the hospital and the University Street
entrance.

The campus is a social border. A U-shape; grey stone buildings, along the perimeter; grass, trees, drive, in the hollow. The
closed end slopes up until it disappears as it becomes part of
the mountain. On the opposite side of the mountain, the ghetto
begins. The open end touches Sherbrooke, then down to St.
Catherine, to Dorchester, to the harbour. In the autumn at a
five o'clock lecture you can hear the ship's horns from the river
and the pigeons cooing near the windows. Hugging the U are
the fraternities, the sororities, the clubs, the apartments. Then
west, on Sherbrooke and Pine, sweeping upwards with the con-
tour of the mountain, are the fine houses, the Presbyterian
churches, the wealth of Westmount. East: the drab sour-
smelling boarding-houses; the shabby apartments; one soon
came to poverty.

For the English-speaking minority in Montreal McGill is a
very important institution. Everyday a reporter comes from the
Montreal Star to the principal's secretary to get some story about
the university, to keep it constantly 'in the news'. The Governors
are among the wealthiest business men in Canada. It represents
wealth, snobbery, privilege. An èlite of Anglo-Scotch and a lesser
number of Jews who will in turn become pillars of society and
send their own children here.

An old man walks up the drive with a cane, stops and looks
around, takes a few more steps slowly and stops and looks back.

I wonder if he was here. The old man has come to the Arts building and rests against the rail. Does one always come back alone? And as I sat on the steps, tired from walking around Montreal, I began to daydream of the generation that one belonged to when one was here. Edouard the Belgium count, Christopher now in Tangier, Mike lecturing in the West, Felicity in England, Leo in Hollywood or New York or London, Ted, Jack, Percy, Sid . . . I watched girls and boys making the same walks as I used to make. The place had not changed.

*

When the war was over the veterans returned and those who could get in went to university, their fees paid by the Government and sixty dollars a month to live on. They also had their gratuities given to them soon after their discharge, sometimes several thousand dollars. With the veterans there was the normal intake from the private schools, the high schools, the sons and daughters of graduates from overseas; the sons and daughters of various diplomats in Ottawa.

One was a 'veteran'. And whatever those war years taught, they certainly did not prepare one for seeing through the conformity that was demanded of the post-war generation. McGill rubbed some of the rough edges smooth. It gave a finish where you could charm, make small talk, be lucid. It gave confidence of the kind that if you wanted to be involved again you had to lose that confidence. It bred the sameness: a continuation of Bishop's, Lower and Upper Canada, Ashbury, Selwyn House, Trinity, Miss Edgars and Miss Cramps. And if you did not come from there you quickly jumped on to the bandwagon, imitated, were 'on the make'.

One had to make a name for oneself. There was the playing field, the political clubs, the student council, the literary magazine, the *Daily*. It was a gay, irresponsible time with few real worries. The going was good. One soon got the hang of the examinations. There were the weekends in the Laurentians; the parties; the dances; the binges; the crap games.

Things were done very much in 'sets' or 'gangs'.

We went to drink at the 'Shrine' or at the 'Berkley'. The 'Shrine' was round the corner from the Union. You could only drink beer, and if hungry have a steak. It used to be full of students who didn't belong; who took Modern Poetry courses; who worked on the *Daily*. I remember one attractive nymphomaniac who had been at McGill a long time taking half-courses,

who spent most of her time at the 'Shrine' getting duller and
stupider as she became tight, going around muttering: 'Has——
been telling you I'm not a good lay?' The 'Berkley' was the cocktail room of the Berkley Hotel further west along Sherbrooke.
We used to come here to drink Brandy Alexanders that were cool
and creamy. It wasn't as noisy as the 'Shrine'. The 'Shrine' had
several small poky rooms upstairs where drinking bouts really
went on. Downstairs there was the large juke-box with jazz and
classical records. You could hear *Peter and the Wolf, Easter
Morning in a Russian Village, Air on the G String, Open the
Door Richard, Ain't We Having Fun* . . . At the Berkley the
fraternity and the sorority crowd, the young alumni, debs, ex-
debs, rakes, and the college boys 'on the make'. A gay rich crowd
who came here from dinners that began with cocktails and continued here with more, until they got blotto, then for three
dollars you could go around the corner to a room in a tourist
house, or else you went to a nightclub, to the 'Samovar', the
'Rockhead's Paradise', the all-negro show in 'fertility dances'; or
back to the fraternities.

The emphasis was on the social throughout the year. The
Plumbers. The Red and White. The Junior Prom. The R.V.C.
Formal. The ritual of the football games at Molson Stadium.
But the biggest blow-up was Convocation Ball that took place
at the end of May or early June.

It was the end of a long week of drinking, eating, dancing,
dinners, class-reunions, stags. In the morning you were told to
come to the Arts building in a dark suit and you rented the
gowns, the mortarboards, the sheepskin hoods in different
colours, and lined up six abreast. Then we marched down the
main drive and sat in the chairs on the lawn. The principal
made a speech, saying what a fine generation we were, how we
fought the enemy of civilization and now we had come to take
our place as useful citizens. He read a letter from a mother of
one of the veterans who was graduating saying this was her
proudest day. And then the honorary degrees were presented to
those on the platform, several heads of large business, those who
would help in the Alma Mater Fund to be launched in the Fall,
and a head from another university. Then the Dean went to the
microphone on the side of the platform and began to call out the
names. The Phys. Ed.s were first; then Agriculture; then the
teachers . . . one after another a continuous stream went from
the chairs to the platform, and, as a name was read out, the
Chancellor stood there with a mortarboard in his hand and, as

you went under, he murmured something in Latin that sounded like 'rhubarb' or 'bacon and eggs'. If a name was followed by honours and prizes there was applause from the relatives and parents and friends who sat on chairs behind the students. But by the time the M.A.s came, and the Ph.D.s, there was no longer any interest. This was strictly an undergraduate performance. And then the guest speaker, the chief of the Boy Scouts, got up and gave a speech; I cannot remember a thing he said. And the Chaplain said a hymn; *Abide With Me* was played by the Scottish band; and it was over.

You returned your rented garments. You picked up the red cartridge cases with the sheepskin inside in Latin. And there was the garden party on the other side underneath the trees, the tame grey squirrels, the tents with punch and food and everyone being very social and friendly, girls in summer dresses and large hats and families taking pictures by the Three Bares; underneath the trees.

For the rest of the afternoon and early evening you went on a series of cocktail parties. You had rented a couple of rooms in a downtown hotel where you left your evening clothes. You had gone to the liquor store and bought several bottles. She had made arrangements with a junior to sign in for her at R.V.C. and cover up. And then with whisky bottles underneath their coats, and wraps, we drove down to the Arthur Currie gym to the formality of the reception line. Everyone knew that the bottles were being smuggled in, but no one would do it openly; it was not allowed. So, while one shook hands and smiled, the girl kept the bottle hidden, but once inside the bottles were brought out on to the long tables, while the reception line, the official chaperons, went to the darkened balcony and watched. They had done the same thing as students.

One sat and drank and talked and danced, and other people came and drank and talked and got up and danced, and the girls laughed and smoked and looked gay and handsome and excited in tight evening dresses and hair carefully set. The ceiling was covered with hanging flags of all the name universities in Canada and the United States. The band played. Around midnight the chaperons disappeared. The lights were put out, except for those on the bandstand, and a revolving light from the ceiling sent flickering shadows on the dancers. And the flashbulb photographer moved from table to table photographing everybody like some documentary evidence that had to be pieced together and sold. Or getting those dancing by a wall.

Whenever his flash went it revealed for a second various couples
in the darkest corners lying on the floor, across chairs; girls and
boys whose fathers owned entire villages and towns in Northern
Ontario and Quebec were quickly getting plastered. Then the
bottles began to run out and several went out and came back
with a new stock.

And later that night in the hotel room we could hear a man
opening a door and walking down the corridor and returning
and shutting the door. Then about five minutes later repeating
the same. And it went on. We named him the hotel detective.
Then she said, 'Listen.' But there was no sound from the corridor. It was the singing of birds. It came from the window. And
then the window went blue. And the birds were singing as I
suppose they do every morning, but never have I heard them as
distinct and loud. And the blue became lighter, and you could
see it growing. And we stood there watching, touched by some
understanding that this was the end of something. Only later
did one draw the blind. And tried to pretend that it was not all
over . . . that it would go on . . . that one would return next
October and go on again to the same enthusiasms, the same
gaiety. . . .

I walked away from McGill with little nostalgia. It was one
of those times when, looking back, one can see at what expense
the good times were had. At its best it was 'borrowed time'. One
knew it would be over at the end of four years, but you did not
believe it. If you wanted to keep on the same way, you could, it
was made all too easy. One had without knowing it joined 'the
organization'. And in those four years it did its work. It sand-
papered the personal rough edges while it continued to dangle
a carrot in front, as long as one toed the line. The boys and girls
from poor homes (it helped if they looked clean-cut, and gave
evidence that they were on the side that organizes, by winning
a few prizes) were given stilts. And as long as they conformed,
they never had to look back.

THE PROFESSOR

I walked down the slope past the willow in the vale, the Three
Bares (did they represent muses or were they just nudes holding
up a hollow stone like an enormous bird bath?), past the grey-
stone Museum, the new library that M.'s father had designed,
modern and anonymous, replacing the more intimate and cold
chapel-library, came out to McTavish Street and went to the

P

Faculty Club. I was to meet my former English professor for lunch at one. He was waiting for me in the lounge.

The place was like a gloomy English club. Sombre leather chairs. A waitress came and he ordered drinks on a piece of paper. We sat there and drank. A man came over and he was introduced as the Canadian Ambassador to Japan, and he went and joined another group of leather chairs. There weren't many people in the large sombre room.

Then we went into the dining-room and, as we were eating, he told me about the petty quarrels, the intrigue, the rat-race, that the university had become. He was a former head of the department, but he had not remained head very long; another professor from overseas displaced him. And he described a tale of deceit, suspicion, betrayal; and his complete innocence of this sort of thing. What could one say? That the world never was the way you said it was. You never bothered, or had to bother, to see what it was like. You received your 'experience' of human nature on the cheap side, through literature. And it served you well as long as you were a junior, lecturing, with enough money. But you became a power; and there were others after power even though you were not . . . He looked beaten, washed out. We could talk no more about writing as we used to. All he could talk about was what had happened to him; and it happened several years ago. He wanted sympathy. How could one give it except by listening. It had taken him longer than others to find out that evil does not have to look like a caricature of itself. That it can be charming, educated, lucid. I remember how he analysed the subtleties of human relationships as he found it in the 'set books'; but now that he was faced with his own, he was at a complete loss. It had completely undermined him. I had lunch with him a week later. He repeated the story, exactly the same as if we had just met.

WRESTLING AND STRIP-TEASE

There was a wrestling match on at the Forum. Usher had a couple of tickets and asked me if I wanted to come along. He said Larry Moquin and Yvon Robert were fighting as a tag team against two Germans. I was to meet him at the 'Honey Bee' at 5.30.

The 'Honey Bee' began as a small store selling pastry and cakes, while in the back they started a catering service. It had now expanded. Beside the original store there was a large banqueting hall, and a plant making delicatessen-meats. When I arrived Usher was busy on the telephone, I went into the kitchen to wait. I used to wash pots and pans here during one summer, then go with the loaded truck to the various places where the receptions were being held and help in getting the set-meals out from the kitchen to the guests. There were new faces making sandwiches, pastry, cakes, preparing fish, chicken and various meat dishes; packaging food cartons that were to go into deep freezes. Most of them came from Europe, a few were French-Canadian. The cook said he was going to warm up a couple of hamburgers: would I like one. He was a tall grey-haired man with a sad expression on his face, a Hitler moustache. We sat by the long wooden tables, well scrubbed, the sweet smell of food and preservatives. He was a Czech and had been working here two weeks. He had come to Canada eight months ago. I asked him how he liked things. 'There is nothing here to like. It is democratic. I'm all right as long as I'm all right. Then everybody nice, want to help me, feel for me. But if I'm down; who cares?'

From the kitchen, swinging doors, to the front part of the store where two salesgirls were selling pastry and cakes from large glass cases. Above them on the wall was an enormous painted bee. On one side it had a sign in Hebrew to say that the food was strictly Kosher. On the other side a golden scroll: 'The Ten Commandments Of Business'.

Usher first drove to several private houses in Westmount to see how the 'affairs' were going. He hired waiters and waitresses while his own staff brought the food from the store, heated it up in the kitchen, and dished it out. There were the usual small crises with everyone rushing. The wine-waiter: 'Where's the ice Mr. D.? I've got the champagne and the glasses but no ice' . . . 'Mr. D., we're running short of ice-cream . . . cut the bricks smaller . . . give them fruit . . . Stop soup . . . I need ten more fish . . .' The rush of the waiters and the waitresses into the kitchen, losing their immaculateness, sweating, dishes falling, tempers. They all called him Mr. D., and he walked around placid, unhurried, only his eyes betrayed the anxiety. Then he would go out and mingle with the guests, greet the person who was paying the bill. Tonight everything was going smoothly, and we stopped off at a delicatessen for a smoked-meat sandwich before going to the Forum.

The ring was built up in the centre of the arena, and Usher had two good seats about twenty yards away. There was a television camera on one of the girders in the grandstand (we were sitting where the ice-rink would be) and opposite the camera, on the other side of the grandstand were several crude placards— white paper on a stick—waved by young boys and girls in the camera's direction. One said: 'Hello, Shirley.' Another: 'See you at the Smoke-Bar.'

No one paid much attention to the preliminary bouts. What these wrestlers lacked in skill they tried to make up by showmanship. Blond hair that came down to the shoulders; bare feet. One of them spent about five minutes glaring at the audience, opening his mouth and snarling, grimacing, showing what he would do to the audience if he could only get at them. Several times he lunged against the ropes as if he was going to carry out his threat. While binoculars were held to the eyes and watched. There was a champion weight-lifter making his debut as a wrestler; he won but he wasn't very convincing; he walked around the ring posing all the time. Then the main bout. The two Germans were very blond, huge, wide chests, and the two French-Canadians looked small in comparison. One wrestler from each team wrestled in the ring and if he could put out his hand and tag his partner by the ropes then his partner took over with the man in the ring. The worst thing was to find yourself in the opposition's corner, going from one man to the other. The Germans were playing dirty. It looked like a lot of punching, smashing elbows, gouging eyes, pulling hair, and one German would come in to help his partner if he was in trouble, even though he wasn't tagged. The crowd howled. Both Moquin and Robert were being roughed-up. Robert's skin around his waist and chest had become pink. Then Moquin got one of the Germans in a neutral corner against the ropes. He jumped up on the lower ropes, one foot on either side of his opponent, straddled him, and pushed him against the post. Then he took the German by the hair and pulled his head back and with the other he raised his fist and was about to hit him in the face when he suddenly stopped, the blow held back, above the German's face. Moquin lifted his face to the crowd. He appealed to the crowd. 'Shall I hit him? Do you want me to hit him?' He waited there for about two seconds, like one of those stills frozen in the middle of its action, then the crowd reacted, it quickly stood up and the arena was electrified by a thunderous rhythmical chant, 'DUN-ZEE MO-KA. DUN-ZEE MO-KA. DUN-ZEE MO-KA'. As he smashed his fist again and again into the face.

The Germans were the better team. They took the first fall,

with a body press. Robert took the next one with his own hold, the whip: the two bodies flapped around the ring going over like treads on a bull-dozer and when he released his opponent he was flat on the mat. The Germans took the final one with a flying mare. And the show was over. The hate of the crowd, the violence, that made all these spectators into participants chanting as one—soon disappeared. People stood up and began to make for the exits while organ music played from the girders and the young boys and girls with the placards kept waving them hopefully in the direction of the TV camera.

I remembered the strip-tease at the Gaiety. The preliminaries here did not matter either. The acrobats, the bad comedian, the tap dancers, the male impersonator. Everyone was waiting for the main event, the last item on the programme.

She came on to the bare stage, a long thin girl, not young, dyed blonde hair, and began to sing badly an old unheard-of piece. Then she stopped singing to the audience and began to hum and sing to herself. The drum began to be more insistent. She began to move about the stage as if she was expecting an important guest and was nervous, tidying things, dusting here, bending to pick something else, very nervous all the time, humming to herself and throwing off piece by piece of her clothing until she was nude except for a G-string and two tiny red flowers on her nipples. A spotlight came on, the rest of the stage was dark. The light tracked her as she went over to the curtain; the drum increased its beat. She took hold of the end of the stage curtain which was drawn halfway across the stage and straddled it. She held with one hand on to the curtain higher than her head and she placed the other hand behind her and took hold of the curtain which was between her legs and pulled it back taut. Then she began to slowly slide up and down the edge of the curtain. She increased the tempo, her thighs thrusting forward as she began to do a back bend moving her head from side to side and occasionally uttering tiny cries from her throat. And there was Moquin standing on the ropes, straddling his opponent, smashing his fist into the other man's face, as she jigged up and down faster and faster, until with a cry she collapsed and the stage went black.

When the lights came on, there was only the buttoning up of fly buttons as the sweating middle-aged men left the front seats; the straightening up of dresses; the putting on of shoes. By the time we came out on St. Catherine all that worked-up feeling was drained away; one felt strangely deflated.

*

I had run out of money again. Usher lent me seventy-five dollars; that would keep me going until I would take the boat, but I needed another hundred and seventy-five dollars for my ticket. I wired my parents and they sent seventy-five. I called up a person who had lived with us when he came over from Poland, as a young man, some twenty-five years ago. He had washed dishes in the Chateau Laurier, peddled fruit, now he was wealthy, in textiles. He invited me up for dinner. He picked me up in his Cadillac and drove me around the mountain until we came to his drive: new large wooden houses with large glass front walls stuck on the slopes. He said, 'This is sometimes known as the B.M. Drive.' I asked him: 'Bank of Montreal?' 'No. Black Market.' He explained how people who made money out of the war in Montreal in foodstuffs, textiles, had to keep two safes, two sets of books. There was a touch of nostalgia in his stories of what went on in Montreal during the war; it sounded like a shabby but happier time. His wife was dressed in striking Oriental clothes. After a good meal with wine and brandy, I asked him if he could lend me a hundred dollars. He gave me a lecture. He did not believe in either borrowing or lending money. That was one of his principles. 'It leads to all sorts of unpleasant situations.' But he wanted to give me a suit. He said he manufactured some of the best men's suits in the country. And it would give him great pleasure if I had a suit made up. He would have one made to measure and get somebody to finish it before I left the country. He recently brought over a tailor from England 'He's made suits for Lords and Ladies (he has a picture of himself holding a piece of cloth and showing it to the Duke of Edinburgh)', and he would make up a suit for me. I needed the money more than I needed a suit; but I could also use a suit. After dinner he took me down to his den and we watched television. A bare room, dark-varnished, goatskin rugs on the floor, no books, though the walls had low shelves, a small bar, and a large television set. We watched a play about an old father who was no longer wanted at home. But he fell asleep within fifteen minutes, completely exhausted, snoring.

THE EDITOR

In a shabby part of Notre Dame was the office of *Le Devoir*. I was to meet Andre L. I planned to go in a few days to Quebec City and spend some time there, but conscience told me that I

hadn't seen any of the 'right people'. All along across the country when I met any of the university lecturers in Political Science
or Economics, and French Canada came up in the conversation,
they said when you are in Montreal go and see Andre L.

Down a dingy back street in the old part of the city, I could
hear the sound of a ship's horn from the harbour. His office was
at the top of old dusty stairs. He was tall, thin, with a neat dark
moustache, very earnest, and presentable in a well-cut grey business suit and a plain red tie.

We talked about language. He said that the French-Canadian
written language was quite different from the one used in everyday life, 'just like the Greeks'. But with TV, the writers were
now using a more direct language and he was convinced that
this would effect the kind of writing that would be coming out,
especially in the novel. We talked about some French-Canadian
poets and novelists. He did not think they gave a good idea of
what was happening now in Quebec. 'French Canada is going
through a crisis. It is becoming industrialized, especially since
the last war. And the whole structure of French-Canadian society
is breaking up. The priest and the lawyer are now not the only
ones getting a good education. Young men and women have
come in from the farms to the towns. They have joined trade
unions. The parish priest has lost some of his power. Of course,
when you have country girls and boys, not well educated, coming to the big city, you get other problems.' I said that on the
emigrant ship there were only two emigrating from France who
would be French-speaking Canadians, that the others were
mainly from Germany and they would all become English-
speaking Canadians. But that did not worry him very much.
'The French-Canadian's strength is that he is not ashamed of
being a French-Canadian. Not long ago I was out West and I
met a mayor of a town. He talked to me about sport, about
hockey, and for my benefit, about French Canada. I knew he
was of Ukrainian descent. I asked him of his Ukrainian background. He was very angry. "I'm not Ukrainian. I'm a Canadian." '

We talked about the coming provincial elections. The paper
supported Duplessis on questions of provincial autonomy, but
it was critical of his social reform. He was sure Duplessis would
get in. 'In the past what has kept us together has been the pressure from the Federal Government to break us up and assimilate.
That has only kept us more conservative and more together.
Now the danger is not from the Federal Government, which

everyone recognizes, but it is in the economic pressure of the United States.'

He looked like a successful young lecturer and editor. He frequently appeared on TV and had his own programme as a commentator. There was a smoothness and self-assurance about him, but towards the end of our talk a note of bitterness crept in.

He had returned from a trip across the country, and he was shocked to see how American much of Canada had become. 'Things have changed in Quebec too but not anywhere like that of the rest of the country. Most of this change is caused by capital invested from the outside, mainly by Americans, who are not very much concerned with our welfare . . . of course there is still the image of French Canada that is advertised abroad. It is what the tourist wants to see. Quaint. Picturesque . . .'

Our neighbour on one side of the yard was Gregoire with eight children. The inside of their house had a different food smell. Sometimes Johnny or Thérèse came in on the Sabbath to make the stove or turn on the lights. Or else Loo or Georgette came in to wash the floors. Across the road was my friend Conrad Hébert. In winter he flooded his back yard and made a rink and brought out an extension light from the kitchen to hang over the rink and we used to go skating at night before going to bed. The hardest street fights were against the Liberty brothers on Friel street. They went to the Separate School in Anglesea Square, with the priests, the nuns, the girls in long black stockings and black tunics, the long crocodiles, the handbell clanging. And I went to the Public School, a block away. I remember when I was six being taken by my mother to the house of the boy I used to play with. He was drowned at Hog's Back. He lay on the dining-room table dressed in his Sunday dark suit, white velvet blouse, his face looking like the wax peaches in my mother's fruit dish. He was surrounded by heaps of real fruit on the table and coloured glasses with burning candles inside. Then during the early part of the war I read about Arcand and his gang going through the Montreal Ghetto one night smashing the store windows, fighting in the streets. Next morning on the side of Dain's grocery on the corner there was a large yellow swastika painted on the brick and beside it *Bas de Juif.*

One was always conscious of the religious barrier and the language. One's parents did not fraternize, and they didn't like it if the children did too much. In the long hot summer evenings the whole street sat on the veranda, on the steps, on the wooden benches, in the rocking chairs, hidden by the Morning Glories. Some spoke French, some Yiddish, a few English. Each veranda talking amongst itself and looking at the other verandas who were doing the same thing.

THE ANGLO-SCOTTISH ELITE

Walking down Peel in a light drizzle. Sun Life Building. Top shrouded in mist. Pigeons with their wings high, like Lysanders, glide down. I was to have dinner with M. (we had taken the same English courses at McGill) but I was early, it was only five past six, so I went into the Mount Royal to have a shoeshine and to kill time. The old man first put on some chemicals to take the dirt off. Then he scraped off the dirt. Then some alcohol. Then he dried that. Finally two coats of polish. I went upstairs and sat in the lobby. There was still a half-hour to wait. Soft orchestral music was piped in. People sat in red leather chairs reading a paper, a magazine, smoking, watching the revolving doors; the same kind of luggage was carried in and carried out. Across the room an anonymous sound of human voices drifted gently with the same indifference as the background music. Sometimes it was pierced by a bell-boy paging a name in that sing-song parody of a child's voice: 'Calling Philip Morris'; or one recognized a background tune. While the eye was continually pulled by small actions that flared up like a cheap firework but failed to burst: the man in uniform behind the desk angrily snapped his fingers; the front door revolved and in walked a tall girl with ash-blonde hair, a dark sun-tan on her face. She watched the eyes on her with complete indifference. A sign like a menu card said: 'Convention of Chemical Engineers . . . Dancing in the Normandie Roof.' A man with a glass eye holding a doll came to where the red chairs were and searched for someone who was not there. A telephone rang. A voice announced 'Trans-Canada Airlines Flight Number . . .'

I went out and walked to Sherbrooke. The drizzle continued. It was the kind of day I liked. The buildings grey and wet; the asphalt black and wet; and the neon of the traffic lights shining through the gloom.

On the corner of Sherbrooke and University a tall brick apartment building rose up against the sky like a box. It stood separate from the cheap café, the tourist rooms, the boarding-houses. On the bottom floor were the offices of doctors and dentists. It looked down the McGill campus.

M. and her mother and a French dressmaker were in the sit-, ting-room. The dressmaker was from Quebec and had come down to make a dress for M. I said that I was going to Quebec tomorrow. Did I know that M.'s father helped to design the centre piece of the Chateau Frontenac? They mentioned Scottish names on the Grande Alle. Then her mother and the dressmaker went out for dinner and M. mixed me a highball and we sat with candles and talked and looked out of the window over the Roddick Gates. The trees, the lawns, were black. McGill is so much part of her experience. I remember one time, going over our notes before an exam, looking out of the window (and seeing the nannies pushing the expensive prams underneath the trees, the young children running through the fallen leaves kicking them up as they ran). She said the first thing she could remember was being taken by her nannie out there. And now she described her father's funeral. How they stopped all traffic on Sherbrooke and how the hearse drove through the campus before going to the cemetery.

We sat with candles and dined on steak and asparagus and strawberries and cream and talked about what has happened since McGill (passing notes during lectures; going to Orme's and pressed together in the narrow cubicle, our raincoats wet, listening to the records of *Macbeth*); she had been engaged three times. The first one was an elder at her church, but he drank; the next two she did not love. 'I want somebody that's going somewhere, that I can push.'

M. is short, attractive, with a round Dutch-like face that makes her look like a schoolgirl. She looks astonishingly young for thirty. Did I know that T. committed suicide? Why? Nobody knows. He put all his affairs in order then shot himself. Maybe out of boredom. This one married an ambassador's son; another one, an international racing driver. J. has worked himself up so that his name is now on the door of the Aluminum Company. Did I see him in London? Yes. I saw him coming out of South Kensington tube station, the rolled umbrella, the bowler hat; he spoke with an immaculate English accent.

We went through the names, where they were, what had happened . . .

They were all much of a sameness. Not only have they inherited money but Puritanism and guilt as well. Their grandfathers came over as emigrants, a few were soldiers, clergymen; they worked hard and left their fortunes to their sons who made more and who 'served' the community as lawyers, doctors, professors, financiers, politicians, on hospital boards, charity drives, universities . . . but they left their children curiously drained. McGill; the few months travelling in Europe, afterwards, was their last fling. They returned 'home' and settled down and they suddenly seemed to have become old, as if they had finally buckled under that anonymous authority of a collective parent who always said: 'No. No.' Those who could went away. They were ashamed of being Canadian. They tried to take on the colouring of either the Americans they met at Murray Bay (who were a little like themselves) or went over to England and tried to fit in there. But they could not fit in anywhere except into the drab, empty, comfortable existence that they inherited and accepted. They stuck together, supporting one another by their own weaknesses, and wasted away. Whatever sense of high spirits they had as undergraduates—I remember W. chartering an airplane to fly him for a weekend with a girl he wanted to see in New York . . . R. staking the borrowed car, that he drove up in, on a throw of dice at a fraternity crap game . . . The punch from the bath . . . the end of an all-night party with the girls in evening dresses and bare feet playing against the boys in a game of softball on the lawn—was dampened by family authority, respectability, and responsibility to the group. One still followed the parents' footsteps to the cottage in the Laurentians in winter, Murray Bay or Tadoussac in summer. There was still St. Andrew's Ball, the Junior League, the game of golf, the charity drive. But they felt inferior to their parents' achievements, they looked ashamed most of the time as if they carried with them a family guilt, that they could not tell anyone, that was eating away from the inside.

*

Before taking the plane to Quebec I phoned up K., and he said he would meet me for lunch at the Mount Royal. He belongs to the same set that M. belongs to. He was one of the wealthiest young men at McGill. Whenever a girl was nice to him he immediately became suspicious that she was going after his money. When he married, the night before, at a stag, he became drunk and tore up dollar bills and threw them up in the air like the old man in *Ring Around the Moon*. He was now a director in an investment company. He helped people with money to invest in the right securities so that they could get the best returns for their money.

We talked about some of the old times (after a lecture in his Plymouth coupé doing ninety on the highway outside Montreal to his aunt's cottage with the antique Quebec furniture, the smell and sound of bacon frying in the large pan on the stove), about C. who was living in Tangier and was accidentally stabbed by a gang of Arabs and had a lung punctured. He wanted to know why we weren't here. But whatever I said, he wasn't convinced. We talked about business, and quickly got into an argument. I said that business was dishonest. He said that business was fundamentally honest. He had to believe in his argument, otherwise his whole life would be a lie; just as I had to believe in mine.

XII

QUEBEC CITY

THE FIRST time I was here was when I hitch-hiked from Ottawa with a schoolfriend. It was August in a hot summer. We had hitch-hiked several times to Montreal, now we wanted to go further. We went into a beer-parlour and had my first glass of beer. I didn't like it. I remember shaving with an electric razor that I received for my birthday. Going to the Plains of Abraham. seeing the statues of Wolfe and Montcalm. Staying in the Y.M.C.A. Taking pictures of the wall around the city; the gates to the streets; the statues; riding in a calèche.

The next time was during the war, waiting to go over to England. About two hundred officers were herded together in an old building right opposite a cigarette factory. It used to be a children's school; the steps were very wide and worn in the middle, but they rose only a few inches at a time.

We were sent to kill time and to learn to behave like officers. The first lot of Canadian fliers were considered too rough and too crude, and they could not allow this kind of representative to go over as a young Canadian officer. So that we pretended. We played at being officers. We took turns pretending we were orderly officers; putting men on charge; being entertainment officers, providing the escort for a military funeral. We were instructed how to use our knives and forks; how to make a toast; how to eat and drink properly. How to dress and behave in public. To see how we finally passed, the Air Force organized a large ball at the Chateau Frontenac and all the eligible debutantes were invited. And we went through that evening, dancing, making small talk, eating, passing the carafe of wine around; the dance band played:

> To you he might be just another guy,
> To me he means a million other things.
> An ordinary fellow with his heart up in the sky,
> He wears a pair of silver wings.

Air Marshals made speeches calling us 'Knights of the Air',
'Captains of the Clouds'; all of which we still believed at that
time.

*

No sooner did the airplane land at the deserted airport outside
Quebec City than the rain started and sheet lightning. Riding in
the taxi the two spires of a church were lit up, two fiery neon
crosses on top of each spire against the black sky. Every time
the lightning flashed, it showed the river in the distance and the
two spires with a golden statue of the Virgin in between. The car
radio was playing a Strauss waltz and the taxi-driver's wife, sitting beside her husband, was humming the tune. But then the
lightning would come and there would be only static, and the
rain pelting down on the taxi roof. By the time we came to the
entrance of the Chateau Frontenac the storm seemed to be
overhead. The other passengers entered the Chateau. I paid the
taxi-driver a dollar and ten cents, took my bag and typewriter
and walked away from the hotel, down the slope. I asked the
first man, who smelled as if he had just come out of a tavern,
where I could get a cheap room. He told me to go down some
steps further down as the hill turned. I followed the road. It was
pitch black. Every time the lightning flashed, it lit up the street
and a statue above me. I saw the stairs. They were wide, divided
into three sections by handrails. Another flash of lightning lit
up the steps; they were steep. At the bottom, opposite the steps,
a man was leaning inside a doorway of an antique shop, the
rain running down the glass. I walked down the steps, my raincoat buttoned tight at the neck, and asked the man if he knew
of a room near here. He said no. There was a hotel around the
corner, if I came in out of the rain he would ring up and save
me walking, maybe for nothing. I entered. A sign inside the
door said 'Studio'. I asked him if he painted. He said he didn't,
but would I like to see the studio while he phoned. He led me
through the antique store with its glass cases, brass and copper
pieces, bits of china, past a hallway with a curtain drawn. I
could see dishes from a finished meal on the table; and into a
back room. It was filled with unframed pictures of Quebec City.
In winter, in autumn, in the sunshine, at night, rain, snow; but
they all had the Chateau Frontenac as the subject. There was an
easel, a sofa, a small table with a large ashtray and several empty
packages of *Matinee* cigarettes in among the stubs. A television
set stood opposite the sofa, and more unframed pictures on the
floor and stacked against the wall. He told me the painter was a

Belgian who was now over in Europe. They sold his paintings to tourists. He told me to look around while he phoned. There were other scenes, picture postcards of Parisian cafès, sailing boats in a harbour, men and women sitting by round tables in nightclubs. He said that they had a room at four dollars and up. 'Is that too much?' I said it was. He suggested that I sit down, take off my coat, would I like a beer? He washed two dirty glasses and poured beer from a quart bottle. He talked about the young Belgian painter. I asked him how did he meet him. He said: 'How does one meet people?'

He filled up the glasses again with beer and offered me a cigarette and I told him where I came from. I asked him if he had a room. No. But he came back with a map and pointed out two streets. 'The Latin Quarter, mostly students live here. You should be able to get a room very cheap. You walk past the City Hall, past Kurhlus' (Yes, I said, I remembered Kurhlus from the time during the war) 'then turn to Garneau and Ferland streets.' I thanked him. He said he ran his shop for his wife. But she was at a political meeting of the Union Nationale. He did not like Duplessis. But he liked the fact that Quebec should remain Quebec. He showed me a poster that he was going to put outside. 'So you see what side we're on. Maybe you come across out west that the English and us don't get on here. We get on well. Let them come down and see. We get on well. This is an old part of the town. I guess we are Bohemian here. Where you are going they are mostly rooming houses for students.' He asked me what I did. I told him. He said his wife wrote poetry, and took down a pile of papers with short poems written in a handwriting which I could not read. I asked him if she sent any out to magazines. He said he did not know any in Canada.

He asked me if I liked French books. I said I did. I asked if he liked Lemelin. 'He is all right, I guess. But the English make more fuss about him than we do.' He hesitated, groping for the right English words. A small spare man, narrow shoulders, a sallow face; he looked ill. 'He is a chronicler, not very important, not much away from—how you call it—gossip. It is a novelty for you about French life, but to us it is not so good. He keeps to the surface, appearance only. He don't go down below.'

We drank another bottle of beer, and I had dried out sufficiently to start back again. He offered me a ticket to take the elevator up instead of walking the steps. I said I preferred the steps. He said he liked them better than the elevator, but maybe on a night like this . . . I thanked him, took the envelope with the directions and the names of Garneau and Ferland and walked out into the heavy rain.

It suddenly became melodramatic. One felt one was odd man out, and strangely happy. There was no one else around. The rain kept coming down, black. The steps were black. The sky was black except when the lightning flashed. I buttoned up, put the collar up and walked with my typewriter and bag back up the hill, by the City Hall, the statues in the square, the churches, store buildings, passed Kurhlus with serviettes and tomorrow's menu framed in the window, a cinema deserted, the empty sidewalk, water rushing down it and the road.

Off the main street, the street lights were out and I could only see the names of the streets by the lightning flashes. By the time I found Garneau I was sweating and wet. I saw a *Chambre à Louer* sign in the first house. I rang the bell and waited. The house was dark. I rang again. The woman who finally came to the door said that she let only for long lets and not for short ones. I tried the next house, also a *Chambre à Louer* sign. The woman left her television set to tell me the same thing. I tried about a dozen houses on that dark narrow street—doors flush to the sidewalk, the street on a slope, dipping down then straightening out before ending in the river—but they all said the same thing. I returned to the start of the street, not a light on anywhere. The rain had soaked through my raincoat and I could feel the bottoms of my trousers, that I had rolled up, wet against my legs. The lightning and the thunder continued. Every time a flash came, it lit up the empty street into an ashen colour.

It was getting late. My watch said twenty past ten and I knew I had to find a room soon. I decided to try the street next to Garneau. The same dark narrow street with the narrow sidewalks and the thick telegraph poles carrying overhead wires sprouting from the sidewalks. All the windows were black. And each dark house had a *Chambre à Louer* sign, in a window, behind the door, peeling on the wall; but I had no luck here either. I decided to try a street running at right angles, Couillard. At the first *Chambre à Louer*, a man came out, a young round face, crew cut, a green plaid shirt. He had left a darkened room that had the door open and I could see several people sitting around the small television screen. I asked, in French, for a room. He called his wife. They debated. How long did I want it? I said I did not know, perhaps a week. They had a huddle. He said two dollars a night. I said that was all right and paid for four days in advance.

The room was on the first floor, up carpeted steps, the large brass vase with dried pussy-willows, the toilet, the bathroom, not a sound in the house; only a sweet musty smell, and silence, as if it was occupied by old people.

I quickly undressed, I was soaked through. I washed, changed, and then I went back into the rain to find somewhere to eat. I walked towards the centre of the city and found a restaurant open, one of those standard horseshoe counters in the centre of a large room. I had an egg sandwich, French fried potatoes, and coffee. Music and static were coming from a small radio above the door to the kitchen. I was the only customer. The waitress, a young plump French girl with large breasts, tried out her English on me and I stuck to the French. She said in English, 'You speak French good'; and I lied right back to her and said she spoke English good. A priest came in and sat down beside me and had some coffee, lit a cigarette, and flirted with the waitress. The radio played a tango. Other people came in, women, to have some coffee, to get out of the rain. I bought an English paper from the steel rack by the counter. It was filled with pictures of the various candidates for the coming provincial elections, like a series of postage stamps. A half-page advertisement: *Duplessis has built 1,510 bridges from Gaspe to La Sarre*. A picture of a small concrete bridge over a narrow river with the French-Canadian village church, the shiny tin steeple on top of the gabled roof visible above the trees. The Queen was going to Russia, rumour said. There were sixteen deaths in Montreal over the weekend. 'Hooligans beat up police in Montreal. Six held down a policeman while the others kicked him in the face and body.' There were more fires across the country. In Woodstock, Ontario, a sixteen-year-old boy was killed. ' "He was fooling with the gun," Gillingwater said, "and suggested, 'How about a game of roulette?' I thought he was kidding," said Gillingwater. Desmond then showed him a shell in his hand and said the gun wasn't loaded. "He fooled around with it some more and pulled the trigger three or four times. I didn't know where the bullet was at the time, but there was only one bullet. I told him that people get hurt that way and quit fooling around. He put the gun to his temple and pulled the trigger." Police are trying to locate the youth's parents, with whom he lived, who are vacationing in Florida.'

I had another cup of coffee. So did the priest. Over the radio a girl was singing:

Q

Il me dit les mots d'amour,
Des mots de tous les jours,
Et ça m'fait quelque chose.

The waitress came back and tried out some more English words; the priest offered me a cigarette, gave one to the waitress, she put it in the pocket of her apron and said she would save it for when she came off work. We talked about the weather. I watched the water sliding down the glass of the restaurant over the sign : PATATES FRITES. I felt tired. I returned to my room. The storm had passed, sometimes in the black sky a flicker of light like that of a shutter, and no thunder, only the rain coming down steadily. I opened the window and closed the shutter, and undressed. Hanging on the wall above my head were two small paintings of thatched English cottages, 'Glorious Devon'; the neat hedge, flowers on the sides, the large chimney. There was 'a sick sweet smell of deodorant in the room, and a yellow paper package of it hung from the toothbrush holder above the sink. In the distance I could hear a railway engine shunting and its bell; the sound of a ship's horn; a church clock striking midnight; and the rain beating down.

*

I was awakened next morning by a pneumatic drill working outside and the sound of children's voices. The rain had stopped. And when I pulled the shutters open I could see men breaking up the road and children playing ball in the narrow street by a greystone building that looked like a school. I went out for breakfast. There was that fresh smell in the streets as there is after a long rain. But the place was empty. I went into the restaurant. It was empty. There was a different waitress, and an old woman washing the floor with a mop. Over the radio a French soap-opera was playing.

I walked around the empty grey streets—plain wooden houses flush to the sidewalk, unpainted telegraph poles carrying overhead wires, *Chambre à Louer* signs, numbers 1, 1 1/4, 1 1/2, 2; they sloped down to the edge of the rock, to the steps, Lower Town, and the river. At their other end they went up to the monuments, the white grey stones of the Basilica, the Place D'Armes, the convents, the hospitals, the churches, the Chateau Frontenac. It had the slowness, the dignity, of an old university town. Everything seemed close together, jumbled up, rarely level; you didn't have to go very far to get anywhere. But there was a deadness, a coldness about it all. Few people walking. Few cars. The calèches with their horses waiting for the tourists. And the white, grey, black, of the stones, the monuments . . . It reminded me of a well-kept cemetery.

The world is arranged
The dead below
The living above.

I walked down St. Jean, down the slope and steps, to Lower Town. Here was something one could understand. The narrow pokey streets (leading off the two main streets like a cross) with the shabbily dressed men and women, the children playing street games, trucks parked on the sidewalk to let the traffic go by. Horses pulled milk wagons, bakery wagons. The cheap stores, the bargain-clothes hung out, the drab restaurants, the religious bookstores. An alligator of schoolgirls went by along the sidewalk with two nuns behind. A church bell tolled. A high grey-stone convent. Men doffed their hats to priests. But even here though it was 'working-life' and it throbbed, there was still something of that white and grey coldness about it. Much of it was flat. Few trees or grass. The river and the side of the rock were not far away. It was unlike any other place in Canada. It was Catholic, seedy, poor.

I went into a small restaurant for lunch. It looked dirty outside. Inside small wooden chairs, by wooden tables. Clean white-and-red square tablecloths. The meal was cheap but not very good. *Pâté chinois* was some minced meat in with potatoes that did not have much taste. On the table by the cash register was a glass jar of pickled eggs in a yellowish green water. A small radio beside them played popular English songs with French words.

I decided to economize again by not eating in restaurants and I tried to find the market. I asked a priest. He turned out to be an English divinity student from Newfoundland, who had two more years before he was ordained, but he said they all had to wear black. He was going back to Newfoundland for the rest of the summer, where he returned every year for his holiday, servicing the airplanes on the transatlantic run. He told me where the market was, across the railway tracks, by the river, but there were only a few farmers selling flowers and potatoes.

It was the end of May, but it was cold. All the houses still had their large double windows up. Rain in the potholes and the hollows of the road. Baby ducks in a window, a huddle of yellow;

in another, baby chickens. A man came out with cardboard box and chirping followed down the grey street.

I decided to do a pub crawl. I went into a beer-parlour. There were only a few men inside, silent. Pickled eggs, very white, in another large glass jar with that yellow green liquid. A sign said 'Smoked Herring, 5 cents'. I put up two fingers and two draught beers were brought. A salt shaker on each table. I had a slice of the smoked herring. It was salty and delicious. There was no need to salt the beer.

Two houses past this beer-parlour was another. No customers. It was five minutes to two. A radio was on loud and a political speech was being broadcast. Again the jar of pickled eggs. A large glass mirror on the wall reflected the two miniature moose carved out of wood, like two book-ends, facing each other on either end of the counter. Cigars in boxes, potato chips, and overturned glasses. Two men came in. The man on the radio was saying that Newfoundland received forty-five cents a ton for its iron. Central America seventy-five cents a ton. But the government of Quebec received only one cent a ton from the U.S. firm that was exploiting it . . . and the man behind the counter switched it off. Two large calendars on the wall had outdoor fishing scenes, all the Fridays had red fish through them. A couple of large arched trout were mounted on both sides of the mirror. More men entered and sat down by the wooden tables and salted their beer. They were all poorly dressed, but they had good manners. One came in wearing a heavy black lumberjack windbreaker. He ordered two glasses. He had a small fair moustache and a round fat face and looked like a farmer. He took out a large leather purse and brought out twenty-five cents and rolled a cigarette and offered me one. We drank beer and discussed the virtues of putting salt or pepper in one's glass. The gadget on the door, that kept it from slamming, was not working. The man behind the counter took off his trouser belt and hooked one end to the door, the other to the transom.

I went into half a dozen beer parlours and each one was much the same: the plain salt and pepper shakers on the tables, the jar of pickled eggs, the dummy stag mounted on the wall with the name of the brewer underneath. In 'Chat Blanc', the place looked gay, the round mirror on the wall was lit with a neon border, but we sat and drank in silence, and watched television. It was depressing.

I returned to the Chateau Frontenac to see if there was any

mail (as my letters were being forwarded on to there) but there wasn't. The staff spoke English; the tourists were middle-aged Americans and they looked very much at home. Outside, the square around a statue, the calèches by the sidewalk, horses with feeding sacks around their heads, and the small drivers waiting.

I walked by the Chateau along the wooden walk of Dufferin Terrace. There was the St. Lawrence below, Levis across the river where we used to walk and run on those cold winter route marches. Two squat ferry boats were crossing each other in midstream. On the benches of the walk people sat taking in the sun. It was very slow and relaxed and silent. Freighters passed by, logs piled on the decks. Old cannons behind me on the grass pointed to the river, and further ahead was the citadel. Children went by with their nannies, a woman in a fur coat with a grey poodle, tourists with cameras. There was no hurry. One was here to relax. The sun shone but there wasn't much warmth in it. Students, boys and girls on the benches, books open, more interested in each other. The walk was wide and it had small wooden umbrella shelters, a flagpole on top of each one. Beside the one where I was sitting a workman was fixing the roof and singing an old French song. Nothing seemed in a hurry. As if its survival lay in its refusal to change. It had not changed much from what I remembered thirteen years ago; nor had it changed from what Henry James wrote about it eighty-five years ago: 'You strive almost vainly to picture the life of this French society, locked up in its small dead capital, isolated on a heedless continent, and gradually consuming its principal, as one may say—its vital stock of memories, traditions, superstitions. Its evenings must be as dull as the evenings described by Balzac in his *Vie de Province* . . . Does it play loto and "Boston" in the long winter nights, and arrange marriages between its sons and daughters, whose education it had confided to abbés and abbesses? . . . Something assures one that Quebec must be a city of gossip; for evidently it is not a city of culture. A glance at the few booksellers' windows gives evidence of this . . .'

That night I lay awake and read some of the poems of Anne Hébert. I had picked up a secondhand copy in a religious bookstore in Lower Town. They had mainly religious tracts and expensive well-illustrated children's books from France. I had read a few poems of hers before and I had pictured someone lonely, isolated, making poetry out of this isolation and provincialism. I had not, until now, realized how close her poetry, personal as it is, is rooted in this place; in the dryness, the sterility, that she celebrates.

> I will give you little towns,
> Sad tiny little towns.
>
> The little towns in our hands
> Are more stern than toys
> But as easy to handle.
>
> I play with the little towns.
> I topple them over.
> Not a man escapes,
> Not a flower, not a child.
>
> The little towns are empty
> And delivered into our hands.
>
> I listen, my ear against the doors.
> I bring all the doors, one by one,
> Close to my ear.
>
> The houses are like silent shells
> Which keep in their frozen spirals
> No rumour of wind,
> No rumour of water.
>
> The parks and the gardens are dead,
> The games lined up
> As if in a museum.
>
> I do not know where they have put
> The frozen bodies of the birds. *

BIOGRAPHY

Next morning I slept in, and by the time I went to the restaurant for toast and coffee it was after ten. There was an Englishman sitting by the counter a few stools away. He was in his late fifties, a handsome full face, but it had become soft and flabby; when he removed his sun glasses there were folds of skin underneath his eyes. He asked me how long I had been here. I said two days. 'It's got atmosphere. Have you seen the churches?' No. He said he had seen twenty-seven churches, 'just French churches'. And he drew out a notebook in a neat schoolboy script; a few sentences, a description of the church, its history, who was buried in it, and a simple sketch of how it looked from the outside.

    We went out and walked towards the Chateau. I wanted to see if any letters had arrived. He knew every statue that we

* Translation by Gael Turnbull.

passed. 'This one is Champlain . . . that's Bishop Laval . . . that's
the Golden Dog . . . have you been inside the Basilica . . . ?' He
lived in Brighton, and he was in religious goods. His wife had
died recently and he was advised to go on a trip. He had been
away six weeks travelling in New England and Eastern Canada,
combining business with sightseeing. He was making notes because he intended to write up this trip for the local paper. But
now he was impatient to get back. 'I have a large cactus growing
in the back garden. It flowers only once in sixteen years and then
it dies. I've had it for eleven years, and the previous owner of
the house said it was five years old when I bought it. Wouldn't
it be my luck to have nursed that thing along waiting for it to
flower these last few years—and then to miss it?'

I thought I could see the detached house on the side of a hill
with the names like: 'Won-o-ate', 'Ayetene', 'Bo-peep'; the pixies
in the front rock-garden with the legs in blue and the red jesters'
caps sitting underneath the stone mushrooms; the high hedge;
the car; golf in the afternoon; TV in the evening; the front curtains drawn in the morning to keep the sun out; the large garden
in the back with the greenhouse, the flowerbeds and vegetables.
I had him down for a character that I would use—but I was
wrong.

There were no letters at the Chateau. We walked along
Dufferin Terrace. It was cool, the sun was out, a workman was
fixing one of those umbrella shelters alongside the rails, singing
'Envois, Envois, ma petite tu vous'.

He said he was a bank manager in India until 1945. 'A third
generation kind of English expatriate. We came home every
eighteen months, but the children had no home. We had to send
them away because in the heat, in the tropical countries, they
mature too quickly, and you're in for trouble. It's better to send
them to a northern country to school.' His time was almost up
when he got malaria and he and his wife came back, bought a
house in Brighton. 'But after the kind of life we had in India,
England was very dull.' He wondered if it was worth it. His two
sons were offered good positions in Malaya and Singapore, but
they turned them down for lesser jobs in England. 'They said
they were tired of not belonging anywhere.' For something to
do he started a small business selling religious goods. He imported the crosses and the figures from the Continent; 'Germany
make the best crucifixes . . . wonderful figures.' And then he
had them mounted, polished up and sold to the religious stores
and private churches.

We decided to have lunch together. He thought it would be better in Lower Town, here it was too commercial. We took the elevator down and walked through the narrow empty streets, deserted, except for other tourists. We were by the waterfront. Children on tricycles, playing ball, pushing with one foot small wooden wagons. Loose papers clogged the street, old magazines, bills. Washing hung across the width of the street. And I could see the steps that I had come down that first night. The backs of houses, fire-escapes, and the squeals of children. Warehouses were on one side of the street, houses were on the other. Children played ball, skipped, hopscotched. It was dark down the streets, there was no grass, just asphalt, but it was safe; the only cars that came down were the large trucks, a few calèches, or a large American car. The Englishman kept on saying, 'Look inside the restaurants. If you see natives in there then you know it's all right.' We went into one. It was empty except for a couple of men in working clothes drinking Cokes. We had pea soup but is was cold and watery. The beef stew was tasteless and full of gristle, the turnips and the carrots looked the same pale dull grey as the meat. And the pie for dessert had very little apple, mainly a thick wet pastry. We went out annoyed. 'That was robbery,' he said. 'It was too small. These small places are out to rook you.' He said he knew a better place and we agreed to meet the next day at the restaurant where we met for coffee then go on for lunch. I walked him back to his hotel, the Louis XIV, at one side of a small square by the base of the rock. Before we said goodbye (he was off on a conducted tour in a half-hour's time to St. Anne de Beaupre) he said that Notre Dame de Victoires was on the other side of the square and he wanted me to see it.

It looked like a shed, a dull maroon outside, a tall sloping tower. We went in. There were six people inside walking around, all unmistakable tourists. 'I always come into a church and just sit in the back for a few minutes,' he said. So we went to the very back and sat in a pew. An old man in an old coat, working clothes, grey hair, came in to worship. He dipped his finger into the font, crossed himself, and knelt in a pew, and prayed. The tourists looked around at the altar, pointed at the red lights, they talked, they took photographs of the stations of the cross. The place glittered in bright blues, reds, whites and golds. The old man kneeling down was moving his rosary. Then he crossed himself, stood up, put his cap back on, dipped his finger in the water, wiped his forehead with a handkerchief and went out, a look of contempt at the others inside.

The Englishman led me to a side chapel. To a plaster statue of Christ, full length, lying down on His sepulchre, a wound in His chest open, showing red, all enclosed in a glass case. 'A wonderful figure,' he said. Then he showed me a small wooden carving of a monk with a wooden cross and behind him a book with a skull on it . . . a glass cross with a small golden Christ. 'A wonderful figure.' He explained the different figures. 'Some like them with the arms straight, others up; some want the legs uncrossed, others the right foot over the left, or left over right. But what doesn't go today is the one showing real suffering . . . it's a wonderful figure . . . the head is turned into the arm, he's all hunched up in agony . . . but it doesn't sell.'

I was glad to get out of the church and into the fresh air. He went to his hotel. I walked to the river. The ferry had just started to go over to the Levis shore. The river here wasn't very wide. It was muddy brown. There was little noise, as if the sound track was removed. I could hear someone hammering, and in the distance a car changed gears. A few seagulls, young birds (their feathers not yet the white grey blue, but a dark brown) flew over. A small boat with logs of wood piled like matches on top of its deck came by silently. The light purple hills in a haze on the far side. I sat on the wood and watched the gulls mewing, the boats passing slowly, and the water made a soft insistent sound as it slapped against the wood.

From there I began to walk back towards the city. I went into the nearest beer-parlour. A television set was showing how women can make their own clothes, in French. Men in windbreakers, overalls, heavy boots, spat on the ground, drank, and watched the television. A sign on the wall:

NOTICE	AVIS
Forbidden to swear, whistle, sleep, sing, pull wrist, in this tavern by the order of The Chief of Police	Defense de Blasphemer, Siffler, Dormir, Chanter, Tirer au Poignet, par ordre Chef de Police

A small boy came in and asked everyone if they wanted a paper, then he hung around watching a young girl in a slip explain how it was made, until one of the beer waiters rushed over and chased him out. The tavern had swinging half-doors, as in all the Western movies. Another boy entered shouting 'Soleil! Soleil!'

*

I was hungry and went into another cheap restaurant to have something to eat, but again the food wasn't very good. I walked by the waterfront towards the main section of Lower Town, by the railway tracks, when I saw bits of smoke coming from the sides of a large building. It seemed to be breathing smoke out from its seams. A few minutes later a fire engine came. A policeman smashed the door, went inside, but came out quickly, as the smoke in thick black gusts seeped out and rose like a cumulus cloud. Firemen smashed the bottom windows with axes and from each one the thick smoke that was inside swirled out. They soon had hoses going. Windows were smashed on the next three floors by the force of the water, and black and brown smoke enveloped the whole building.

It became an inferno. Hoses were all over the ground like so many snakes, more engines came. The water that was poured into the windows came down the stairs like a waterfall. Now you caught the sight of flames at the centre of the black, then they were hidden by the smoke. More hoses, more long arrows of white forced upwards to the building and the water cascading down the front steps churning in a froth. A large crowd gathered, police roped off the area. It had become cold.

Then something extraordinary happened. Two small birds, they looked like sparrows, suddenly appeared above the roof. They flew in to the smoke and went in under the edge of the roof. A rainbow appeared by the building over the water that the hoses were pushing in. It seemed fantastic. A rainbow, the birds, the force of white punching in the arrows, the billows of thick black smoke, and the sky lit up in greens and scarlet, as the sun was setting. There was something horrible yet terribly beautiful about it all. Ladders were pushed automatically up from another ladder, a fireman climbed it carrying a hose, photographers went in closer and kept taking pictures. Then the bricks began to fall as the water from the hoses played on the roof, ripping off the ornamental top of the building. Water was going in from the side and back windows, and coming out of the front. The windows were all black. Everything looked black; sometimes a fiery glow, a small red eye, stared out from the inside. The sky remained a light blue. The wind was cold. It was now eight, and the fire had been going on for three hours without showing any signs of easing up. A rainbow continued to appear in front of the building. Twelve hoses kept punishing the front and there were others on either side. The sound of the water was louder than a wave breaking. The crowd was quiet.

Priests were there, and nuns. People drove up in cars to see it. The wind had carried the smoke across Lower Town like a sign.

I returned next day to the fire. The smell of burning wood reached me long before I came near the building. During the night it had fallen below zero and the building was a frozen shell of ice. There were icicles everywhere: from black pimpled pieces of wood; from ripped pieces of tin hanging like newspapers; a staircase dangled in space like an accordion, swaying silently in the wind, the wood covered in ice. Icicles had boarded up the windows, they hung down from the sills. Down the front steps, where the water had poured out, there was a thick, solid, slab of ice.

The sun was shining on a side of the building and there the thaw had started. A pipe was burst and the water trickled up and curved down like a toy fountain as it fell to the floor. The ice on the floor was thawing slowly, it cracked into large pieces, like broken pieces of glass. It was grotesque. The ice, the frost, the cold, had made motionless and tidy all the debris, and now it started to be released. Pieces of a wall, of wood, of stairs, floated in it. Adding machines lay on their sides the key faces burned off; boilers, boxes, bits of machinery, tin trunks. It had been a warehouse storing luggage on the ground floor and television sets on the others. Now all that remained was a black hollow shell with swaying, dangling pieces of wood, tin, and hundreds of icicles dripping down. A policeman stood inside in the middle of all this on a wooden plank to keep his feet out of the water and to prevent looting.

I walked to the restaurant to meet the Englishman. He wasn't there. The waitress gave me an envelope. There was an American five-dollar bill inside, a card with his name and Brighton address and phone number. 'Sorry about lunch. Have it on me. Chance to get passage back from N.Y. Had to leave this a.m. Come and see my cactus[1]—if it's still there.' I felt disappointed. Had a couple of western sandwiches in the restaurant and several cups of coffee. Then I called at the Chateau, still no letters. I was expecting to hear about my passage and about some money to pay for it. There was nothing to do but wait until the evening delivery.

[1] He came back in time. The cactus flowered the following summer (like a huge green banana with several skins peeled back and the centre part forced out like a telegraph-pole for about twenty feet in the air—red flower on top). He died three months later.

252 CANADA MADE ME

I walked around the ramparts; cannons and cars were there.
Down a small deserted side street, smell of cooked cabbage. I
saw a sign *Musée Historique* and went in.

The admission was a dollar which I thought expensive—
and a sign said to go upstairs. It was a house. A notice said a
record in French and English would explain the exhibits. I went
up and the record began. I was the only customer. It first said
welcome and what fine specimens these were and what great
artists they were who thought it up and that all the figures I
would see were life size and they all had natural hair.

They were in glass cases, except for the first one that showed
Columbus trying to convince Isabella. The next one had the
Mayflower, and there was a mother breast-feeding a child. The
martyrdom of Dollard at Long-Sault spared nothing, the angelic
severed head stuck up on a stake, the daggers entering the
Indians, the blood. Wolfe was shown writing a letter; Montcalm
dying a hero's death. Then a special case showed French-
Canadian soldiers, mouths open, leaping over the top of a trench
about to bayonet the German soldiers caught on the other side.
The next floor was devoted only to 'Great Men'. Edison, Curie,
Bell, Einstein, Paderewski, Toscanini, were jumbled in one case.
Next was Mackenzie King, Roosevelt and Churchill at the
Quebec Conference. In one glass case was Field Marshall Mont-
gomery, another of Cardinal Villeneuve, then the Pope. And
the very last glass cage had, as the record repeated in two lan-
guages, 'the greatest man, the great car builder, Henry Ford'.

If you followed the record it did not allow you to look at
things but kept you moving along. Of course the whole thing
was a big swindle; it was provincial. I felt cheated and walked
out angry.

I decided to go down to the antique store and see if my friend
was there. He wasn't, but his wife was. A short, plump woman.
She showed me around the store. From the window I could see
those steps that I came down the first night. I asked her if they
shot the Hitchcock film *I Confess* from near here. 'Yes, right
from the doorway,' she said. 'I hate those steps, they make me
sick. The drunks come down, especially in winter. And I get sick
every time. I thought now I am cured. But no, a couple of weeks
ago someone goes plunk and tumble down. I watch and I get
sick like a dog.'

The bell above the door jangled. Some Americans came in.
The men with high-trousers, flannels, in their fifties, with that
boyish fat face, crew cut, and the movie camera slung over their

shoulders. They looked around. They asked about prices. They whispered amongst themselves. They offered a quarter of what she asked. She refused. Children were outside waiting by the window and when the men came out the children surrounded them. One man handed out coins to the children and smiled while the other took a movie of it. 'They think we are still the backwoods' the antique woman said indignantly. 'They come here expecting bargains; that they will pick up something cheap, because we are ignorant.' A priest came down the stairs, the wind lifted his habit. Two women entered the store and looked around. 'Did this vase come from my sister's house?' The antique woman said she did not know. 'I'm sure it must have come from her house, because I've got the other.' I left them arguing.

Outside in the narrow street a young boy came running out from a door, his mouth still chewing food. He put his hand out.

'Mister, five cents. Mister, five cents . . .'

I refused to give him any. He continued to jig alongside, his food had now been swallowed so that he just grinned confidently and kept repeating: 'Mister, five cents . . . C'mon give me, Mister, five cents . . .' He followed me to the river like a dog jumping up and then suddenly ran away to a woman with a camera.

There was a restaurant built on wooden logs at the water's edge. I went inside and had another cup of coffee. It was large, clean, empty. The waitresses were bored; they stood behind the cashier's desk staring out to the water. The cashier played a game. She followed with binoculars every ship that went by and called out its country or origin. If she did not know the markings she consulted a book beside her.

I tried to find a political meeting but there wasn't one. It was all being done by radio and television except in the country villages. I went along Ferland and Garneau and Couillard. Grey, blue, emptiness. Nobody in the street. Telegraph poles stuck up in the sidewalk. There was no sign of life. Large double windows. I felt I was continually walking by large houses with empty rooms. It was cold again. I bought some groceries in a shabby store on Couillard and brought them back to my room and ate. I still had an hour before the mail would be in at the Chateau Frontenac.

I went out and walked to the river again. I saw two young girls in black windbreakers and blue kerchiefs go down a steep turning hill on bicycles. As far as I could see, it led right into

the rock. I followed them and came to a narrow alley with a
large clean nameplate SOUS LES CAP. On one side of the alley
were wooden outhouses flush with the rock that sheered upwards
to Hautville. On the other side were the dilapidated backs of
wooden houses showing the kitchens with connecting wooden
bridges between the house and outhouse. The wooden bridges:
it was like walking under a lot of trestles with pieces of sky
breaking through the spaces. In the kitchens newspaper hung
on the walls, iron stoves with the fat stovepipes going along the
ceiling. Children played softball in the alley. The ball was a
cheap piece of battered rubber, the bat an old leg of a chair,
home plate a flattened tin can, there was only one base and
that was a brick. Other kids rolled old car tyres. Small mongrel
dogs, rubbish piled high, newspapers torn, washing hung underneath the wooden bridges. I turned at the end of the alley from
the backs of these houses to their fronts and there were, across
the road, large stone bank buildings: Imperial Bank of Canada;
Toronto Dominion . . . You would never know the mess that was
behind from walking along the sidewalk by the small grocery
stores, the banks, the houses with the plain grey fronts.

Back to the Chateau; no letters. I decided to return to Montreal tomorrow. My flying pass was finished and I went down
to Lower Town and bought a ticket on an Express bus. A car-
penter was nailing boards to the windows of the burned-out
building; a policeman still stood there. At the main intersection
men dressed as bell-hops and commissionaires were selling tags.
I walked back up Couronne, passed the beer-parlours that I had
drunk in during the day, by the faded mural posters along the
sides of the slope showing Quebec history. There was a small
snack bar open. I had a couple of hamburgers and coffee. The
small radio on the counter; the glass jar of pickled eggs. Two
men in leather windbreakers were drinking Cokes and talking
about the wrestling they had seen on television. At another
round wooden table two old men were playing dominoes.

Outside it war dark and cold. Lower Town had only a few
lights. But the Chateau Frontenac was brilliantly lit up. A train
wailed in the distance, those two deep melancholy notes. I was
again alone in the street. By the statue of an Archbishop, down
the slope to Garneau. Empty, dark, deserted. And it was only
10 p.m. Down Ferland, also dark, newspapers and loose straw
and cold fried potatoes on the road. All the houses were dark,
locked up for the night. And the emptiness and the cold
soaked right through. I returned to the house where I was

staying and had a hot bath and felt better. I took out my notebook ('Quebec is all steps and, at the bottom of the steps, poverty') and wondered if I was sorry or glad to leave Quebec. I didn't know. But unlike the rest of Canada, where the places seemed to be just part of the same thing; this was different. But the price it paid for clinging to it. And I wondered if it was so strange that the two places in the country that tried to go against the grain were both at the ends: the provincial English in Victoria and the provincial French in Quebec. I imagine, not long from now, people will come here to see this as something out of a museum, a museum piece, when the rest of the country has been swallowed up into a sameness.

I thought of Leo pretending he had a guitar; the man in the torn jeans, I wish I was somebody; Mr. McKay waiting for his gear to turn up . . . Do I look good to you, tell me? I've got a car . . . If You're So Smart Why Ain't You Rich? I wondered why I was attracted to the failures, to the seedy, to the new-comers who could not fit in. They appealed to me far more than the Babbits on Main Street or the dull Anglo-Scotch or the immigrants who were quickly corrupted.

I had gone looking for some photographs to illustrate this book. But I could not find anything like what I saw. Canada was busy selling. Places like Fort William, Port Arthur, were only represented by photographs of grain ships and grain elevators. Ottawa had the Peace Tower, the War Memorial, the miniature Japanese Garden along the Driveway, a snow scene in Rockliffe. Winnipeg, the width of Portage Avenue. Vancouver, the Lions, Burrard Inlet, sunsets by Stanley Park . . . In selling one puts the best thing on top, what the customer wants to buy. It was landscape, machinery; it was 'a way of life' that showed large cars, gadgets, comfort, good food. It's poetry was in the advertisements and statistics. They were like the photographs that one takes from a height, where depth is eliminated, where the cracks are covered up, just showing Nature, landscape, machinery, statistics; but hidden away somewhere underneath was the human being.

'DON'T WORRY, YOU'LL NEVER LEAVE THIS WORLD ALIVE'

I returned to Montreal by bus feeling anxious and depressed. And now looking back I cannot understand why. For I con-tinually kept meeting people I had known; there were the chance

encounters with strangers; I would go often to the Classic Bookshop on St. Catherine and browse around . . . I cannot remember
why everything at the time seemed particularly hectic. Perhaps
it was my anxiety over money again. The only cheap passage
available was on the same line I had come across, and I had to
raise the passage money quickly. It meant going around, telephoning, sending letters, being taken out by people that one
knew; before the evening was over I would have to ask—'Can
you lend me . . .?' But my luck held. I was able to get my ticket
and forget about money for a while.

The place was hot and sticky. Men walked around in shirt
sleeves, girls in summer dresses, streetcars clattered by with
their windows open. On the side of the mountain across from
Fletcher's Field, bodies lay on the grass sunbathing. I went down
to St. Lawrence and picked up my new suit. It was very comfortable and cool and fitted well. The tailor from England
beamed. He was a large man, going bald; his lower lip jutted
out, his top lip was a fine line across. He had a picture of himself and the Duke of Edinburgh holding a piece of cloth. There
were others in the photograph but they had been blocked out.
The owner came in. 'You look like a million dollars,' he said.
But he did not like the blue shirt I was wearing nor the dark
blue tie and he sent out an office boy to 'get something smarter'.
I left his office all dressed up and feeling comfortable and cool
and gay. And as I walked down to St. Catherine I walked across
plate glass windows of the men's clothing stores with the dum-
mies wearing suits similar to the one I had on, they were framed
like oil paintings and beside them were small cards: 'California
inspired. New classic notch with 90 degree opening, new neater
slimline lapels, a lower waistline, straighter fronts, free easy
centre vent. Open a charge account. 26 weeks to pay. 26 *semaines
pour payer.*'

On St. Catherine East the restaurants and stores had French
names. I went into one and had a couple of fat smoked-meat
sandwiches and a cup of coffee. The waitress was French, the
records piped in were French, but they still served smoked meat.
How often during those first two years in London, in a pub,
especially on the wet, cold winter evening sitting by the coal
fire, drinking bitter and eating a dry roast-beef sandwich did I
think back longingly to Montreal. There would be snow. And
then going into a warm delicatessen and having smoked meat
in slices on a plate or thick in rye-bread sandwiches. Smoked
meat belongs here, to the European, cosmopolitan part of North

America. I did not find very much of it out west or on the
Pacific Coast. The salt beef that one gets in London, in the
Nosh-bars opposite the Windmill Theatre, is tasteless compared
to smoked meat. But like all good food it has deteriorated. It
costs more and the meat is no longer smoked. They still soak it
in the large wooden vats with brine and spices. Then hung up
on large hooks—all that was left of one's fishing worm after
the fish had bitten off the part that wriggled—in a room that
is like a low-burning oven, and are slowly done by the heat. Until
the hide turns a dark mahogany, as if it was covered in warts.

Outside, by a Laura Secord store in the centre of all those
candy boxes was a large framed card:

> More things are wrought by prayer
> Than this world dreams of.
> TENNYSON

A trinket store. 'Miss Germany dances when she sees herself in
the mirror.' Playing cards of nude women. Burnt-out signs in
wood. 'If you fight with wife all day you won't have peace at
night.' The luminous musical altar with a glass cross and the
figures of the Last Supper: (Please Do Not Overwind Me).
Totem Poles. Indian heads hollowed into the shape of mugs.
Pillow covers with Mounties, Maple Leafs and Montreal embroidered on them.

Until I had been away I did not notice the worship there is for
personal publicity and amateur advertisements. You would think
that underneath each one here was the secret wish to be a copy-
writer.

There was a half-page add in the *Star* to advertise secondhand
cars. A car lot is one of the dullest sights imaginable: it occupied
the centre of the ad. Around the borders, like a graduation
photograph, were the heads and shoulders 'of the boys': Les,
Dick, Robert, Marcelle, 'The Boss' . . . or if you came from a
smaller town you went to Montreal for an exciting bang-up time
and you visited the newspaper store on Peel and St. Catherine
and for a dollar they would give you a front page of a dummy
paper with your own headline, BUNNY BRILL HITS MONTREAL,
thick and large and black, while underneath were details of a
murder, a fire, a robbery, to make it look real.

I went into the *System* where you could always see three full-
length pictures cheaply, where you could bring your lunch,
where I used to go whenever I wanted to skip lectures. People
asleep, people kissing, the place half empty and the cowboy

R

pictures rolling on and on. Morgans and the three arches of Christ Church Cathedral. The Dean in whose house I had that basement room on Guy and Sherbrooke, going to hear him at Easter and Christmas. The organ with the bad echo. The gloom. The ex naval Officer coming in and helping himself from the offertory whenever he was hard up.

And then that part of St. Catherine that one had taken for granted, used, that was the background against which one walked, ate, and loved. That one knew and no longer paid any kind of formal recognition.

The neons of The Astor and The Cosy Café. The Eatons Big Deal, the two movies, the Honey Dew, and the same beggar sitting without legs on the flat piece of wood with the baby carriage wheels, the pants neatly folded over, and thumping away, his fingers on the wood, holding up laces, pencils, match boxes, the hat beside him and people crowded thickly past Woolworths, Macys, The Royal Bank, a nightclub with a neon snake flashing on and off, a woman's corset store, a shoe store, another movie, Murrays, Simpsons, another bank, another Honey Dew, Banque Canadienne Nationale, Mappins, Burtons, a florist, another Laura Secord. At Peel and St. Catherine a boy and girl kiss on the sidewalk under the clock that says 'Players Please'. Streetcar tracks curve and branch out like the mouth of several rivers. Here A's father used to stand selling papers in winter in that canvas hut with the small stove. 'The Greatest Guy In The World. The man who takes his family out to dine at Murrays. It's a Happy Family Habit to eat out once a week.' The boy sees the girl get on a streetcar; they both wave as the lights change and the car goes down Windsor. Bankruptcy sale, going out sale, fire, smoke, damage sale. The chickens and spare ribs turning on the spits at Dinty Moores. A joke store.

God could not be everywhere
∴ he made moths

———

God Bless Our Mortgaged Home

In a drugstore: toothpaste, bubble bath-soap, cameras, and painted across the window front in white:

24-Hour Service
Urine analysis . . . $2.00
Pregnancy Test . . . $4.00
Pre-natal sex determination

A poster in another store:

> ZWEITES GROSSES DEUTSCHES VOLKFEST
> IM BELMONT PARK. AM SONNTAG DEN
> 28 MAI 1956
> VON 2 UHR MITTAGS BIS 12 UHR NACHTS
> DAS GROSSTE FEST DES JAHRES DER
> DEUTSCHSPRACHEN IM MONTREALS
> VERJAHR KAMEN 5000

On a streetcar a bank was advertising, telling everyone to BE A GOOD CANADIAN. An armament firm told why it was necessary to go to church to preserve 'our way of life'. A brewery said: 'Let's All Work Together For A Happy Prosperous Canada'. Another brewery had: 'More and More Canadians Have Time To Enjoy Baseball'. In large black letters on a yellow background in a store window was the sign:

> DON'T WORRY, YOU'LL NEVER LEAVE THIS WORLD ALIVE

And higher than the buildings on the street, on a hoarding, against the sky, was an enormous neon bull with neon tears falling steadily from his eyes.

A HIGH STANDARD OF LIVING

On this my last night I was invited out for dinner. It was over an hour's drive from the city to the smart residential area of the Town of Mount Royal. The house was very new. It stood in the hub of half a wheel with the spokes—tree-lined streets—all converging to this one house. In front of it was a circular drive with grass and trees.

My host was in his early thirties. He was a small stout man, pugnacious, but with a sad face. His fair hair was receding and he had a little paunch. His father emigrated from Roumania just after the first world war and became a rags pedlar in the Ghetto. When he died he left a profitable junk business (scrap metal and rags) for his son who expanded it into larger yards, a railway spur, at Lachine. He was very proud of the house and the gadgets. We went into the den. It was in Honduras mahogany, a TV set, a Hi-Fi, a bookcase, but no books. An all-encased built-in bar, black marble counter, stainless steel sink. There was a tap, but no handle. You moved the spout to the right, it gave cold water; you moved it to the left, hot water; in the middle it was off. The back of the bar was in turquoise and gold mosaic tile. There were cigarettes in black paper and gold edges, three kinds of brandy, several sherrys, whiskys, vodka, liqueurs, and a tiny refrigerator for ice-cubes. We sat there and drank and smoked and talked about cars. His wife's brother (in textiles) had driven up in a large new yellow-cream car. We went out and looked it over. He was very excited. He had taken delivery of it that day. My host said he was tired of American cars; he intended to buy a Rolls.

His wife showed me around the house. She was also very proud that all this was hers. Dark handsome Jewish features, the large brown eyes in deep shadow, a small spare body. She was brought up in St. Urbain Street and met her husband at Baron Byng school. They moved to this house five months ago. Since then they had changed their names. 'For business reasons,' she said.

She showed me around the kitchen. The large electric stove with its clocks, like the inside of a cockpit, all spotless white: automatic clock, bake dial, bar b/q dial. There was a fan on top so you didn't get any odour or grease; beside it was the automatic dishwasher, the garburator that disposed of the garbage, bamboo curtains, lamps on a spring loader from the ceiling (you pulled them to any level and they stayed), air-foam seats on the kitchen chairs, refrigerator on 'eye level' (everything inside moved out when you opened the door), a deep freeze. In the living-room: the candelabra, the wool carpet, gold and white walls, light Swedish furniture, the room was divided by a flower box built of natural stone, indirect lighting; a miniature evergreen was in the copper box surrounded by white marble and gold. In the vestibule there was a Paris scene complete with park bench. The staircases were of wrought iron, the wallpaper in the hall was gold with fleur-de-lis. Nightlights were sunk into the walls at ankle level.

The bathroom was magnificent. Large, shiny, glittering with polish and chrome. Green and pink toilet paper, the same colour as the wash basin and the toilet.

I thought of the time we lived in Sussex in between the Downs. Old cottages facing a busy main road, then fields with cows, and behind the cottages were the gardens. Twice a week I would dig a hole in the garden and empty the lavatory bucket into the earth. And when one had made holes all along you came back to the start and opened the earth again. I could see the others digging their holes, emptying their buckets. This had gone on for generations. The ground was rich. The fruit, the vegetables, the flowers, growing in it were the finest I have seen in England. We had large raspberries in late November, but most of our backyard was covered with nasturtiums, thick masses of them, enormous in size, their fleshy stalks pushing out horizontally, the brilliant orange and yellow of the flowers against the large light-green leaves. And one was continually surrounded by the smell of human excrement decomposing and the luxurious growth of the nasturtiums, the cabbages, cauliflowers, and beets. How simple one's pleasures were. I remember how I looked forward to taking the bus to Horsham, going to the public lavatory in the Carfax, inserting a penny, getting a cubicle, sitting on the seat, reading the words underneath the pictures on the walls, watching the feet of the pigeons above the glass tiles, then flushing the bowl.

We ate barbecued chicken which was picked up at the 'Chicken Coop'; all one had to do was re-heat it. Then we went back into the den and drank and their eight-year-old daughter came and gave a recitation. It was a parody. The expressive movements of the hands, the mouth, the eyes, were exaggerated and not synchronized to the words of a little squirrel waking up in the morning and looking for acorns. When it was over she bowed very stiffly. The parents were proud, they said they had an offer from TV of a fifty-dollar-a-week contract for her. But when she went out of the room they admitted they were worried. She did not like school and she could not make friends. They had her take ballet lessons, painting lessons, and elocution. Then they decided to take her to a psychiatrist. After three months he told them that she was sensitive.

She was a nice little girl with a round sallow face, straight black hair and brown sentimental eyes. She behaved just like any girl of her age until they had her do another recitation . . . when she finished she went to her room and played with her dolls.

We went out on the porch, in the front, and sat on the stone steps of the balcony as I had done often on the veranda steps on Murray Street and they on St. Urbain. In the centre of the drive, on the grass between the trees, two boys in jeans and T-shirts were throwing a ball. We went for a drive in the new yellow-cream car and they drove through the silent streets of the suburb and stopped in front of a friend's house. Two men in shirt sleeves were playing cards, and the women were watching television and eating chocolates. They all came out and admired the car and said, 'Wear it well,' and laughed.

We returned to the house and went to the back porch and sat

there drinking. There was a pool sunk in the lawn for goldfish, water lilies were open on the surface, a few trees, birds were singing. The sun had gone down and above us where no clouds were the sky was green, towards the horizon there were patches of clouds, their bottoms a flesh red. Suddenly the hostess said, 'Look, we're all going to have good luck.' A black cat was going slowly across the grass towards the fence. Birds began to make a continuous noise. I could see only part of the cat as it was hidden by a tree. A blackbird had flown down and was only a few inches away from the cat's tail. But the cat did not move. When it did, it had a large blackbird in its jaws, one wing dragged across the grass as the cat began to go towards the end of the lawn. Two blackbirds were flying over it, following it and making a continual urgent chatter. 'It's got a bird,' the husband said. And he got up to go after the cat. But she stopped him. 'We're going to have good luck,' she said. 'It didn't cross our path.' The husband sat down, upset. And for about the next twenty minutes, until it got dark, the trees were black and you could not see the pond, I could hear a solitary soft low 'cheep'. Then silence. Then that recognizable 'cheep' again. The other birds had stopped. 'Cheep. Cheep. Cheep.' And all the while we talked about cars, about money, about liking the negroes and hating the Germans, about what a good country Canada was, why go back to England . . . And the 'cheep' continued, then stopped, as it got completely suffocated by the emptiness and the darkness.

THE TOURIST SHIP

HOW DOES ONE SAY GOODBYE?

IT HAD rained during the night. By morning the rain had stopped. And riding in the taxi to the docks, the streets wet, there was that pleasant early-morning feeling of a hot day. Inside the wharf-shed it was dark, a section of the wall was open, the light from the outside entered the gloom, showing the thickness of the mud on the floor. Men were sprinkling sawdust on to the mud then scraping the mud off with large shovels. I could hear a band playing *O My Poppa* and the sound of shovels against concrete. It did not take long to get on board. I returned down the gangplank to make a few last-minute telephone calls, but no one was in. An old man with a shovel stood by the phone box, unshaven, a French-Canadian. He held out his hand, put on a sad face. 'Some money for me. Give some money for me.'

A woman in her forties, heavily made-up, drunk, began to do a Highland Fling, shouting out 'whoops' as the four-piece band played *Auf Wiedersehen*. The ship's photographer kept taking pictures. By the wooden rail a young attractive girl (black hair, a fringe, high cheek bones, a small scar on one cheek) held a handkerchief to her face and watched the wharf. On the wharf was a young negro, tall, gaunt, a white Panama hat, a coat over his arm, you could see vividly the white patches of his eyes. They stared at each other. The ship began to be pulled away. The negro raised his hand to his lips and brought the hand down again. The girl tried to get the handkerchief tighter to her face. She lifted her hand above her head and, as if in slow motion, bent her wrist. The negro did the same. He lifted his hat above his head and then back again. He held his hand up. It was all done slow. And then the girl began to weep. The woman with the heavily made-up face continued to jig around and to sweat; the band repeated *Auf Wiedersehen*. The girl buried her face in her handkerchief and sobbed—the other passengers had cleared a space on either side of her; she embarrassed

263

everybody—until a woman came and led her down into a lounge.

Landmarks. Bits and pieces that were only starting points begin to go backwards.

The twin towers of Notre Dame. The smell of incense burning. Bright red glasses with flickering candles. Listening with her to the Messiah. Then back into the thick snow. The cups of coffee and crumpets in the 'Honey Dew'. The early morning meetings for breakfast. She waited for me underneath the clock in the Arts building after the last lecture. Then the meal out, the Saturday night film, and at Christmas ski-ing at Mont Tremblant. Her mother, a widow, had brought her to McGill after the war, after Labour had come into office. She told me about the people she knew who were leaving England, those who had their children down for Harrow and Eton, of friends in Kenya and Southern Rhodesia. She told me about an old house in Suffolk with earwigs coming out of the taps, of her nannie, of hunt balls, of being presented at Court. And here in the anonymous cubicle of a room in Royal Victoria College was 'a home from home'. The black wooden tuck-box under the bed; the box Kodak with the rough canvas case and *St. George's, Harpenden*, marked in India ink; the small brown teddy bear lying on the pillow; a copy of *Winnie the Pooh* with a child's crooked lettering inside. Then walking in winter through the silent frozen streets; in spring through the mud and the slush watching the shoots push out like small hands through last year's dead grass; or in the car driving to the Laurentians; to St. Adele, St. Sauveur, Piedmont, walking to the lake, bitten by mosquitoes, in the magnificent decay of the Fall—she was homesick for Ivor Novello . . .

> We'll gather lilacs in the Spring again
> And walk together down an English lane.

A home from home. *The Times* calendar on the wall; staying up all night to hear the B.B.C. broadcast of the Royal wedding; the crumpled copies of *Punch*; *The Illustrated London News*; crumpets in the 'Honey Dew'.

We pass freighters leaning against the sides of the banks. Bergen, Helsingfors, Glasgow. A clock says it is 12.30. Quai Jacques Cartier. Another journey. How does it begin? Does it begin with a girl crying? Or is that its end? We pass Great Lakes boats, freighters with logs piled high on the deck, tankers. Under Jacques Cartier Bridge, an elaborate Meccano. Thirty years have gone by. And what does one think about?

Faces. 'Old faces, faces hated, faces loved, alive or dead . . .' Faces that have gone. Things left unfinished. The pretence, the lies one told. The things one had wanted, one had loved, admired, and abandoned.

Across this bridge, by bus, to Ile-aux-Noix. The French-Canadian village near the United States border. A church steeple. The hotel with the badly spelled English name. The good highway running through, built during Prohibition. Tutoring three boys from Guatemala and one French-Canadian to speak English. Tutoring meant going out in the sailboat, dinghy, or canoe, while they read from Thackeray and I explained the meaning of words and corrected their pronunciation. We slept in the large stone house, cool, dark, silent. A line of poplars at the end of the lawn hid the place from the highway. Madame de Rostaing, a Huguenot, looking like one of those late photographs of Colette, fluffy, dyed, blonde hair, faded yellow, piled loosely on top of her head; writing in a huge curving script; playing Chopin on the piano in the evenings in the dark. Surrounded by Balzac, Hugo, piles of old *Vogues*, *Geographical Magazines*, goat-skin rugs, old photographs of nudes with long hair wading into the shallows of a river. Isolated. Living off her past. Telling me about the good times with Tyrone Power (senior). How he had his cottage by theirs on the river, then it burned down. Then down the dusty dirt road by the low fields that are flooded every spring, by the tall telegraph poles, to the cottage beside the Richelieu River. Water-snakes, reeds, blood-suckers. The spinning-wheel, the old piano, and a sour smell of things not used. Outside old Lacosse in his rocking chair and fireman's braces, spitting tobacco, complaining about the old-age pension, teaching me how to spear carp at night with a light. Fishing. Sailing. Writing. Going with Lucien in his 'model T', delivering and collecting the farmer's letters, mostly mail-order catalogues, in the tin letter boxes stuck crookedly to the wooden posts. A cold night, late September, an orange harvest moon. The three Guatemalans staying up outside all night to see their first snow. And the frogs coming from the river, across the low fields, to the highway to be crushed by the thousands. Whenever you walked, whenever a car went by, dead frogs, live frogs, frogs drying. Saturday afternoons, and the farmers going with sticks whacking the frogs and filling up sacks for the Montreal restaurants. The hotel filling up with American businessmen who have brought their secretaries for the weekend. While the priest in church cursed the crops because the village girls wore shorts in the summer.

S

Going under this bridge on another hot June day. Standing on the freighter's smelled deck. A gramophone playing from the first mate's cabin. Going under this bridge for the first time, borrowing the fare, wondering if I would return, but not looking back.

A heat haze behind us and through it Mount Royal. Tree-topped like a picket fence: light green, yellow, flaked with black. The squat cross against the sky dwarfed by a red television mast. Listening to a symphony orchestra on top of the mountain, lying on one's back, in the dark, watching the stars, while couples try to find a piece of earth where small boys with flashlights will not find them.

We swing and turn and the Sun Life Building turns with us. Down the cobbled hill, by the Windsor Station, the wind blowing as the street turns. Burns in the square and the pigeons, calèches around it. Autumn: leaves blowing across the empty square like small frightened mice.

The shore-line was like a Lowry landscape but without human beings; again it was all mathematics. Industrial chimneys, storage tanks, B.A., Esso, freight cars standing by long warehouses. Haze, Smoke. Mist. And through it a splash of crimson of waste burning like a tattered flag at the top of steel derricks. Below: green leaves, grey streets, car-parks, junk piled in yards. There was hardly a wind.

Then the river widened and a cool breeze came across the water. Marker buoys with small evergreens tied to their tops indicate the channel. Very flat, very green land on both sides; a few trees, a bungalow with a coloured roof painted red, green, blue; and the white sides. At the water's edge cows graze, further inland above a clump of trees the shining silver church spire. As we go by, the waves we send back break gently against the shore.

We came to Quebec at night and let the pilot off. Lights. Rock. And on top of the rock like some advertisement for Mr. Atlas posing with his chest out holding a deep breath was the overpowering centre piece of the Chateau Frontenac. Below it the narrow waist: the dark; the wooden steps; the drab narrow streets leading to the river. You expected the top to come off and there would be a smaller Chateau Frontenac underneath; then that one came off and there would still be a smaller one beneath. And underneath the last one: poverty, religion. Fitzgerald was right, it is 'a tin soldier's castle'; the kind one made with cards; but those castles always fell down. On the Levis side of the river a large neon sign kept flashing:

Union
DUPLESSIS
National

I watched the two ferry boats crossing in the middle of the river.
From somewhere a ship's whistle, and then its echo against the
rock. American girls came to the rail and looked at the Chateau
and the lights.

'That's the capital of Canada.' They were holding guides to
Britain, to Austria, to the Low Countries.

'Ain't it cute?'

It felt odd watching the lights of Dufferin Terrace, the darkness of Lower Town, go behind. Regret. Nostalgia. How quickly
one wants to forget the unhappiness, the emptiness, the boredom.
The ship turned, blotting out the lights, leaving only the river
and the sky and the ferry boats; two lit-up pumpkins moving
slowly apart in the black.

I AM A ZERO

I share a cabin with a Hungarian acrobat. He looks like a jockey.
His name is Lazlo Lossan, but he tells me to call him Poobie.
He is going to Germany to work for fifteen days at the Metropole in Stuttgart then he intends to round up some of his friends,
form a circus, and bring it back to Montreal. 'Very good artiste.
Very cheap money in Europa. I get together.' A smile, a slap
together of hands. 'So, I have circus for all Kanada.' He says
proudly that he is a Canadian. He has been seven months in
Canada and has earned five thousand dollars working in a
Montreal night-club. Short, stocky, with a sun-tanned lined face,
blue eyes, in his early forties. He looks muscle-bound. On his
arms are tattoos of a snake, a parrot, an anchor. He showed me
his scars: a snake bit him in the arm, a monkey in the leg, his
chin had a sharp cleft where a lion mauled him. We speak partly
in German, partly in English, and partly in pantomime. Often
conversations consist entirely of verbs. Everything about him is
neat. The small black chamois shoes, the Scottish cap, the green
corduroy trousers, the brown suede jacket with a leather fringe
hanging down the zipper front and along the seams under his
arms as if he was an Indian scout in some cowboy film.

Our table steward tells us his name is Alfred and anything we
want he will try to get for us. He is tall, lanky, stooped, with long

thinning hair combed slickly back. He sniffs continually. He fawns over us. He looks after two small tables facing the wall. At the table I am at, there is also a couple of young Americans in their early twenties. They show me their farewell 'Bunny Cards' sent to them from home with 'tips for world travellers'. They keep on asking, 'It this the right way to use your soup spoon? Is this a fish knife? What's this thing?'

This is their first trip away from the States. They come from a small town in the Mid-West. Her name is Murt; and his is Don. They worked as a waiter and a waitress for the past two years so that they could save up enough money, mainly from tips, to come over. They intend to hitch-hike and bicycle ride around England and the Continent.

At the next table is a Jewish woman with a dark inquisitive face, very nervous. When she smiles, spaces show between her teeth. She is with her young son and they live in Toronto. She came over from Germany to London in the 1930's and after the war emigrated to Canada. From her ears hang tiny flashing Maple Leafs. She is going to visit her sister in Hendon. The other person at the table is an architectural student from Mississippi. He is older than the other students on board. He says he was in the Navy. He speaks in a clear Southern drawl. Alfred quickly attempts to get into our confidence.

'We had such a rotten trip coming over.'

'Was it rough?' Don said.

'Not so rough. But it was emigrant boat. Pigs. No different. They come down and eat like pigs. I am not used to work on emigrant boats. I tell the chief steward. He says for this one Alfred you can have military. I tell him I prefer to have tourists.' And he gives us a grin which says clearly: I know I can trust you to tip properly.

At the other tables were youth hostelers, college boys and girls, crew cuts, sweaters, a studied casualness, an open proclaimed innocence and vacancy in their faces. There were also some Canadian soldiers and returning immigrants from Canada and the States. The home port of the ship was Bremerhaven and most of the older passengers were German. They wore, for the first few days, large plastic buttons with their names and their home-towns on them. Some had silver Maple Leafs pinned to their lapels: 'So they won't mistake us for Americans.' The women resembled hausfraus, well-fed, dumpy, with expensive-looking haircuts and infinite patience. They sat quietly in the empty lounges and played bridge. The men in shirt sleeves, hand-painted ties, crew cuts, cigars. Amongst themselves they spoke German.

In the river the second day. Calm. No sound except the dull vibrations from the engines. On deck, the slap-slap of water against the sides.

In the lounge I met the girl who had wept by the rail as the boat was pulled away. 'I am a Zero,' she said. She did not know when she would see her husband again. They had been married two months and after seeing her off he was going to a hotel in St. Agathe to wash dishes for the rest of the summer. She went to her cabin and brought up a copy of the *Montreal Herald*. On the front page was a large picture of them both, telling their story. She said that she was German, had come over to Pittsburgh for a visit and married an American negro she met at a club. Her husband decided to go over to Canada, to McGill, he wanted to become a teacher. The Canadian Immigration would not allow her to come in and stay, until he established residence in the country. She could not go back to the States. She had lost her German citizenship by marrying an American. 'I am a Zero,' she said.

But there was so much vitality in her wanting to burst out. You could see it even as she sat in the lounge, in jeans and a tight white sweater, writing letters to her husband that she could not send off, but making sure that everyone could see what she was doing. Her eyes wandered around the room. She repeated her story to every young man who came and sat beside her. And her tears made sense, just as her wandering eyes, now. She couldn't be faithful to anything except the immediate experience. She couldn't say 'no' to life.

Next morning, a slate sky, a smooth sea, not a ripple, gulls criss-crossed hopefully. It felt as if we were sailing on a lake. We passed Newfoundland; a shape in the mist; rock, pine-black trees, grey-blue spaces, emptiness. Then the sun came out and the students sprawled on deck sunning themselves. They lay with their pocket books on Freud, Kierkegaard, 100 *Best Poems in the English Language, Time, Life, Reader's Digest, Movie Screen*. It was all part of the same thing. Question: Is it true that Anna Magnani is 46 and wears falsies? Answer: No. She doesn't wear falsies. The star system operates in everything. 'Did you know Die-lan Thomas? Did you know him *personally*?' They talked about ethnic dishes, psychology, cameras, and very earnestly sang *On Top of Old Smoky*; *Jimmy Crack Corn and I Don't Care* . . . They wore the same casual clothes and worried about the correct way of doing things. Nothing, so far, has bitten them deeply; there was not a line in any of their faces. They walked around continually optimistic, healthy, wanting to be liked, and looking in the mirror.

Routine settled in, and the luxury in this boredom of just being a passenger, of not having to worry about food or a place to sleep for the next ten days. A young boy with chimes woke us in the morning, then we waited to hear him again for lunch and dinner. Before meals the pacing up and down the deck, like animals at the zoo at feeding time. In the evenings Poobie and I lay awake in the bunks. He told me about his life in Hungary, how to cook Hungarian dishes, how to read hands. He told me how he threw away all his European clothes when he received his first cheque and bought all Canadian clothes. 'I am Kanadian. I must dress Kanadian, moderne.' He lay in the bunk in a white T-shirt with Daisy Mae and Lil Abner on the front. And hanging up were the hand-painted ties, the loud diamond socks, the suede windbreaker with the fringes. He had an unquestioning faith in Canada and in things Canadian which he saw around him where he lived on St. Lawrence and in the cheap advertisements. The only English song he knew was the one he had as his cue for his act in the nightclub. He sang it often. He knew the tune, but he did not know the right words. He tried to fit some in. In his innocence and ignorance they made a kind of sense.

> Maybe you fall in love with me, no money.
> Maybe tomorrow night the sun will shine.
> I change my name from Johnny to Giavanni.
> If we are sent no money, you'll be mine.

When he woke up in the morning he sang sad Hungarian songs.

The Gulf of St. Lawrence. A bright blue sea with patches of black and the occasional iceberg. Small yellow-green birds flew on to the deck. There were hundreds of them. The American architectural student thought they were wild canaries. They flew in the bars, into the lounges. They hopped around the deck, on to the rigging and the rails.

The boat itself was old and had a seediness that appealed. It did not try to look different than it was. None of the lights had shades and they only used the smallest bulbs. On the sixth day it was foggy and everyone was driven inside. The canaries got cold, puffed out, and hopped slowly around the damp deck.

They did not touch the bread or the water left out for them. Children (playing with them) kept chasing them until, exhausted, the birds died.

Fulmars follow us, banking in the low troughs and gliding beside the ship. The ship cuts through the slow swell, pushing back the water to break white with the green like a smoke underneath and the dark blue around.

The young Americans at my table always came late. They were both very much 'in love', especially the boy. He kept dropping hints how they spent their time in the cabin. This was their first affair. He was simple, tall, husky, easy going, not worried. She was small, a tight little mouth, unattractive, a sad pinched face, she hardly smiled. They deliberately teased each other one minute then the next they would be silent, frozen in a pose, of holding hands, looking into each other's eyes, and staring, not eating, just staring. Whenever they came to the table they brought the smell of bed with them.

Time passes. The girl who wept when the boat left Montreal had found herself a boy-friend. She joined the others at night carrying blankets, hiding in the darkest corners of the deck, on top of the hatches, or in a lifeboat. And in the dampness of the early morning watching the Greek sailors wash down the decks.

LAZLO LOSSAN: ARTISTE

Poobie had become like a bodyguard. At 10.30 he came and looked for me in the bar, in the lounges, on deck, and waited until I was ready to go to the cabin. Then we lay awake and talked. One night neither of us could fall asleep. He got out of bed and washed some handkerchiefs, then hung them up on a hanger by the mirror to dry. I tried to read. But it was no good. We both decided to get dressed and walk around the deck for a while.

A warm night, no wind, the stars above us. The sea was black and we watched it turn white as we went through it. We walked. A loudspeaker was bringing recorded music. *Ramona. Lady Be Good.* We stopped by the rail, looked at the sea and sky and where they met: black. Poobie indicated with his hand a jump over the side and into the water. 'Oops and feeneesh.' A shrug of his shoulder. 'Easy.' We returned to the cabin.

He told me of the poets and the novelists he knew in Hungary. 'Hard work,' he said, and shook his head sympathetically. He told me that when he had made a lot of money out of his circus in Montreal (and he was convinced he would) he promised to send for me wherever I was to come and stay with him as his guest. I agreed.

Back into the bunks and still not able to sleep. 'I tell you,' he said, 'about my life. Maybe you write someday . . .'

'My family for 800 *jahre* in circus. In Hungary, Germany, Roumania. *Alle* circus director and acrobat. The uncle from Momma, a horse rider well known in England, Mihal Schmidt. In Budapest I was born in circus. When I was three I see my *Mutter tanzen*. I come from bed, my eyes crying. Momma, Momma. I sleep in wagon. When six years old, my uncle come. We need money. "You do handstand." I do handstand. After that I must practise every day. In two months I can work for children to see. By the time I was ten I was very good making handstands. I like. It was small circus and we all do other job. We had twenty horses. I look after them, give out tickets. Then I learn ride horses, trapeze. At 12 years my Momma died. Father not good. I leave home. I no earn enough from acrobat, so I do for seven years wrestling. For two years I was the best wrestler for my weight in Hungary. At twenty I marry a girl also from long family from circus. I work for her father. I now star. I perform Russian dance, Hungarian dance, with horse riding, jockey, trapeze, acrobat, and wrestling. For four or five year I work like that. We live very good. I work for my father-in-law. He had the circus. I star performer. I see my father-in-law take in big money. I ask for some more. He told me to take my wife, his daughter, and go. I go to my sister in Budapest. She has big heart. I ask for five hundred dollars to start circus. She gives me. Then my father-in-law comes where we are and says to my wife, "Where is your crippled bad man?" I hear. I am strong, strong like five men. She says to me, "You are a good man, I go with you." I only have a shirt and one pair of trousers. I make a bundle of a few things, my wife go down from wagon, I give my boy from the wagon to my wife and I see my father-in-law drinking and leaning by the wagon. I come down and close the wagon door and my father-in-law hit me on the neck and side. My wife turn around. She sees me full of blood and laughing. She knows when I laugh I am very angry. She come to me. "You no hit Poppa."

'All my life I have been beaten. I am small. When I was a child and I don't do something right, like ride horse or acrobat I would be whipped by my father. I buy a horse for hundred and fifty *pangu*. I put my son and wife on horse and I lead the horse one hundred kilometre. I need money. We must eat. I go in a *Dorf.* I go to tavern. But man not interested when I say I work tonight. I go to *Burgermeister.* I ask for drum. He give me drum. I go in square and make with the drum. People come. I tell them tonight in the tavern I work. December. It was cold. Snow. In the evening four or five people come. I have not enough money for food or pay the drink in tavern. I go beg for bread for my wife and son, I no eat. People go at eleven o'clock. I speak to boss; I go on street with wife and child. I give my jacket to my child, and I go in sleeves. I stand in street. Looking. Looking. *Alles* sleep. *Kommen* a *jungen Mann.* He look. "What is this?" I tell him I work in circus. Have no money, no bed. He tell me go to other tavern, they have horses, and there you sleep. This is half past twelve. My child sleeps in my wife's hand. I go to boss at tavern. He laugh. He says it is cold. No much straw. I say I come. I go and take my wife and child and use straw for them and I let them sleep. And I think I good acrobat. I no have costume. No have money to go to Budapest. I understand circus business, no other kind of business. In the morning I go away from here. It is no good. Put my wife and son on horse and walk. After five kilometre I see circus wagon on road, the horses are no good, there is an old man and one girl. I talk to old man. He say he work in winter in tavern. Little show, some money. I say I big artiste. We make bargain. Partners. I give my horse. Three horses pull. We make good money. Two weeks I buy little wagon and then I want to work for myself.

'I work myself. I go from *Dorf* to *Dorf.* I take drum. I drum and people come. I do acrobat and pass the hat. I go from *Dorf* to *Dorf.* Then I see Hungarian gendarme. Where is my paper for work? I say my father-in-law sent you. He say no, but laugh. I know. So I go to the next *Dorf.* Again the drum, again the people come. Again gendarme. Say no paper, no work. I must go to Budapest. I go to Budapest and get paper. I also do work in Budapest, lots of money. Then 1939 everyone must be soldier. I tell them I'm artiste. I must work for my wife and children. I sell my wagon and five horses to my Uncle Schmidt. He is big circus director, lots of money, he has Royal Orpheum in Budapest, nice villa on America Street. He say to me you are big artiste, you are crazy to go from *Dorf* to *Dorf,* you come and work for me. I work a *Monat.* He give me big money. I go to the Minister, I tell him me no good soldier. I good acrobat. Give me passport to other country. He say O.K. I work in Zagreb, Bratislava, Prague, Budapest. I then must go to the army. My wife I leave behind. I go for a year, entertain troops. When I come back my wagon is here but my wife is no here. I find her live with other man. She think I dead. She come back and live with me. And then she die, bad heart.' And here Poobie broke down and wept. 'After that I come to Kanada with my boy. Soon I work in nightclub, make good money . . .'

We were invited to the Captain's cocktail party the second last night aboard. Poobie went through his case asking my opinion what he should wear. On top of his clothes was a steel stick with a small steel cross handle. He had that for thirty years; that's all he needed for his act. Then he went through his wardrobe. Besides his clothes there were lace panties, blouses, slips, high-heeled shoes, silk stockings. 'For my girl,' he said shyly. He was going to Germany to work in the Metropole, to get a circus together, and a new wife.

The last time I spoke to Poobie was in the cabin just before disembarking. He asked me to address an envelope to his son in Montreal. He wanted to send him a photograph that the ship's photographer had taken of the wharf just as the boat was leaving. In the picture a cluster of faces, some waving handkerchiefs. The only one I recognized was the tall gaunt negro. I typed out his son's address, while Poobie complained that he wasn't eating well. 'Four days now without toilet. At home I cook myself. I feel the strength come in my body. I feel like a bear.' I asked him about a return address. 'Lazlo Lossan, Artiste,' he said. I typed that out in the lefthand corner of the envelope. 'What else?' 'Lazlo Lossan, Artiste,' he said, 'no else.' He took the envelope. '*Prima.* Good.' A chuckle. 'Now I go try toilet again.'

On the last day the Jewish woman began to worry about the correct tip to give Alfred. It was obvious none of us had money to spare. The American student from the South and I said we would give four dollars, she said she would do the same. Murt and Don said they didn't have much money and they didn't think they could afford to give a tip. We put the bills in an envelope and the Jewish lady handed the envelope to Alfred. 'From the two tables.' He smiled, gave a bow, and disappeared into the kitchen. He returned quickly and came up to me.

'Have you been satisfied with my service?'

'Yes.'

He went to the American at the next table.

'Have you been satisfied with my service?'

'Yes.'

He asked the Jewish lady.

'Have you been satisfied with my service?'

'Yes.'

'Then why did I only get twelve dollars from two tables?'

He did not wait for an answer but began to shout in German. 'Look at them sitting there like Kings and Queens . . . they're no better than those damned emigrants.' Another steward said in German, 'Alfred don't make so much fuss. I have twelve people and I only got seventeen dollars.'

Neither Murt nor Don showed up.

Alfred said he would complain. This wasn't enough. The American and myself said we gave him what we thought the service was worth. The Jewish woman was so upset over his performance that she gave him another dollar. But this did not calm him. As he served us he kept on muttering 'Emigrants. No better than those damned emigrants.' Then he would break into English. 'The chief steward told me at the start. "Alfred, take military, you are sure of three dollars each from the military, it is paid by the Government." But I said no. I will have tourists!'

He returned to my table. 'Where are the other two?'

'In the cabin.'

'Is theirs included?'

'Yes.'

I guess he was counting on having four or five dollars from each one and he counted the small boy as a place.

WHEN THERE'S NOTHING AT STAKE

A tender came out the mist and we went into a Whistler landscape to the dingy shabby customs at Southampton. The small grubby train with dust. And the Americans excitedly snapping pictures as the train went through the slums. 'I wish I had sixteen more rolls of this.' Snapping poverty as they would snap at almost anything. This was new. 'O look at their purty little cars. Ain't they cute?' Then they solemnly did their money tables. 'How many shillings to the pound . . .?' 'Whose got a florin . . .?'

Back to London. Nothing seems to have changed. Has one been away? The houses falling into decay; the red buses in the grey evening light; Joe Lyons; grey stone; grit in the mouth. One felt pleasantly anonymous again.

Next day I went to Canada House to see if I could find some accommodation—into that empty room filled with provincial papers, a business man's sentimental journey; on the dark-stained tables pamphlets with photographs of war cemeteries in Europe beside them the blue sheets with the latest stock market quotations—and met Hector B., who was on his way to Hanoi to become the Canadian representative there; the last one was recently shot.

We sat in the room and tried to talk, but it was too noisy. Every few minutes people would come in and ask for mail at the reception desk. The phone would ring. In the background there was the sound of girls with little children's voices, the sing-song talk, impersonal, as if they were elevator operators announcing floors and merchandise. We decided to try an Expresso. I knew a large one in the Haymarket. We sat by a small table in a corner and had two cups of coffee. A fountain in the centre, slabs of coloured glass, the water running down. He was looking forward to Indo-China. He had been in the diplomatic service since leaving McGill. A distinguished leonine face, greying hair, a clear resonant voice that could not completely lose its public platform tone even in private conversation. The last time we talked was in the Union at McGill. I knew he had been a bush pilot, and I said that of what I had seen in Canada I preferred the bush and the interior.

'Only rejects go into the bush,' he said. 'They're the failures.'

I said that failure in Canada is something that appeals to me. We talked on about the people we knew, about what he had done, about some of the things I had experienced, how I felt about them.

'The trouble with you,' he said, 'is that you hate your country.'

What could one say to that? Love and hate, hate and love, they get mixed up all the time and I have been held by one just as much as by the other.

That evening I was to meet a friend of mine, a painter, in a small pub at the start of Kensington Church Street, but I was late and he wasn't there. The pub was hot. A light drizzle was falling outside. It was close. The pub door was open and a curtain was drawn across. I decided to wait, and went into the far side of the pub, away from the bar.

A young boy and a girl were sitting by a table in front of the Ladies. They sat there, tense, not saying anything. Again I was struck how slow, how silent, the face of so much of human unhappiness is. She was very nervous and kept fumbling with her handbag. He looked embarrassed. They were having a lovers' quarrel and she did not care who heard it. She started to weep, her make-up ran down underneath her eyes. He tried to console her. He said that everything would work out. He said that he loved her. That seemed to have some effect for she stopped crying, but you could see she was hurt. 'When there's nothing at stake,' she said grimly, 'that's when you say, "I love you".'

I left the pub and went out into the light rain and walked along the High Street towards Kensington Gardens. I wondered why I felt so bitter about Canada. After all, it was all part of a dream, an experiment that could not come off. It was foolish to believe that you can take the throwouts, the rejects, the human kickabouts from Europe and tell them: Here you have a second chance. Here you can start a new life. But no one ever mentioned the price one had to pay; how much of oneself you had to betray.